MW01296053

# Accounts Payable

*In the 21st Century Business Environment*

The most current and advanced

Accounts Payable practices and procedures

*A fully revised and updated 2019 edition*

# Constantin Levi P, CPA

New York 2019

Barnegat Lighthouse Business Publications

Eleventh Edition

Originally published in March 2013

Accounts Payable in the 21st Century Business Environment

Barnegat Lighthouse Business Publications
P.O.BOX 33695
Bay Ridge NY 11209

Book design and production: Emily-Liz Daniels / Barnegat Lighthouse Business Publications

Editors: Moses Netherlanders and Julia Knobloch

**Library of Congress Cataloging - .in - Publication Data**

Constantin Levi P, CPA 1969 –

Accounts Payable in the 21st Century Business Environment

Includes appendix.

ISBN – 13: 978-1481989374

ISBN – 10: 1481989375

*This book is dedicated to Iryna and our children*

*and*

*to my past and present Accounts Payable teams:*

*Bruce R.*

*Charlie S.*

*Darcy L.*

*Hilton L.*

*Keisha R.*

*Loleng G.*

*Jennifer D.*

*Elizabeth G.*

*♡ Rosa S. ♡*

*Shuxiao W.*

*Steven L.*

*Brian K.*

*Teri DL.*

*Greg H.*

*Carminia R*

# Other books by Constantin Levi P, CPA

1099 Compliance

Nonresident Alien Taxation for AP & Payroll

# Content

- Payment methods
  - Checks (125)
  - EFTs (127)
  - Wire transfers (136)
  - Commercial Cards payments (142)
  - Remotely created checks (146)
  - EFTPS (149)
  - Direct debits (150)
- Tracking payments (151)
- IWRP (Interactive Web Response Portals) in Accounts Payable (156)
- Processing form 1099 and form 1096 (158)
- IRS Notice CP-2100/*B*-Notice and Back-up Withholding (194)

## Nonresident Alien Tax Compliance in AP operations (199)

- US tax residency (201)
- Substantial Presence Test (202)
- IRS exemption codes (206)
  - *IRS code exclusion [§117 & §274] (199/203)*
  - *Foreign source income exclusion (212)*
  - *Income tax treaty exclusion (215)*
- Tax treaties forms 8233 and W-8BEN (226)
- Processing forms 1042-S and 1042 (230)

## Purchasing Cards operations

- Purchasing Cards purpose (236)
- Purchasing Cards accounting (239)
- Purchasing Cards use (243)

## Other Accounts Payable concepts and processes

## Processing Accounts Payable in PeopleSoft

**General Principles of the AP-related processes and application**

**Managing the Accounts Payable Department (385)**

## The Accounts Payable philosophy
## & *A.S.P.I.R.E.* concept

*When in doubt, mail it out* – I used to advise tongue in cheek my Accounts Payable department specialists when they came to me with errors on processed checks. We, the Accounts Payable team, have a sense of humor and "mail it out" only emphasized the rule to never release a doubtful payment.

This is not a book to read once. This is a manual, a reference guide to keep on your work desk. It speaks in real terms about the real world – the 21st century Accounts Payable environment and your place in it. The material covered in this book is not meant for easy reading: there are complicated and not so well legally-defined processes and concepts in the Accounts Payable department operations, which (AP operations) are often presented in simplified *no-brainer* terms of the back-office activities. I will also argue in this book against many established Accounts Payable misconceptions and outdated ideas, which are no longer valid and applicable in the 21st century business environment.

Are you an Account Payable professional, or someone who oversees the AP operations? Yes, you are; no person in the right mind opens a book named *Accounts Payable in the 21st Century Business Environment* unless she is an Accounts Payable professional and wants to be a top-notch Accounts Payable expert. It is the custom and attitude to insinuate how dry, tedious and less important than other financial operations the Accounts Payable is, and I strongly disagree with this attitude. It may appear boring to the outsiders, but not to me. And one reason why I like the

Accounts Payable is because *I am* an Accounts Payable professional myself. This is what I do and this is what I am good at.

I like it so much that I decided to write a book about it. Well, you may ask, isn't there some *circular reference* in your reasoning? I say, What circular reference? - This is a book on Accounts Payable and not excel! I like it because I do it, and I do it because I like it. You get the idea, – reading an AP book can also be not so dull and humorous, at least in the introductory section.

On a more serious note, the Accounts Payable is an integral part of any business operations. It may have a varying degree of importance within a company, but there is no possibility that any company can do without it. A foundation of the largest national university system that I have been working for in the past ten years as Manager of Payables and Tax Compliance *is* an Accounts Payable company. We are responsible for managing the university's grants and research funds – disbursing those funds in compliance with the spending purposes and limits and other fiscal accountability objectives; processing hundreds of millions of dollars every year, making thousands of payments of any imaginable type weekly. The AP operations within my company get attention and respect, since they have been our main purpose for being "in business" for the past fifty years.

This was not the case with the previous business that I worked for. A global manufacturing company, Tyco International, and more specifically, its plastics division, depended much more on its sales force. The salesmen and the sales department was the driving power behind the company's growth, since there were numerous competitors on the market selling almost identical kinds of products. A smartphone company, I can imagine, has designers and developers as its key-asset. There is no problem selling a new and *hot* smartphone model to customers once it is developed and released. You get the idea.

What I am getting at is the question of the Accounts Payable department's place within the business hierarchy and the resulting organizational philosophy about it. Let us be honest, most businesses do not have the Accounts Payable activities as their key operation. It has been said many times that the Accounts Payable is a back-office operation, a supporting function of business. Offices will not go dark, cold and without coffee in case that the whole Accounts Payable departments suddenly quits today. A reasonable replacement will be found sooner than for the sales department under the similar circumstances. This is the reality and it should be understood and accepted.

There are other departments that bring in business, customers, contracts, grants and thus, ensure cash inflow. And this is what counts for any business – new clients, more cash, higher income and higher returns for shareholders. Other departments, not the Accounts Payable, by definition, make the cash flow in. But, my fellows Accounts Payable professionals, do not lose good spirit and pride in what we do just yet. There is another variable in the business equation to think about that makes the revenue into net income or net loss. And this is where the Accounts Payable comes into play. How the hard-earned company's cash is being spent?

This is what the Accounts Payable is charged with and held accountable for: assuming the responsibility for orderly disbursement process and its contribution to the company's operations, preventing fraud and managing cash flow. Performing the Accounts Payable functions responsibly, paying for rents, equipment, supplies, materials, liabilities and employees' reimbursements, allows all other departments to operate without friction and perform optimally to ensure higher financial returns or meet other business mission goals. Inefficient Accounts Payable operations can drag any business down, allow for vendors' frustration, fraud and embezzlement, create internal tensions and get the IRS's attention (consider poor 1099 and 1042 reporting). You get the idea; Accounts Payable is not rocket science, but still a 'must-have' business function.

Where you manage the Accounts Payable, work makes a big difference in you AP attitude. You're may be employed by a vibrant and exciting business; you can relate to Michael Bloomberg, founder of the Bloomberg News and a three-term New York City mayor who said (in his book *Bloomberg by Bloomberg*) that he *loves* Mondays. I do like coming to my office on Monday mornings, too.

But, if you find yourself in a business environment, which is *not-so-dynamic*, dull and boring, reading this book may give you another perspective on your daily routine and allow you to change less-than-exciting ways of the AP processes into dynamic and up-to-date operations. Your newly acquired advanced Accounts Payable skills will prove you an irreplaceable asset to your company, since you are now the one who knows how the AP business is run best and who assures the continuous and orderly operations of the Accounts Payable process within your company. Make AP a department of confidence for your bosses – they will appreciate it.

My passion for my Accounts Payable work made me engage in a laborious process of writing an Accounts Payable book, which I envision to be the best Accounts Payable book ever written. Reading *Accounts Payable in the 21st Century Business Environment* will help you to make your company's AP operations better and more efficient by offering new ways of running the Accounts Payable operational segment of your company, adjust your current policies and procedures, foresee possible pitfalls or just compare your current practices to the ones presented in this book and realize how good and up-to-date you are, I guarantee it

In this book, I will present six **A.S.P.I.R.E.** principles, listed below, to apply them in your Accounts Payable practice and philosophy:

-**AP**: Aspire to be the best AP professional one can find: read, research and attend everything that applies to the AP profession. Improve your professional image in substance and appearance.

-**S**ystems: Strive to work with an ERP or AP systems that approximate the ERP's functionalities.

-**P**aper: Eliminate paper processing where possible.

-**I**maging: Use easily-accessible imaging system for storing the AP documentation.

-**R**educe paper checks processing to the absolute minimum.

-**E**rr on the side of under-paying and over-reporting when in doubt.

## A.S.P.I.R.E. to be the best you can be!

Let us think about it again, the way I think about it daily: I am a part of a business - what I do is important for my company and the outside customers. I know and do my work well. I use the cutting-edge Accounts Payable technologies, practices, systems and processes. I am proud to be a professional and contributing member of the society in which I live. 'All in all, you're just another brick in the wall' (Pink Floyd) – *and that's a lot*; I am proud of it. I am proud to be a professional and contributing member of the 21st century American business environment, doing my share of work to assure that the world is functioning in orderly and organized fashion and progressing towards a better future for all.

# What kind of business do you work for?

Do you work for a public utility or construction company, online retailer or hospital, web-design company or university, airline, bank, local government, supermarket chain, transportation, or publishing company? For any Accounts Payables person, it matters -  and it doesn't. It matters in a sense that there are different company styles and dynamics within different industries, different types of peoples, work ethics and attitudes. There are very different kinds of demands to your Accounts Payable skills within a web-retail company and a municipal office. A web-retailer wants you to be quick and proactive. A municipal government environment calls for thoroughness and conservatism. Working for an investment bank requires fast action on any Accounts Payable issue, even if it takes placing a phone call to a colleague at two o'clock in the morning. *Closing the month* in a construction company may require staying a few hours later after five o'clock, while getting out of the office at five *on the dot* is the undisputed right for some other organizations.

And it doesn't matter because your functions as an Accounts Payable specialist remain the same no matter where you work: your job is to pay bills and process T&Es on time, provide internal and external reporting, administer corporate cards accounts, do the 1099 and 1042 reporting to payees and the IRS, monitor  and withhold taxes form US temporary residents (NRA's), administer back up tax withholding, manage Accounts Payable systems (online e-payment modules, *front-end* AP reporting, e-vendor portal of your company's website), write and update Accounts

Payable policies and procedures, just to name a few AP functions.

It goes without saying that you, as an Accounts Payable professional, is more satisfied with what you do in an office where your personality and work style fit best. Happier people make better and more productive employees. And you do want to be happy and satisfied with your professional life. Isn't it a good idea to analyze and re-access whether you are doing your best and getting the best returns working where you are?

It is great if you are. And, if you think that your company is not the best fit for your personality, make the move. It is not easy. The years that you have worked for your present employer have made you entrenched in your ways. And this is another danger for any kind of individual's professional development – complacency and routine. Change it! Easier said than done? Yes, it is easier said than done - true. The cost of living and other increases has probably taken your pay higher than what similar positions pay in the beginning. But you will do good service to yourself and your family by beginning to look for a better fit for your Accounts Payable talent. The "old" company will be better off too, finding a more felicitous individual to fill your big shoes.

The forgoing may not always be true, since any successful business operation requires certain degree of *good* hostility within a company to prevent self-assuredness and complacency. But, again, this tension produces the best results only when like-minded people work together and when differences in personalities do not hinder cooperation and collaboration within a company.

*Birds of feather flock together*; the old saying often holds true even for the most of mid- to large-size companies being the Affirmative Action and Equal Opportunity Employers. There must be a sense of Us working Together towards certain goals, a Mission that individual employees of your company must find themselves united by.

What kind of individuals should you desire to be professionally associated with? Intelligent, educated, hard-working and mind-challenging people who demand high quality work results, innovative approaches, and *outside the box* thinking from themselves and others around them. Bingo! Like you and I am. Do I attempt to flatter you? It's beyond the point: you're already "in the club" of the intelligent and curious by the virtue of reading this books at this time and not another issue of the *People* magazine.

# What system(s) does your company use?

What accounting system does your company use? Is it PeopleSoft, QuickBooks, SAP, Intacct, Oracle, or MIP Abila? That, of course, depends on your company's size and what your company can afford to buy and maintain. But having worked for the past ten years with a cloud-based (accessible via the Internet) ERP system myself, I can attest that the quality of the AP work that you get using the ERP cannot be compared to the quality of the legacy accounting systems. It's just that all the information that you need to do your AP work productively is there, under your fingers with one log in, in one system – all *under one umbrella*. The *Wikipedia.org* describes the ERP as following:

*Enterprise Resource Planning (ERP) systems integrate internal and external management information across an entire organization-embracing finance/accounting, manufacturing, sales and service, customer relationship management, etc. ERP systems automate this activity with an integrated software application. The purpose of ERP is to facilitate the flow of information between all business functions inside the boundaries of the organization and manage the connections to outside stakeholders.*

I had once counted all the *fractured databases* (a term coined by Larry Ellison (Oracle Corp.), who had pioneered the ERP research and development) that I used before my ERP days. I counted eight databases: my main accounting system, online AP system, imaging system, front-end reporting system, *Cyborg* payroll application, *nonresident alien database* system, corporate cards bank's website, and then the new ERP system to which the company was transitioning at the time. You can add the email system as one of the important Accounts Payable system tools, of course.

What is the big deal about the fractured databases? Just write the passwords down and keep on logging-in and timing-out all day long. The problem was bigger than the numerous daily log in's. Our AP information was indeed all over the place and "fractured". At times, I could be "chasing down" a payee with an incorrect (as reported to me by the IRS) social security number, not knowing that the person has an old and correct record in the nonresident alien system, having been paid fellowship in earlier years. Later on, I learned to check and synchronize all databases, which was a time consuming and prone to human error task; under this scenario, the AP information was stored in too many places - not always correctly copied from one system to another, since the data entries were done by different people, maintaining various sets of records, systems and databases, all within one company.

But here comes the ERP system: PeopleSoft, SAP, NetSuite, MAS500, Lawson and other – one system that houses all relevant to the business process data in one place and it is often accessible online. Your vendor may send an invoice electronically to you; it is uploaded into the ERP - all relevant documents in required image format are attached to the e-records and routed from person to person within a company (the proverbial *workflow* process). If you have a question to anyone involved, there are email links, ERP "chatter", and phone numbers listed, as well as the audit trail, showing the progress a payment is making through the ERP's AP system. You can no longer lose a document *en route* to..., well, there are just too many places where a piece of paper can get lost or languish on someone's desk. The ERP systems are the AP's present and future and you are lucky if you are using one such system now.

Otherwise, companies with older systems (e.g. Abila MIP) are trying to mimic the ERP's capabilities by adding separate functionality systems to the main accounting system. Scanning of all processed AP documents, which is a huge step forward compared to the paper archiving and retrieval (think of the 1099 review and you'll know what I mean), is one such advancement, short of the ERP capabilities. A process to have all source documents imaged, indexed and available on your computer, be it within an ERP or a separate imaging module, is the best improvement that affected the Accounts Payable operations in the early 2010s. It made my daily office work and customer service so much quicker, *in real time* and less frustrating for all parties involved in the Accounts Payable process.

Another system improvement, unless you are already using an ERP, is online paperless invoice processing. There may be separate web-based AP modules attached to the legacy system, which allow for the collection of AP information online and routing it to users-processors for their review and approval. After passing all the workflow authorization points, the AP information, i.e. payment vouchers, are uploaded into your central AP system.

The cost centers, various locations, offices, departments, colleges, and other reporting units submit all their AP information online and thus perform the AP data entry for you instead of completing non-system payment requests of various kinds. No paper is mailed around and, sometimes, lost; this is one of the most frustrating situations for any Accounts Payable professional to face: an invoice has been input, but a resulting check cannot be released, because there is no supporting documentation for it to be matched with. I used to joke through my tears in all such cases back in the dark ages of the paper-only days: *We never lose payment documents - we just sometime forget where we left them.*

I do suggest that, unless already in use, the processes of digitizing of all AP documentation and online AP invoices submission should be the next two system additions to your current accounting applications. I will discuss both processes later in the book.

# Internal controls and segregation of duties

The Accounts Payable department is the most closely scrutinized place within a company with regards to having documented and promulgated internal controls and segregation of duties documents. The Accounts Payable is the most fraud-tempting operation and must have clearly written internal control rules about the disbursement process. What is the purpose? Fraud prevention, first and foremost. Internal controls and segregation and duties' main goal is fraud prevention. The proper term for 'fraud' being stealing of money or tangible assets is 'misappropriation of assets'.

What is segregation of duties? The process involves assigning different people the responsibilities of authorizing transactions, recording transactions, and maintaining custody of assets. Segregation of duties is intended to reduce the opportunities to allow any person to be in a position to both perpetrate and conceal errors or fraud in the normal course of the person's duties (source: AU-C 315).

It is an old Accounts Payable adage that most fraud is committed by old-time employees. It is not true. Individuals who steal from their employer do not last long in any Accounts Payable position. But a lesser degree of fraud, such as cheating on reimbursement requests or buying disallowed items, is indeed committed most of times by the old-timers, since they keep the positions that allow to request and approve payments for goods, services, and T&Es; they are well connected with one another to have second party's *rubber-stamp* approval of payments or reimbursements.

Other reasons for establishing comprehensive internal controls and segregation of duties are appropriateness, correctness and budgetary compliance in the Accounts Payable process. It is easier to achieve a higher segregation of duties within a larger company. In a smaller company, many otherwise disallowed intertwined Accounts Payable functions may be performed by one person. But it has been my observation, based on experience, that there is much greater attention by business owners or managers to the cash disbursement process in small businesses, which (attention) compensates for the lack of the available segregation of duties.

Large business or small, it is prone to fraud and it is your duty to assure that all the reasonable and standard for the industry processes are in place to prevent fraud. Leaving aside purchasing department's internal controls and segregation of duties, I will begin to analyze the disbursement process with a vendor's invoice reaching the desks of the Accounts Payable department, physically via mail room or electronically, or third-party data-entry service provider.

The invoice must be approved and coded by the appropriate department. It is a good practice to have the payee providing (on the invoice) name or department within your company that had requested the invoiced goods or services. Or, the invoice must list a PO number. Some companies require all invoices to originate in a PO. The invoice is routed to the ordering department (physically or via the ERP workflow) and returned with the approval and accounting coding information. While the invoice is being approved by other department(s), the Accounts Payable must begin processing of payee's form W-9, in cases where the invoice is a first payment to the payee and set up of a new payee in AP system. Based on the number of licenses available for a software, departments can enter invoices themselves and thus initiate the payment process, my preference – give departments the power to start up the process instead of sending *ad lib* documents to the AP.

A person who creates new payees' AP records must not have the ability to input invoices into Accounts Payable system. It is advisable to have the purchasing department responsible for all new payee set up. This, however, is not possible for types of businesses, since the Accounts Payable department may be responsible for processing many other non-PO-based payments, such as utility, T&E reimbursements, honoraria, scholarship, and out-of-pocket reimbursements types.

Once approved by department, invoice is routed to the AP department and entered into the AP system for payment (unless already in AP system), which results in what is often called **payment request** (associated with purchase order) or **disbursement voucher** (from here on I will use one "catch all" term - *payment voucher*). Entering an invoice into the payment system may entail a two- or three-way matching. Two-way matching is often described as *Invoice to Receiving Document* matching. In real life, the two-way matching is most often *Invoice to Purchase Order (PO)* matching process. Note that AP terminology varies greatly – in Intacct lingo a 'payment request' is an open invoice selected for payment. Most of time 'payment request' is what intuition tells us – a request to issue a payment, which may take many different forms.

Three-way matching brings together invoice, receiving document, and purchase order (PO). Payee's name, items codes, quantity, and price (appears only on Invoice and PO) must agree on all three documents, which (documents) are generated in three different and duties-segregated departments and verified/matched in the Accounts Payable department.

The input payment voucher is now ready to be paid, based on the payment terms. The person who posts/pays open payment vouchers in the accounting system must not be involved in the invoice approval or input processes, printing of checks or pre/post-printing review of checks and bank-processing of EFTs and wire transfers.

A person responsible for checks printing must not be involved in invoices data entry process. Check processor obtains blank checks (which are stored in a safe) from a person outside of the Accounts Payable, but most likely a member of the same finance department. The custodian releases blank checks to the checks processor who documents the pre- and post- checks printing reconciliation based on the number of blank checks used (using blank checks stock numbers printed on blank checks (different than check numbers) and the printer report of the number of checks printed. After the checks are printed, the remaining blank checks and printer reports are returned to the auditor who reconciles the count of checks printed and printer reports, reviews and verifies the amounts paid and performs other checks processing controls (e.g. quality of printing, aligning of the *MICR [Magnetic Ink Character Recognition]* line, etc.). The printed checks are then released for the final review before mailing. Smaller companies simply print checks which are reviewed by the signor – the whole approval process may happen when checks get signed, it's not unusual.

The final review is still often administered after checks are printed; I advise to make all attempts to change the last review process *before* the printing of checks. This will eliminate voiding of erroneous checks and correcting of information on the checks' remittance portion (invoice numbers, remittance addresses). Voiding of checks is undesirable without questions and pre-payment review reduces checks voiding to, practically, zero. *Remittance Advice'* correction is wrong in a way that the Accounts Payable system will not have the corrected information within, such as adjusted on paper check invoice numbers (think of possibility of duplicate payment) or remittance address. Do the final review before payment vouchers are posited and paid.

The internal controls must have, as additional auditing requirements, second signing of checks, based on payment amount thresholds (e.g. audit review of all checks over $5000, higher level audit review and second signing of all checks over $10,000, department's head audit review of all checks over $50,000, executive level audit review of all checks over $1,000,000). The same auditing rules for issued payments must apply to the EFTs and wire transfers. ERP may have a built-in workflow that routes all high dollar payments for additional controller or CFO's review.

To avoid collusion, the invoice processing and payment vouchers data entry processing must be performed in the Accounts Payable department, but review and posting of batches to AP Ledger and GL posting performed in a separate area of the Finance department.

All ACH payments, which are more properly called the EFT payments (electronic fund transfer payments) are processed online, based on a system (AP) created bank file, which is generated by the Accounts Payable system after posting/paying of open EFT payment vouchers, performed separately from checks payment, based on the EFT payment method criteria. A bank file that is created must be unalterable and must be saved to a secure shared-drive with restricted access. An individual who posts and pays open payment vouchers must provide a report (payment register) to the person who uploads the bank file to the bank's website for banking processing through the Automated Clearing House (ACH). Different banks have different methods of processing the EFTs and it is, generally, a process of secure login, uploading of the AP system-generated (based on "paid" invoices) bank data file (XML or *flat-file* type) from a secure shared-drive, validating and releasing the file.

A person who posts and pays EFTs (selected based on the payment type – *EFT*) must know how to select the correct banking date, based on the bank holidays schedule and timing of weekends (see Bank Holiday Schedule for years 2019-2020 in the appendix). The general industry advice is to assign the payment date two business days ahead. Practically, you can assign as the payment date the next business date and have your EFT batch processed if you release it before 10 p.m. on the processing date. The cut-off time may vary depending on your bank. The process of (1) posting/paying EFTs, (2) uploading and validating the bank file and (3) releasing the EFT file should be handled by three different persons, or, at minimum, No. 3 must be processed separately from No's 1 & 2.

Bank transfers to foreign payees: given the difficulty of retrieving wired-out funds from foreign locations, this process should have a heightened level of segregation of duties and pre-processing review. A senior level manager should receive (AP-processed) wire transfer information (payment register, payment documentation, bank transmittal information) and input banking information manually in a designated place of the company's bank website. Another senior level manager should release all input wires.

The following are the areas of concerns when and should be addressed and documented (email train, not phone calls):

1. Alteration of documents and records
2. Missing approvals or signatures (on paper documents)
3. Excessive purchases with company purchase card
4. Missing invoice information such as address or items description
5. Discrepancies between PO and invoice (match-exception)
6. Vendor remittance the same as employee's address
7. Same remittance address for two or more vendors
8. Use of generally available email domains (e.g. Google.com) by vendors
9. System controls 'turned-off'
10. Frequent management overrides related to PO and invoice processing

The idea behind the internal controls and segregation of duties is to insert as many as reasonably possible verification levels in the cash disbursement process to prevent the possibility of monetary loss or fraud and assure an orderly cash disbursement process. To make the segregation of duties process more practical and less disruptive to the Accounts Payable operation, it is important to have the senior management's full support of the AP processes and controls to support a delays-free processing on every level and overall processing compliance.

I want to give you a couple of real life examples of what shape and form fraud can take. These two are examples of external attempts to gain illegal access to the company's funds by not too intelligent swindlers and scam artists. Good internal control must be designed to prevent both internal and external fraud attempts.

One day I received the following email from an unknown person (in the quote I only changed the names and kept the orthography and punctuation):

*To whom it may concern, I'm reaching out to let you know that I was sent over a check from a so called employer by the name of CCC Technologies. I was job-hunting when I was reached out by a Mr. David who's sent me the check over letting me know that I would need to money to buy required equipment for the position which I've been considered for. What made it weird was that David was more focused on when I'm going to be depositing the money than the "Offer". So, I smelled something fi hay which is why I'm reaching out to you guys. PS: The check was a (your company) check.*
*Sent from my iPhone*
*Name*

A copy of the check was enclosed. It was my company's check with the sender's name (as a payee) and a $9,000 figure typed on it. What made this case (and there've been similar others) so memorable is that my company's

10036 zip code typed on the check was 100306 – one digit too many for a valid US zip code. It was obviously a forged check, which the AP system records confirmed as well. I've had few more email exchanges with the person who was asking me in different ways, - What do you think of it? - wondering what he really wanted from me. Did he expect me to say: "The check looks so real! Please don't take it to a checks-cashing place – it will surely get cashed"? I had reasons to be convinced that the sender was trying to get more information of our checks processing. I restricted myself to advising that the check was a forge and that the person should contact the law-enforcement authorities to address the situation. It is a prudent approach when dealing with con artists to stick to a very formal, rigid, and succinct communication that includes the law enforcement as the only possible mean of resolving any illegal activity.

Another example is a common fraudulent request for a loan that I provide below with no modifications to the original email I received. I do get this kind of communications on a monthly basis and it's interesting to note similar patterns in all of them. I'm amazed how some people have the time to plan, customize and distribute these lame fraud attempts and what the 'success rate' is.

*Good Day,*

*Sorry for any inconvenience, but I'm in a terrible situation. I came down here to Moscow (Russia) for a program, last night on my way back to my hotel room I was robbed at gunpoint, my wallet and other valuables were stolen off me, leaving my passport and life safe. My luggage is still in custody of the hotel management pending when I make payment on outstanding bills I owe. I called my bank for a wire transfer but it has proven almost Impossible to operate my account from here as they made me understand international transactions take 7 working days to be effective which i can't wait. I need you to help me with a loan to pay my hotel bills and get my self home. I will reimburse you soon as I get back Home. I will appreciate whatever you can assist me with.*

*Let me know if you can be of help*

*All hopes on you.*                    *Thank you,*

*(Signed - real name of one of my company's managers who was not in any troubles in Moscow at the time.)*

# Policies and procedures

So much was said about the Accounts Payable policies and procedures. This may not sound like a primary concern for your Accounts Payable day in the office. But the Accounts Payable policies and procedures must be written, approved, and made available to all concerned before you can engage in any kind of Accounts Payable activity. They are the Accounts Payable department's road map, reference book and legal protection. The Accounts Payable department must have its policies and procedures periodically updated for any new situation or process that takes place in the course of the department's operations. All AP operations, processes or workflows must be described in the policies and procedures: how to create new payees, how to process invoices, how to pay invoices, how to store documentation, how to handle returned or lost payments, how to process forms 1099 and 1042-S, how often internal audits are conducted, how often employees must take vacations and who performs their duties at that time. And if a certain situation has never happened before, it must be brought up and analyzed, formalized, and incorporated into the Accounts Payable department's policies and procedures.

The policies and procedures serve many functions: they may be used as manuals and instructions on various AP processes in case there are absences or change of personnel. There must be no exclusive technical and procedural knowledge within your Accounts Payable department which is a possession of a single individual. The procedures must establish the frequency of payments processing; you must process checks, EFTs, wires, credit card payments according to a schedule with a very limited allowance for exceptions. Otherwise, the payment process becomes hectic and disruptive, based on ad-hoc requests for payment.

The approved written policies and procedures will protect you, when you have followed them, in adverse situations. You will be well served by them if requested to do something outside of the accepted processing routine; an improper "rush" demand or any other kind of request that will conflict with your professional consciousness, possibly requested to be done by a senior company employee. The policies and procedures will provide a legal protection in conflicting situations arising within or outside your department or company.

Policies and procedures must be updated any time a change in process arises and no less frequently than once every year. Current policies and procedures must be stored (besides your computer) on your department's shared-drive, company's (restricted access) website, and in printed format available to all authorized users.

# Accounts Payable Accounting

## Journal Entries

As an Accounts Payable professional, you should know the Accounts Payable inner-workings of what you are doing and how your activities affect the company's financial reports and operations. There are three basic financial statements used by any business: *Balance Sheet, Income Statement* and statement of *Cash Flows*. Accounts Payable data processing has an impact on all three statements, although decisions on (accounts) coding of payments are made most of the times outside of the Accounts Payable department. The usual Accounts Payable operational effect on the financial statements is increase of *expenses*, which reduces *cash* via *Accounts Payable* account. Keep in mind that the *normal* account balances are **debits** for balance sheet accounts (e.g. cash, prepaid expenses, machinery and equipment, raw materials, etc.), debits for Income Statement expense accounts (office supplies, travel expenses, rent expenses). And **credits** for Accounts Payable accounts (Accounts Payable, back-up tax payable, NRA tax payable, unclaimed checks payable, etc.) and revenues. Example:

*Payment voucher entry to an expense account and payment of it:*

**Expense**          X *(GL code provided by dept. or PO match)*
**Accounts Payable**          X *(General Accounts Payable)*

**Accounts Payable**          X *(Balance removed/zeroed out)*
**Cash**          X *(Reduced)*

This basic accounting journal entry, generated in the AP journal by payment voucher input, shows paid for *expense* (expired period cost with no future benefit) that is fully allocated to the current accounting period and presented on the Income Statement, which shows operating activities for a given period.

Another similar AP data entry, but different from the accounting stand point, is capital purchase processing or pre-payment of a future expense:

*Payment voucher entry to a Balance Sheet account:*
**Equipment (Machinery, Equipment)  X**
**Accounts Payable (system offset)              X**
Or
**Pre-Paid Expense (Current Date – "accrual")  X**
**Pre-Paid Expense (Future Date – Reversal)              X**
**Expense (Future Date – future expense)              X**
**Accounts Payable                                              X**

*Payment voucher payment:*
**Account Payable      X** *(Balance removed/zeroed out)*
**Cash                              X** *(Reduced)*

This kind of AP transaction appears on the Balance Sheet statement and usually has a larger dollar amount to pay. Information about the GL accounts (expenses or balance sheet accounts) to code invoices to, is provided by other departments or included on purchase orders (POs) (during the matching process, POs coding translates into AP accounting coding). It is a very good idea to understand the accounting principles of coding of invoices as opposed to the mechanical *keying-in* of the provided information.

Purchases coded to the *Balance Sheet* accounts are used over longer than one accounting period terms (as opposed to expenses, which appear on the *Income Statement (also called, P&L – Profit and Loss Statement)* and are attributable to one accounting period) and thus they are carried from period to period on the Balance Sheet until fully used (prepaid expenses), depreciated (equipment, machinery) or depleted (natural resources). You will present yourself in a good light if you are able to spot an error of payment coding provided to you by another department.

Let us review a more complicated Accounts Payable scenario now. In cases where you need to withhold taxes on a non-payroll payment (back up withholding, nonresident alien taxes) the following journal entry results, based on the tax rate assigned to the payee's payments (I will use dollar figures for better clarity of presentation):

*Payment voucher entry:*

| | | |
|---|---|---|
| **Expense** | **100** | |
| **Accounts Payable** | | **76** |
| **Accounts Payable/Back-up withholding (24%)** | | **24** |

*(Tax liability to the IRS)*

*Payment voucher payment:*

| | | |
|---|---|---|
| **Accounts Payable** | **76** | |
| **Cash** | | **76** |

*(Only $72 is paid to payee)*

You need to process another payment based on the 24% tax withheld to "clear" (pay) the IRS liability account via the regular payable account. This is done periodically according to the IRS' requirements based on the total amount of taxes withheld. Payments to the IRS are made via the EFTPS (electronic federal tax payment system) or wire transfer.

An AP entry resulting from such payment first reduces/zeroes out the IRS liability account (when you enter a payable entry with debit to *AP/Back Up Withholding* account and second, reduces the cash account reverses the *Accounts Payable* account balance.

*Payment voucher entry*:
**Accounts Payable/Back-up withholding** *(cleared)* **24**
*(Removes the tax liability to the IRS)*
**Accounts Payable**                                                    **24**

*Payment voucher payment (to issue payment due to the IRS):*
**Accounts Payable**          **24**
**Cash**                                      **24**

Payroll tax liability accounts balances (FICA, Federal or State taxes) which originate in the Payroll department, are often cleared (paid) by the Accounts Payable department.
*Payment voucher entry:*
**Federal Tax Withholding** *(to zero out/pay)*  **1,234**
*(Last payroll processing created new balances in tax liability accounts)*
**Accounts Payable**                                          **1,234**
*Payment voucher payment:*
**Accounts Payable**                      **1,234**
**Cash**                                              **1,234**

When you enter a *Credit Memo*, a negative, or credit side expense, is entered. A credit memo cannot be used until there is a sufficient amount in regular/debit invoices accumulates to pay (to the same payee), which exceeds the credit memo's amount. If there are no invoices to apply against the credit memo, the payee should be contacted with a request for refund.

*Credit memo entry*:

**Expense**                      **X** *(Credit-reduced)*
**Accounts Payable**    **X** *(Debit-reduced)*

Another journal entries example will touch on yet another accounting concept. Let us say that you have a telecommunication company's $1000 invoice to pay: $500 applies to the current month and $500 for the next month. A correct journal entry is to *expense* $500 and code the next month's portion to the balance sheet's *prepaid expense* account. This is called *full accrual accounting* – current expenses are matched with current revenues (on Income Statement (I/S)), and future expenses are *accrued* (coded to Balance Sheet (B/S) accounts) to be matched with future revenues to calculate income accurately.

| | | |
|---|---|---|
| **Prepaid Expense (B/S)** | **500** | |
| **Expense (I/S)** | **500** | |
| **Accounts Payable (B/S)** | | **1000** |

Why then the same kind of two accounting periods invoice is fully *expended* by a different business – a municipal office or a city hospital? Governmental and not-for-profit businesses have other than income generation purposes for existing. They are in business to serve the public and assure fiscal and operational compliance. Therefore, all disbursement amounts are *expended* fully in the current period – there is no income to calculate and be concerned with. Below is an example of a city hospital's purchasing of a cat-scan machine to be used over the next ten years. There is no Income Statement in the not-for-profit accounting or governmental accounting:

**Expenditure**            **100,000**

**Accounts Payable**                 **100,000**

Governmental and other fund accounting is based on the *modified accrual basis of accounting* that aims to assure operational and fiscal accountability rather than accurate income computation, which is the case with the commercial *full accrual accounting*. Modified accrual basis is a blend of accrual and cash basis of accounting – all Accounts Payable transactions are expended in the current fiscal period. Even purchasing of very expensive equipment (e.g. a fire track) is fully expended in the current fiscal period. However, all capital assets are coded as such, amortized and presented on the Balance Sheet statement.

These are the basic accounting transactions behind most of the work that is done in the Accounts Payable department. There are purchase orders (POs) and associated encumbrances (in the not-for-profit and governmental accounting), corporate cards accounting operations and nonresident alien AP processes and related accounting journal entries, which I will talk about in later chapters. There isn't much of elaborate accounting in the Accounts

Payable operations; the primary attention is given to managing of the workflow and adherence to the AP policies and procedures, vendors' relations, maintaining internal controls and assuring internal cooperation, which actually makes for a more exciting AP work day than the advanced corporate "bean-counting".

# You need to pay an invoice: step one – form W-9

You need to pay an invoice. You have the invoice on your desk with all the necessary authorizing signatures and accounts coding, or you have it in the electronic format in your e-Accounts Payable system. This is your first invoice from the payee, and before doing anything else you must obtain a properly completed form W-9 (with exceptions) from every new payee that you make payments to (I frequently use the word *payee* and not *vendor* since it is an all-inclusive, businesses and individuals, AP term). I make exceptions on W-9 requirement for governmental, nonprofit, and reimbursement payees.

Every new payee must furnish form W-9 to you; true or false? It is both, true and false. A US business or person must supply form W-9 (the current W-9 was updated by the IRS in October 2018). *A foreign payee cannot sign form W-9* and the most recent version of form W-9 has an important clarification about the W-9 filing requirement, asking to certify that the person or business, named on the W-9, is a "US citizen or other US person" and requiring a "Signature of US person".

Further in the W-9 instructions you can find the following: "If you are a foreign person, do not use Form W-9". Why can't a foreign person who possesses a valid US social security or other tax ID number sign the W-9? Paying foreign payees requires a statutory 30% tax withholding, unless one of the IRS tax exemption codes can be applied (more about paying a foreign businesses or persons in later chapters). Not determining a proper residency status may cause tax liability, which adds up close to half of the payment amount if processed improperly under the US residency assumption.

*Example:*

A payment of $100 was made, with an assumption of US tax residency based on completed form W-9. 30% tax was not applied. *Gross up* the amount to what it should have been to issue a net $100 check after withholding 30% tax. $100 / 70% (100/0.7) = 143

Back-tax owed to the IRS is $43 plus fees and penalties.

Keep in mind that many times, form W-9 is completed by foreign businesses or individuals that have valid US tax IDs. This is improper unless you can establish that such businesses or individuals are US tax residents.

For all domestic businesses and persons, form W-9 has two options for the name – *Name* (as shown on your income tax return) and *Business Name* (that is, DBA – *Doing Business As*, not the tax name). This may be confusing for many; *Business Name/DBA* may be the same as the *Tax Name*. But many times, *Business Name/DBA* is not the *Tax Name* and since there is no tax ID for *Business Name/DBA*, you will end up supplying technically incorrect information (if 1099 filing is required) to the IRS. The IRS will ask you to correct this discrepancy by mailing you Notice CP-2100.

It is very important to understand, based on the completed form W-9, what form of business ownership the payee is formed under (Corporation, Partnership treated as Corporation, Partnership treated as Partnership, Individual

Sole Proprietorship). The appropriate box must be checked. If the *Individual/sole proprietor* box is checked, a person's name must appear in the *Name* box, and a social security number provided. For all other forms of business ownership, the *EIN* (employer identification number) must be provided. A *Limited Liability Company (LLC)* may be treated for tax purposes as a 'disregarded entity', corporation or partnership. This is an important distinction to keep in mind, since the corporate treatment does not require you to file form 1099; corporate exemption does not apply to medical and legal LLC/corporations and corporations (Inc.) LLC's Partnership treatment does require the 1099 filing. This is a fine point to understand and apply. I believe that given the importance of practical W-9/1099 corporation-partnership classification, it is worth a more in-depth analysis. Nathan M. Bisk, JD, CPA provides an excellent description of this partnership-corporation selection in his books "CPA Review: Regulations":

*Under the 'check-the-box' regulations, an eligible entity may elect its classification for federal tax purposes. An eligible entity is an entity that does not meet the definition of a corporation under the regulations, and is not a single owner entity, trust, or otherwise subject to special treatment under the IRC. If the entity fails to elect a classification, the regulations provide a default classification. The use is broader than the common law meaning and may include groups not commonly called partnerships. (a) A partnership is a syndicate, group, pool, joint venture, or other unincorporated entity through which a business is carried on, and which is not a corporation, trust, or estate. (b) Mere co-ownership of property is not a partnership. However, if the entity provides services in conjunction with the use of the property by the lessee or licensee, the entity may be characterized as a partnership. (c) Limited partnerships are subject to the same rules as general partnerships. (d) Limited liability entities may be classified for federal tax purposes as either corporations or partnerships. Limited liability companies (LLC), limited liability partnerships (LLP), professional limited liability companies, etc. are frequently designed to take advantage of the pass-through tax status of partnerships and limited legal liability of corporations, but the partnership tax status is not automatic. Unless a limited liability entity meets conditions that require it to be taxed as a corporation or it elects to be so treated, it is treated as a partnership for tax purposes.*

Governmental, not-for-profit, and other tax-exempt businesses and organizations must enter the *Exempt Payee Code* if one is available from the list of codes found in the instructions for form W-9 revised in October 2018. [Note that 501(c)(3) not-for-profit organizations fall within Section 501(a), Exemption Code 1].

The following codes identify payees that are exempt from backup withholding: 1 - An organization exempt from tax under section 501(a), any IRA, or a custodial account under section 403(b)(7) if the account satisfies the requirements of section 401(f)(2). 2 - The United States or any of its agencies or instrumentalities. 3 - A state, the District of Columbia, a possession of the United States, or any of their political subdivisions or instrumentalities. 4 - A foreign government or any of its political subdivisions, agencies, or instrumentalities. 5 – A corporation. 6 – A dealer in securities or commodities required to register in the

United States, the District of Columbia, or a possession of the United States. 7 - A futures commission merchant registered with the Commodity Futures Trading Commission. 8 - A real estate investment trust. 9 - An entity registered at all times during the tax year under the Investment Company Act of 1940. 10 - A common trust fund operated by a bank under section 584(a). 11 - A financial institution. 12 - A middleman known in the investment community as a nominee or custodian. 13 - A trust exempt from tax under section 664 or described in section 4947.

There are boxes on form W-9 for address, account number and signature. Having properly completed form W-9 on file fulfills your responsibility to collect the payees' tax ID and business ownership status information. You may find it useful to register with *Dan & Bradstreet* services (http://www.dnb.com) to validate companies' names and validate other relevant for your Accounts Payable purposes information.

It is a good practice to have an internally-created *New Payee Questionnaire,* to be completed by all new payees. This form may have additional payee information, such as contact names, phone numbers, fax numbers, email addresses, company website, remittance address(s), bank account information (ABA/routing number, account number, account name, accounts receivable contact information and email address). Bank account information may be provided on the payee's dedicated form and supported by a copy of the vendor's check usually marked "void". The *New Payee Questionnaire* must require immigration status, tax residency, and foreign business or individual's US tax ID information and certification, something that form W-9 is not designed to do.

Failure to furnish form W-9 to you triggers back-up withholding at the rate of 24% (for years 2018-2025). The back-up withholding is reported to the IRS on form *945* and to the payee on form 1099-MISC. I have not processed one such 24% withholding in my career, although had set up many payees for back-up tax withholding. All payees comply with your W-9 requirement once you explain what the noncompliance may trigger: back-up taxes and, possibly, IRS audit.

Foreign persons cannot by IRS regulation sign form W-9. What form do the temporary residents sign to certify their possession of a US tax ID number? You may often hear the advice to "sign the appropriate form W-8". This is wrong. There may be no appropriate form for a temporary visitor to sign, and second, those forms W-8xxx (W-8BEN, W-8BEN-E, W-8CE, W-8ECI, W-8IMY) are not used for the purpose of collection nonresident alien tax IDs. Those forms serve other purposes: W-8BEN (the form was updated by the IRS in July 2017, the new form W-8BEN-E is now used by business entities) to certify foreign status of beneficial owner for United States tax withholding, W-ECI to certify foreign person's claim that the income is effectively connected with the conduct of a trade or business in the United States. The bottom line is that any form W-8xxx (W-8 has been out of use for more than twelve years) cannot be used with the temporary residents instead of form W-9. The AP professionals who suggest using form W-8 just do not know enough about the nonresident alien taxation. Also, allowing the foreign persons to use forms W-8xxx may give them a false impression that they may be eligible to certain US tax benefits when, in fact, they are not. You can read more about forms W-8xxx on the following IRS web-page:

http://apps.irs.gov/app/picklist/list/formsInstructions.html?value=w-8&criteria=formNumber

If you need to collect a US tax ID from a temporary US visitor, use your internally developed *New Payee Questionnaire*, on which you should also ask about the visa status and other nonresident alien-related questions (history of priory US visits, copies of various immigration forms (visa, I94, DS2019, I20, etc.).

The most recent updates to form W-9 were officiated in October 2018 to reflect the final amendment to the Income Tax Regulations commonly known as the Foreign Tax Compliance Act, or FATCA. FATCA targets tax noncompliance by US taxpayers with foreign accounts; the focus is on reporting by US taxpayers their foreign financial accounts and offshore assets and reporting by foreign financial institutions money accounts held by US taxpayers or foreign entities in which US taxpayers hold a substantial ownership interest. FATCA is designed to better track worldwide income of US persons by requiring much greater information sharing by the US and foreign financial institutions. Certain payees are exempt from FATCA reporting. There is a list of codes (A through M) provided in the instructions to form W-9.

The new W-9 form has the former "Exempt Payee" section, which was used on all previous forms W-9 by not-for-profit organizations, United States agencies, etc., renamed "Exemptions" and separated into two sub-sections: the familiar "Exempt payee code" and the new *Exemption from FATCA reporting code*". The completion of FATCA exemption code section does not affect your company's new payees or 1099 processing unless your company makes payments to financial institutions which are required to report income payments to account holders who are US persons under FATCA regulations.

| Form **W-9**<br>(Rev. October 2018)<br>Department of the Treasury<br>Internal Revenue Service | **Request for Taxpayer**<br>**Identification Number and Certification**<br>▶ Go to *www.irs.gov/FormW9* for instructions and the latest information. | Give Form to the requester. Do not send to the IRS. |
|---|---|---|

1 Name (as shown on your income tax return). Name is required on this line; do not leave this line blank.

2 Business name/disregarded entity name, if different from above

3 Check appropriate box for federal tax classification of the person whose name is entered on line 1. Check only **one** of the following seven boxes.

☐ Individual/sole proprietor or single-member LLC  ☐ C Corporation  ☐ S Corporation  ☐ Partnership  ☐ Trust/estate

☐ Limited liability company. Enter the tax classification (C=C corporation, S=S corporation, P=Partnership) ▶ _____

Note: Check the appropriate box in the line above for the tax classification of this single-member owner. Do not check LLC if the LLC is classified as a single-member LLC that is disregarded from the owner unless the owner of the LLC is another LLC that is **not** disregarded from the owner for U.S. federal tax purposes. Otherwise, a single-member LLC that is disregarded from the owner should check the appropriate box for the tax classification of its owner.

☐ Other (see instructions) ▶

4 Exemptions (codes apply only to certain entities, not individuals; see instructions on page 3):

Exempt payee code (if any) _____

Exemption from FATCA reporting code (if any) _____

*(Applies to accounts maintained outside the U.S.)*

5 Address (number, street, and apt. or suite no.) See instructions.

Requester's name and address (optional)

6 City, state, and ZIP code

7 List account number(s) here (optional)

**Part I** Taxpayer Identification Number (TIN)

Enter your TIN in the appropriate box. The TIN provided must match the name given on line 1 to avoid backup withholding. For individuals, this is generally your social security number (SSN). However, for a resident alien, sole proprietor, or disregarded entity, see the instructions for Part I, later. For other entities, it is your employer identification number (EIN). If you do not have a number, see *How to get a TIN*, later.

Note: If the account is in more than one name, see the instructions for line 1. Also see *What Name and Number To Give the Requester* for guidelines on whose number to enter.

Social security number

or

Employer identification number

**Part II** Certification

Under penalties of perjury, I certify that:

1. The number shown on this form is my correct taxpayer identification number (or I am waiting for a number to be issued to me); and

2. I am not subject to backup withholding because: (a) I am exempt from backup withholding, or (b) I have not been notified by the Internal Revenue Service (IRS) that I am subject to backup withholding as a result of a failure to report all interest or dividends, or (c) the IRS has notified me that I am no longer subject to backup withholding; and

3. I am a U.S. citizen or other U.S. person (defined below); and

4. The FATCA code(s) entered on this form (if any) indicating that I am exempt from FATCA reporting is correct.

Certification instructions. You must cross out item 2 above if you have been notified by the IRS that you are currently subject to backup withholding because you have failed to report all interest and dividends on your tax return. For real estate transactions, item 2 does not apply. For mortgage interest paid, acquisition or abandonment of secured property, cancellation of debt, contributions to an individual retirement arrangement (IRA), and generally, payments other than interest and dividends, you are not required to sign the certification, but you must provide your correct TIN. See the instructions for Part II, later.

| Sign Here | Signature of U.S. person ▶ | Date ▶ |
|---|---|---|

*(Form W-9, last revised in October, 2018)*

## SSNs, ITINs, EINs, and Other Numbers

When you receive information of a tax ID number on form W-9, you accept it *in good faith*. But, as an Accounts Payable professional, you know that all US tax ID numbers have nine digits. If there are less than nine, you should inquire further and not process the W-9 information. A social security number (*SSN*) is assigned by the Social Security Administration to US persons and, often times, to foreign persons (http://www.ssa.gov/online/ss-5.pdf ). **Possession of a valid Social Security Number does not establish or indicate US citizenship or tax residency status of an individual**.

*ITIN* is an individual taxpayer identification number; it is issued by the IRS upon completion of form *W7 - Application for Individual Taxpayer Identification Number (http://www.irs.gov/pub/irs-pdf/fw7.pdf)*. It is more proper for a foreign person to have the ITIN than the SSN. The ITIN always begins with number "9" and has numbers "7" or "8" in the fourth place. You are not required to know this or verify form W-9 or other tax ID source information based on this rule. But, if you spot possible errors, based on this information, and inquire further to correct the tax ID provided, you will improve the quality of your 1099 and 1042-S reporting and avoid possible IRS inquiry about wrong tax IDs later on. Both SSN (issued by the Social Security Administration) and ITIN (issued by the IRS) are structured in the 3-2-4 format (xxx-xx-xxxx).

*EIN* stands for the Employee Identification Number. The EIN is issued by the IRS and is structured in the 2-7 format (xx-xxxxxxx) (http://www.irs.gov/pub/irs-pdf/fss4.pdf ). Here too, you must be experienced enough to notice that different states (especially the state where your company operates) have identical first two-digit numbers of the EINs. A deviation from the rule should not trigger further inquiry once a payee has properly completed and signed form W-9, but may call for your own action to verify the correctness of the information.

The best process to verify US tax IDs is to register with the IRS for the online TIN Matching using the following web-address:

https://la1.www4.irs.gov/e-services/Registration/Reg_Online/Reg_RegisterUserForm

The online IRS TIN matching is an immensely useful tool for any Accounts Payable professional. There are just too many scenarios when you want to check the accuracy of tax IDs on file. The service *does not* allow to find out what tax ID for the name or name for the tax ID are, but to verify the correctness of "tax ID / name" combination information that you have. Too many attempts to verify similar information will lock your user account and require a phone call to the IRS or registering online to have the account re-activated (you will need to wait for a letter from the IRS in the mail with a new activation code).

Once I had a case when a person, who was reported to me by the IRS on form CP-2100 as not having a correct tax name or ID, would provide the same name and tax ID again and again. I tried to validate it using the IRS TIN matching system, but would always get the same erroneous results: *TIN and Name combination does not match IRS records*. I did not want to report a very significant current year's dollar amount paid to the individual again using the same tax ID, having been made aware of the past discrepancy. I requested to see the person's SSN card and lo and behold, his last name was a two-part last name and the person was only using the second part, thinking that the first part of the last name is the middle name. It looked like this – John Paul Jones, with the *Paul Jones* being the official last name, while the person always used Jones as the only last name (intentionally or not, at least with my organization). I had matched the first name and the two-part last name to the same SSN successfully using the IRS TIN matching system, and was able to untangle the mystery thanks to my access to the IRS's TIN matching tool.

Any foreign tax ID cannot be accepted or used (other than as reference) for your US operations and tax reporting. One notable exception under the new FATCA-related regulations is the permission to process tax treaties with foreign tax IDs. *There will be instances when you accept reportable to the IRS payees with no US tax IDs into your Accounts Payable system.* It is normal to pay a foreign service-provider in the US, who earned fees for services and got paid without possessing a US tax ID. Such payment must be taxed at a 30% rate and reported to the IRS on form 1042-S with an affidavit that certifies your inability to obtain a tax ID. The IRS will accept your reporting only when you support it by the withheld and remitted taxes; otherwise (without taxes applied) it will highlight your non-compliance and assess past due taxes, fees and penalties.

Most of today's Accounts Payable systems validate the tax numbers' 9-digits format, but not any other rules and standards built into the SSNs, ITINs and EINs structure. You can perform the analytical test yourself, based on the publicly available information. Social Security numbers are structured as follows:

i. *The first three digits indicate the State where the Social Security Number was issued.*
ii. *The two middle digits approximate year when the Social Security Number was issued. "00" was never used.*
iii. *The last four digits is a sequential number.*

The following are the first three-digit ranges assigned by state where SSN was issued:

| | |
|---|---|
| **001-003...** | **New Hampshire** |
| **004-007...** | **Maine** |
| **008-009...** | **Vermont** |
| **010-034...** | **Massachusetts** |
| **035-039...** | **Rhode Island** |
| **040-049...** | **Connecticut** |
| **050-134...** | **New York** |
| **135-158...** | **New Jersey** |
| **159-211...** | **Pennsylvania** |
| **212-220...** | **Maryland** |
| **221-222...** | **Delaware** |
| **223-231...** | **Virginia & West Virginia** |
| **232-232...** | **North Carolina** |
| **233-236...** | **Foreign nationals** |
| **237-246...** | **North Carolina** |
| **247-251...** | **South Carolina** |
| **252-260...** | **Georgia** |
| **267-267...** | **Florida** |
| **268-302...** | **Ohio** |
| **303-317...** | **Indiana** |
| **318-361...** | **Illinois** |

| | |
|---|---|
| 362-386... | Michigan |
| 387-399... | Wisconsin |
| 400-407... | Kentucky |
| 408-415... | Tennessee |
| 416-424... | Alabama |
| 425-428... | Mississippi |
| 429-432... | Arkansas |
| 433-439... | Louisiana |
| 440-448... | Oklahoma |
| 449-467... | Texas |
| 468-477... | Minnesota |
| 478-485... | Iowa |
| 486-500... | Missouri |
| 501-502... | North Dakota |
| 503-504... | South Dakota |
| 505-508... | Nebraska |
| 509-515... | Kansas |
| 516-517... | Montana |
| 518-519... | Idaho |
| 520-520... | Wyoming |
| 521-524... | Colorado |
| 525-525... | New Mexico |
| 526-527... | Arizona |
| 528-529... | Utah |
| 530-530... | Nevada |
| 531-539... | Washington |
| 540-544... | Oregon |
| 545-573... | California |
| 574-574... | Alaska |
| 575-576... | Hawaii |
| 577-579... | Washington, D.C. |
| 580-584... | Puerto Rico & Virgin Islands |
| 585-585... | New Mexico |
| 586-586... | Guam, Samoa & Pacific Territories |
| 587-588... | Mississippi |
| 589-595... | Florida |

| | |
|---|---|
| **596-599...** | **Foreign nationals (old issues)** |
| **600-601...** | **Arizona** |
| **602-626...** | **California** |
| **627-699...** | **Foreign nationals (new issues)** |
| **700-728...** | **R-type Retirement** |
| **729-999...** | **Other purposes** |

Individual Taxpayer ID Numbers, ITINs (issued by the IRS) have the following format, no matter where or when they were issued:

**9xx-7x-xxxx**

**9xx-8x-xxxx**

## New Payee Set Up

Now that you have your policies and procedures written up and approved or updated, forms W-9 submitted by the payees, you can begin processing invoices (this is highly theoretical, since it's unlikely that you begin your company's AP operation from scratch). To create a new payee, you need to submit the *New Payee Setup* requisition form to a person who, according to the segregation of duties concept, has no other Accounts Payable function but the creation of a new payees. You must have an established payee IDs creating system which is logical, understood and consistent. The AP system may assign vendor IDs in numerical sequence, which is my preferred method of assigning IDs to payees. All modern Ap systems allow for pay IDs sequencing.

Otherwise, I believe that using a combination of letters and numbers is the next best system to unitize, where technically feasible. Using letters gives you more room to create new payees in the years to come, since there are 26 letters and only 10 numbers (0 to 9) to use in each place. If you are using a "numbers only" payee IDs system, it assigns the next sequential number for each new payee (six digits payee ID format will allow for 1M less 1, i.e. 999,999 vendor IDs to create. Think if this will be enough). With the alpha-numerical system, I advise to use letters in the first eight places and digits in the remaining two. Following is an example of the alpha-numerical system:

Payee name: **First American Brewing Company, Inc.**
Payee ID: **FIRSTAME01**

Payee name: **First American Consulting, LLC**

Payee ID: **FIRSTAME02**

You may find it a good practice to eliminate the connecting conjunction "and" (or "&") from the payee ID structure:

Payee name: **Levi and Struk, LLP**
Payee ID:   **LEVISTRO01**

There may be certain Accounts Payable reports, depending on the system that your company is using, where only vendor IDs are showing against other AP data. It is impossible, using the "numbers only" payee IDs, to have a quick understanding of the payees' names without translating the payees' IDs into the names first. It does save time during AP data entry as well, to understand which payee is being processed by just looking at the payee's ID.

A system for coding individual names may be as following: use the last name in places 1-7, first initial in place 8, sequential digits in places 9-10. Use the Xs for short names or use remaining spaces for the first letters of the first name:

Payee Name: **Denny Laine**
Payee ID:   **LAINEDXX01 or LAINEDEN01**

Shorten the last name if it is longer than 7 characters:

Payee Name: **Ashley Poindexter**
Payee ID:   **POINDEXA01**

Never allow for space(s) in the payee IDs:

Payee name: **Jazz Van Burren**

Vendor ID: **VANBURRJ01**

If business name is different from legal name, use the name under which the business normally operates and shows in its invoices. Add a different tax name, if necessary, in the *Legal* or *1099 Name* field in the payee set up. The legal name may be very unfamiliar to people involved in the Accounts Payable process – making the legal name the main search criteria may delay the search process or, worse, lead to an assumption that the payee is a new payee, which results in (attempt of) duplicate payee creation. Duplicate payee creation is one of the big no-no's in the Accounts Payable. One way to avoid this is to run duplicate payees tax ID report or "flag and stop" new payee tax IDs entry (upon new payee creation) as a duplication of the existing one.

A payee may have a number of different "remit-to" addresses. Usually, these multiple-remittance addresses payees are large corporations, such as AT&T, Verizon or various IRSs processing centers. Large companies process different locations' invoice at their different offices around the US. What is more critical is to realize, where applicable, that "a new remittance address" for identically sounding business name is not a new remittance address at all, but the remittance address for a different business altogether, possibly a *franchise* which operates under the same brand name. Franchise is a right to operation under a well-known business name, such as McDonald's, with each franchisee being a separate business for all other purposes: *"McDonald's continues to be recognized as a premier franchising company around the world. More than 80% of our restaurants worldwide are owned and operated by our*

*Franchisees" (quoted from the McDonald Co. website, below).*
http://www.aboutmcdonalds.com/mcd/franchising.html

Again, form W-9 provides the information about all the critical data in this less than clear situation, such as Business Name and tax ID number.

The default remittance address should be the most frequently used remittance address. Any remittance address that is no longer used should be inactivated, but not deleted or overwritten with a new address, to preserve the historic records in the Accounts Payable system.

Any update to the payees' information must be performed by someone independent from the Accounts Payable cycle, preferably using an internally-created Payee Change Form (this form may be combined with a New Payee Setup form) supported by documents that justify the request for change. There must be another person within the Controller's or Finance department who is familiar with payee setup or change process and who can perform the task in the absence of the primary responsible individual.

There may be an added layer of internal controls when any change made to the payees or payees' addresses automatically puts such payees on hold and must be reviewed and approved in order for the payees to become active again.

Bank information is entered in the payee's remittance address or in a separate payee EFT/ACH setup module. It is crucial to obtain correct vendor's banking information from an authorized individual within the vendor's company and have the banking information correctly entered into the AP system. Pay attention to the Account Name, ABA (American Banking Association) number (same as *Routing Number*; always a nine-digit number used only for domestic EFTs), account number, accounts receivable email (most of times a general accounts receivable email address, such as AR_remittances@Business.com). You can validate the ABA numbers on the website address provided below. A sound advice is the practice to test all new bank accounts by remitting a penny and get a feedback from the payee – you may think this is an overkill, but SAP Concur always does this to validate new direct deposit accounts.

http://www.routingnumbers.org/bank_routing_number_0210 00021.html

For a quicker and less detailed search result, one can just type the ABA number in the web address bar (https://) of your web browser and hit "enter" – Google's Chrome is my personal preference for any search right off the web address field. For individuals, the best bank account collection method is a copy of personal check marked VOID.

The order of segregation of duties is without a doubt best handled by the ERPs, which generate immediate email alerts for the next person to act on any change or creation of a new payee. ERPs have audit trails that reflect all payee modification actions. With the legacy accounting systems still in wide use, paper forms are filed and routed from individual to individual; reports must be run periodically to find out any possible *on-hold* situations and emails or phone calls initiated to remind responsible individuals to do their part in the process.

A new payee initial setup information and supporting documents (form W-9, *New Payee Questionnaire*) must be digitized and accessible in the *Payees/Vendors* records for future references and verifications.

## Invoices, invoices

Invoice number: why does it matter so much if you know that you are paying the correct dollar amount to the correct payee? It is not important when processing a travel reimbursement (and there is no genuine invoice number to begin with) to a person who expects to receive this payment. Other than that, the invoice numbers processing is crucial to efficient and accurate operations of the Accounts Payable department (and its counterpart, vendor's accounts receivable).

The invoice number communicates to the payee, who may be receiving thousands of payments daily, which exact invoice is being paid, properly apply your payment and eliminate a possible disruption of services by putting your company on credit hold. Invoice numbers for payments made are supplied on paper checks remittance stub, or embedded within EFTs transmission bank files as addenda records (and with EFT email notifications, generated by the AP system or manually). The EFT addenda records (invoice numbers) appear on the vendors' daily cash logs, but informational transfer integrity varies from bank to bank, so EFT-email alert is often crucial in the process.

Many vendors still ask to have the remittance portion of invoices detached and sent along with checks. Do not do it – we did it back in the 20th century. First, it takes time to detach and stuff in envelopes those remittance portions of invoice. It is not possible to do this "bottom-portion-of-invoice mailing" with the EFTs, which are replacing the check payment method everywhere. And this 'tear off' business is not needed since most vendors use an orderly for all company billings *unique number* invoicing system and your Accounts Payable department is entering and verifying the correctness of the invoice numbers (this accuracy is not needed when vendors' feeds are uploaded into your AP system since it is the payee's billing system that "talks" directly to your AP system). **Vendors' accounts receivable application of your remittances must be sufficient based on just two criteria: invoice and/or account number and payment amount.**

I had a very interesting experience with a rather large vendor whose invoices began to be flagged by my AP system as duplicate invoices. When I researched, I found out that the numbers on invoices sent to my Accounts Payable department now, had been paid many years ago. I called the vendor and was informed that the company was *recycling* the invoice numbers. Vendors' recycling of invoice numbers is void of any logic; it is a bad practice still used by some large American corporations. A mere eight digits' invoice number format allows for one hundred million (less one) invoice numbers made of the numbers alone. Invoice numbers that contain letters allow for even greater invoice numbers data bank (as stated earlier, there are 26 letters versus 10 digits to use in one place – Dell Direct and UPS use this system).

Vendors should know not to use letters that may be confused for numbers (O or I), just like it is the case with the Vehicle Identification Numbers (VIN) used by car manufacturers. The repetitive use of invoice numbers causes confusion and delays in the AP processing; the Accounts Payable processor must assure that the repeated invoice number is not a duplicate invoicing and then *modify* the new, but reused, invoice number, which is a bad practice. Recycling of invoice numbers also creates uploading issues (rightfully so) with the e-invoices submission for vendors who employ the recycling invoice numbers practice.

When communicating invoice numbers (or other codes) to vendors and business counter-parts, you can use either the *NATO* or *English* phonetic alphabet listed below:

| Letter | NATO | English |
|--------|------|---------|
| A | Alfa | Andrew |
| B | Bravo | Benjamin |
| C | Charlie | Charlie |
| D | Delta | David |
| E | Echo | Edward |
| F | Foxtrot | Fredrick |
| G | Golf | George |
| H | Hotel | Harry |
| I | India | Isaac |
| J | Juliet | Jack |
| K | Kilo | King |
| L | Lima | Lucy |
| M | Mike | Mary |
| N | November | Nelli |
| O | Oscar | Oliver |
| P | Papa | Peter |
| Q | Quebec | Queenie |
| R | Romeo | Robert |
| S | Sierra | Sugar |
| T | Tango | Tommy |
| U | Uniform | Uncle |
| V | Victor | Victor |
| W | Whiskey | William |
| X | X-ray | Xmas |

| Y | Yankee | Yellow |
|---|--------|--------|
| Z | Zulu | Zebra |

It is very important to receive accurate invoice information from vendors and feed it back unaltered to vendors along with payments. Invoice numbers must be entered _exactly_ as they appear on vendors' invoices (some vendors use space in their invoice numbers. You need to follow, but this is not a good invoicing practice). **I strongly believe that vendors' invoice numbers modification must be avoided during payment vouchers entry into the Accounts Payable system.**

If you delete leading zeroes in the invoice number, it will shorten vendors' invoices by one, two, three or more characters, thus making your open payment vouchers or history reports looking awkward due to the misaligning of the invoice numbers' lengths. Any dash, underscore, or text (e.g. _INV_) that appears in vendors' invoices as "invoice number", must be preserved. Following of this invoicing system accurately and consistently will allow for immediate AR payment applications, prevent time-consuming inquiries from vendors' accounts receivable departments or requests to provide your customer account number as a reference to each payment and eliminate credit hold issues with your vendors.

What do we do when there is no invoice number on invoice? Some examples may be telephone company bills, recurring rental and lease payments, T&E payments, payments to the IRS. Procedures for assigning "invoice numbers" (where invoice numbers do not exist) must be developed, documented in the AP guidelines, and followed uniformly by all involved the AP process. These invoice-assignment rules must be literally *set in stone* to prevent duplicate invoice payments and to allow for better understanding of the AP-system information. Some disagree with the idea of assigning internally invoice numbers where they do not exist, preferring to see blank fields instead of internally created invoice numbers, and provide description of payment in the payment reference. Given that the six basic criteria of the Accounts Payable information used in AP reports are *(1) payee name, (2) invoice number, (3) invoice amount, (4) invoice date, (5) payment number and (6) payment date,* and *reference information* is not one of the basic AP data, it is a much better practice to have invoice numbers generated internally than leaving "invoice number" fields blank. See a sample of a payee's payment history below and decide for yourself:

(Invoice numbers assigned internally)

John Lee – NRA Conf., LasVegas/NV, Oct'17 - 1,000.00 – 110116 – CK123456 - 111016
John Lee – Concur lunch meeting // Oct'17   - 156.45 –   120516 – EFT4564 -  121916
John Lee – New Year party suppl//Dec'17     -  43.50 -    122516 -  EFT4670 – 123016

(No invoice numbers assigned)

John Lee – (                    ) - 1,000.00 –  110116 – CK123456 - 111016
John Lee – (                    ) -  156.45 –  120516 – EFT4564 -  121916
John Lee – (                    ) -   43.50 -  122516 -  EFT4670 –  123016

You will never create invoice numbers internally for the vendors that do use invoice numbers on their invoices – there is no possibility of mixing the two processes for one payee.

The invoice numbers for telephone companies' bills must be based on telephone account numbers and statements' dates:

*Account number and Statement date:* **(212) 123-0000 January 21, 2018**

*Resulting invoice number:* **2121230000-01212018**

For the T&E reimbursements, the internally-assigned invoice numbers may contain abbreviated description of reimbursements, that is, invoice number "*ABC Conf., NYC, December 2017*". There are fewer T&E payments made to any given employee than invoices paid to vendors – it is easy to see from the open and paid invoices report what was paid or entered as a payment voucher and what was not processed yet; a discrepancy in personal reimbursement invoicing is not as crucial as in vendors' invoices' records. Travel processing systems like Concur have a logic to identify possible duplicate entries in user's reports.

Payments to rental and lease companies may have internally assigned invoice numbers similar to the telephone companies' bills with your account number first and payment period second. Again, use the same format at all times:

*Lease account number and period:* **1122233, June 2018**
*Resulting invoice number:* **1122233_June2018**

A similar system of invoicing may be created to suit your company's specific needs. If you are required to provide extended information about payments, you can use the payment reference field for both checks and EFT payments. I am reluctant to submit any additional remittance advice other than the invoice number, unless specifically required by the payee (recall IRS requirements for EIN, tax period, tax form number).

Utility and telecom bills with no invoices numbers on them is still a big challenge to all extensive and distributed AP operations; for many years my New Year wish has been that all business and individuals I deal with use invoice numbers. Alas.

What should you do with the statements sent in by vendors? I reconcile them to the invoices paid and open in AP system and contact vendors or ordering departments within my company about any discrepancy between the statement and my Accounts Payable information. I never *pay statements*. I request the invoices from the statement to be sent to me. A statement number should never be used in place of invoice number.

By the way, always enter your company's account or customer number in the payee's record (if the function is available) so the number appears on each check or appended to each ACH transmittal. Notice that there may be multiple accounts with the same payee – do not duplicate vendor IDs for the sake of having an account number assign to a vendor ID, leave account number blank: invoice number and dollar amount will allow a proper payment application.

With paper invoices, I am very reluctant to process a copy of an invoice, a faxed copy or anything else other than the original invoice. Using copies may be allowed in exceptional cases, but the original payment documents must always be submitted later and be attached to the payment documents. Again, with the common place inroads that the ERPs and online Accounts Payable systems are making into the 21st century Accounts Payable business environment, it becomes a non-issue for you, since you are working with the e-invoices, imaged copies of invoices and other supporting documents, while the original documents are stored by the originating departments, locations, offices or colleagues. Again, the use of a unique invoice identifier (invoice number) is crucial for AP processes that do not utilize the PO-matching functionality.

An instance where even the best invoicing system may be circumvented is when a corporate card is used to make a purchase from a vendor. Since the corporate cards information is uploaded into your general ledger periodically or in real time, manually or by 'pressing the button, (more about corporate cards accounting in later chapters) and invoice numbers being not a part of the bank feed (but transaction amounts, merchant names, and transactions dates), there is no possibility to flag a duplicate AP invoice entry against a posted corporate card transaction or *vice versa*. In the past, I have seen AP checks returned to my Accounts Payable department marked "already paid by corporate card." This was a problem. A corporate card policy must be established to forbid use of the commercial cards with Accounts Payable vendors paid by check, EFT or wire and only out-of-pocket, travel and other T&E types of expenses allowed. Many billing systems of vendors generate invoices even though such invoices have already been paid by commercial cards. It is a good practice to assign a particular payment type (check, EFT, wire, credit card) to each payee.

If there are lost invoices, in transit or internally, they must be identified during your monthly statements review; that is, if all vendors send statements to you, and, more importantly, if you have the time to do it. Usually, even those vendors that do not normally issue monthly statements will do so once their accounts receivable aging reports begin to sound alarms about your company's payments. Being put on "credit hold" may highlight problems in the invoice processing chain within or outside the Accounts Payable department, but it is always a situation requiring your immediate attention. This is the time to pick up the phone and call your vendor, discuss the problem and promise a quick resolution. Process such emergency payments as soon as possible, requiring all involved to attach higher importance and quicker approval (not sacrificing the quality of AP work), process payment and call the vendor with payment information, be it check number or EFT or wire transfer information. Causes of your delayed payments must be identified – within the AP department, other departments or between your company and the vendor's company – and analyzed. Take actions to change the current procedures where needed to eliminate the possibility of this happening again with this and other vendors. If problem lies outside the Accounts Payable department, the issue must be communicated on inter-departmental or inter-company managerial levels.

When entered into the AP system, an invoice gets assigned a system payment number (transaction number, payment voucher number, trace number). The number will come in handy in future reviews and reports. All entered invoices are sent to a person who reviews and approves (posts) entered transactions. I had switched my AP department to conducting the final payment review before posting/paying open payment vouchers during the times of the EFTs transitioning from paper checks. I realized that **performing the final open invoices (payment vouchers) review prior to posting/paying them is a much more accurate and efficient process than doing the final review**

**of the already processed payments, when the open payment vouchers have been posted/paid.**

I have already said that the ERP systems are here to eliminate all other types of legacy accounting applications for all businesses, large or small. The AP data entry activities performed in the Accounts Payable department are reduced (depending of your AP payment types make up) when using the ERP, since invoices are sent as data feeds by those of your vendors which are technically equipped to do it, or entered remotely by users in different offices, cost centers, colleges, or other reporting units. Departmental approval is performed first, and once approved the invoices immediately appear in the Accounts Payable administrators' system (with email alerts marking every next processing step generated by the ERP). Usually, there is a three-step review and approval process of all e-invoices in the EFTs AP workflow (besides the data entry): departmental, Accounts Payables, and final review before payments are paid and released. There may be added processing layers in cases when payments exceed certain dollar thresholds (senior management review), payments made to nonresident aliens (nonresident alien tax compliance manager's review) or capital assets purchases (general accounting manager's review).

All ERP systems have payment documentation imaged and attached to the respective AP records – it is available for immediate review, based on relevant reference criteria: payment number, payment voucher number or invoice number. Imaging of payment documents used with the legacy AP systems is one huge benefit the accounts payment departments are reaping since early 2000's. I cannot praise the imaging functionality more than I have been doing since I started having access to it before my switching to the ERP system use. All older AP systems can be equipped with a separate payment documents imaging system, which must be updated with all newly processed payment documents; scanned after processing and indexed to allow for search based on payment or invoice number.

You will immediately realize how outdated and cumbersome the paper processing is, once you get the taste of having the AP documentation digitized and available on your computer screen. There is no greater embarrassment for the Accounts Payable department than losing a not yet scanned and indexed paper payment request and not being able to release a processed payment or retrieve an AP document because of that.

# Payment Types

## *Vendor Payments: Supplies, Equipment and Materials*

Paying for supplies, materials and equipment may be your Accounts Payable department's primary payment activity. There are usually a limited number of preferred vendors that companies deal with. Such business relationships are well established and routine. It is a duty of your purchasing department to make sure that your company is getting the best market deals and is not lulled into inertia by long-lasting business relationship and personal connections. Description of purchasing department's operations is beyond the scope of this book, with a few AP-related exceptions. You, as an Accounts Payable specialist, can be happy or bored working within the established routine with familiar business counterparts, if this scenario is applicable to your Accounts Payable department.

This situation however is suited best for the e-invoicing process: the established relationships create a stable environment for the process (more about e-invoicing platforms in later chapters). Upon uploading of e-invoices feeds into your AP system, all invoice information is now input in the AP system; data entry error-free, identical to the source information that originated in the vendor's billing department. The uploaded e-invoices can now be routed by the AP system's workflow through the proper channels of reviews and approvals. There is no room for errors related to the e-invoices information other than vendors' rare billing errors or corrections, which you may find necessary to make during your AP review. In case where remote users submit invoices electronically, possibility of errors is present and such invoices much be checked carefully (but not entered) during the AP review. If there is no e-invoicing or web-based remote invoices submission capability, paper invoices are mailed to your company for processing the old-fashioned way. Paper invoices may also be mailed to a remote data-entry center, often outside of the US.

There is almost always at least the two-way matching done when processing vendors' invoices. The two-way matching that I have been exposed to has always been *PO to Invoice matching*. Not *Receiving Document to Invoice*, as most Accounts Payable publications present it. Three-way matching is used when all three documents, *Purchase Order, Receiving Document and Invoice* are required for processing to assure proper procurement internal controls of what is being ordered, received, billed and paid for.

Sales tax and shipping is included on vendors' invoices. If your company is a not-for-profit organization, it may be exempt from the sales and use taxes in your home-state and may be exempt from sales and use taxes in certain other states where it has sales tax exempt status. You must apply with each state to obtain such sales and use tax exemption. The process may be more or less vigorous: easy in Ohio and difficult in Rhode Island. New York, New Jersey, Pennsylvania, Illinois, Tennessee, Missouri, Florida (and other) allow out-of-state not-for-profit organizations to receive sales and use tax exemption, while the DC or Virginia require the physical presence in the state or order to qualify for sale and use tax exemption. CA has a very narrow allowance for sales tax exemption – practically, speaking, no allowance.

Value-added tax (VAT) is used in the European Union. Read a brief description of the VAT below:

*A type of consumption tax that is placed on a product whenever value is added at a stage of production and at final sale. Value-added tax (VAT) is most often used in the European Union. The amount of value-added tax that the user pays is the cost of the product, less any of the costs of materials used in the product that have already been taxed.*

*(source:*
*http://www.investopedia.com/terms/v/valueaddedtax.asp )*

All imported goods (for which you may process invoices) are not exempted from the VAT tax unless your company is registered as tax-exempt organization in the exporting country.

A word about the *AP to AR settlement*; this is a process of netting (or offsetting) of the AP invoices that your company receives with the billing that your company does with another company that is both the vendor and the customer of your company. In other words, when you buy from and sell from the same business, it is possible to net the payables with the receivables. I call this process a good example of mixing apples and oranges; AP is not AR and the processes must be run separately. There may be issues with incoming and billing invoices, the netting of them makes the AP and the AR intertwined and interdependent to the point where more issues are created than solved by this process. Do not use the *AP to AR settlements* process.

### Payments to Independent Contractors

Who is considered an independent contractor? Can one choose to be an independent contractor if it is more beneficial for individual tax purposes rather than becoming a company's employee? ***Who is an employee and who is an independent contractor?*** The following is the IRS approach to this crucial determination, which is often made in the Accounts Payable department and cannot be decided by any other than the IRS mandated method:

*The general rule is that an individual is an independent contractor if the payer has the right to control or direct only the result of the work and not what will be done and how it will be done. The earnings of a person who is working as an independent contractor are subject to Self-Employment Tax.*

*It is critical that business owners correctly determine whether the individuals providing services are employees or independent contractors. Generally, you must withhold income taxes, withhold and pay Social Security and Medicare taxes, and pay unemployment tax on wages paid to an employee. You do not generally have to withhold or pay any taxes on payments to independent contractors.*

*(http://www.irs.gov/Businesses/Small-Businesses-&-Self-Employed/Independent-Contractor-(Self-Employed)-or-Employee%3F)*

An independent contractor is an individual or business providing services free from direction and control of performance including the means and methods used. Independent contractors fall into two categories: a company or firm providing service or individuals who are clearly in business for themselves such as doctors, computer programmers, accountants, lawyers, architects, electricians, performers, and other. It is the responsibility of the department that hires independent contractors to make *initial* determination as to whether to classify an individual as an employee or an independent contractor.

The IRS has issued general guidelines rather than more specific regulations on the employee/independent contractor distinction. Each contract with an independent contractor must be evaluated very carefully. There is no single criterion which determines classification one way or another. Extra caution must be taken before signing contracts with individuals not ordinarily in the consulting business, or with past company's employees.

The general IRS rule is that if an individual is subject to the control or direction of another merely as to the result to be accomplished by the work and not as to the means and methods for accomplishing the results, such individual is an independent contractor, rather than an employee. Most of the IRS's criteria for determining the status of a service provider hinge on the idea of *the degree of control the employer exercises over the individual*. Keep in mind that for the IRS, it doesn't matter whether or not this control is actually exercised, just that a relationship of control exists. In each case, it is very important to consider all the facts - no single fact provides the answer.

I still sometimes find requests to make a payment to an independent contractor directly (e.g. Mike Lee) instead of paying the business shown on the W-9 (Lee's Lawn Services). Make sure that payee name (remit to) is the 'Business Name' or 'Name' as they appear on the W-9.

The IRS developed the *20-Factor Test* to determine whether a business controls and directs a worker or has a right to do so. The factors (questions), applied to each individual circumstance under which services are to be performed, determine the individual's classification. The questions must be objectively and consistently applied to determine the individual's correct status. To be classified as an independent contractor, answers to question 1 and question 2 must be "No". If the predominance of answers to the remaining 18 questions is "No", the individual is an independent contractor. If answers to question 1 or question 2 is/are "Yes", the individual is an employee; otherwise, predominance of "Yes" answers for the remaining 18 questions is indicative of the individual's employee status.

Answering the first two questions provides the answer to the employee or independent contractor determination based on the basic test: whether a business directs or has right to direct a worker as to *how*, *when* and *where* the work should be done.

**The 20 questions are:**
1. **Is the individual directed by someone in the company where and how the work is to be done?**
2. **Is the company providing detailed instructions or training to enable the individual to perform the work in a particular time-frame or manner?**
3. **Can the individual perform the work without any risk of direct economic loss to himself/herself?**
4. **Are the services provided by the individual an integral part of company's operations?**

5. Must the services be performed specifically by the individual (rather than by someone else employed by the individual)?

6. Will the company hire, supervise or pay others to help the individual on the job?

7. Is there a continuing work relationship between the individual and the company?

8. Is the work schedule set by someone at the company?

9. Is the individual required to devote his/her full-time work to the company?

10. Is the work required to be performed on the company's premises, or in specific places designated by the company?

11. Is the sequence of work set by someone at the company?

12. Are regular oral or written reports required to be submitted to the company by the individual?

13. Is the method of payment based on hourly, weekly or monthly fees (as opposed to commission or by the project/job)?

14. Are business and/or travel expenses reimbursed?

15. Does the company furnish the tools, equipment and materials used by the individual?

16. Can the individual perform the work without making or having made any investment in equipment or offices?

17. Does the individual perform services exclusively for the company rather than working for a number of companies at the same time?

18. Does the individual make his/her services regularly available to other businesses?

19. Is the individual subject to dismissal for reasons other than nonperformance of contract specifications?

20. Can the individual end his/her working relationship with the company at any time without incurring liability for failure to complete the job?

## *Utilities Payments*

These are payments for electricity, water, telephone, internet, office maintenance and other recurring overhead and office and administrative expenses payment. They are paid monthly and care must be taken to pay them on time, because many utility companies routinely assess late payment fees, which they do not reverse the way one of your vendors may do, based on your business relationship. A small amount late fee occurrence may mushroom into an issue of the Accounts Payable department not being on top of things. An argumentative executive from another department, who approves the utility invoices for payment, may blame your lateness beyond reasonable circumstance, especially if your AP track record is otherwise impeccable. This is how life is – don't fret too much about it.

Often time there are no genuine invoice numbers on utility monthly statements – you must utilize your internally developed and consistently followed invoice generating system. It is best to have all such recurring utility and telecom expenses pre-approved for a fiscal year and set them up as auto-payments on a company credit card or as direct debit on checking account. Once utility or telecom account is set up there is little or no review and adjustment of the charges which are based on period contract terms, meters or usage readings.

## Travel & Entertainment and other §274 Accountable Plan reimbursements

I wish this chapter was as short as the previous one. But it is as longer as the time you spend processing the T&Es compared to your processing of utility payments. This is an area where you may make enemies or friends. Travel and Entertainment payments (T&Es) are often a point of friction between the Accounts Payable and other departments. The confusion starts right with the abbreviation, T&E: the original meaning is "Travel & Entertainment", while the modern and evolved one is "Travel & Expenses" (which sounds redundant to me).

You must be factual and professional about processing T&Es – this is the best approach. You need to develop (often in team with the HR) and uphold a regulations-based and familiar to all involved system of reimbursement requirements for submission and processing of the second largest controllable business expense (T&E). This is the area where policies and procedures, and not individual employees' opinions, requests or demands, must dictate how T&Es are handled.

Why processing of T&Es is such a sensitive issue? Well, these are dollars owed to the people who work next to you. And who gets to spend companies' money on travel and entertainment? Most of time, higher level management and executives. What you hear very often when a request for reimbursement is submitted is this: my credit card bill is coming due soon – I need my travel reimbursement as a manual check *today*.

Another aspect of the T&E, which is not discussed frequently in Accounts Payable publications, is the *income component of the T&Es.* It is an unpopular and unwelcome topic with all involved, save, probably, the IRS. There is *no* income component in the T&Es reimbursement by definition, you may knowingly point out. This issue had been taken up by the IRS and later dropped. It was agreed that there is no income component. The *Accounting Plan* concept establishes that incurring expenses while on business assignment by the employer is fully reimbursable and free of any tax obligation. I do agree with the accounting plan concept professionally, but analyzing the situations impartially, I believe that the T&E payments or reimbursements *do* carry income element within and this is another reason why many people are only too willing to incur reimbursable expenses and are so impatient to have their reimbursements processed as soon as possible.

Let us review a simple hypothetical example. An executive engages in a one-month business assignment in Las Vegas, NV, of all places, and incurs the following (simplified) travel expenses (all on credit card, as usual):

*-$4500 hotel*
*-$2400 food*
*-$1000 transportation*

**$7900** is on the credit card statement, which is later reimbursed to the employee and remitted to the credit card company by the employee. The fiscal effect on the traveler is net zero expense for the month.

Now, in the same hypothetical one-month period, an employee, who does not travel, incurs the following (simplified) living expenses:

*-$1000 housing rent*

*-$1000 food*
*-$400 transportation*

**$2400** to spend requires $3200 of gross payroll to earn (assuming 25% effective payroll tax).

Net $2400 monthly expense compared to no expenses on a month-long business trip to Las Vegas, NV.

I am not being sarcastic, but realistic. Of course, there are other considerations and elements to keep in mind when thinking about being *on the road:* the traveler is away from family and is still paying rent or mortgage expenses. But, there are sumptuous meals, hotel rooms with nice views, per diem payments for the days when one doesn't feel like eating much, frequent flyer miles and cash bonus points on credit card accounts, which are not officially considered, but never the less exist. For my part, I take any opportunity to travel on business matters, because it just feels good, both financially and emotionally.

Now, that we have established the absence of income component and tax liability in connection with T&E reimbursements, it is understood why the unchecked *"bad T&E behavior"* is still a commonplace occurrence. Often times it is the disallowed expenses claimed to be reimbursed. Sometimes, it is actually T&E *fraud*, although many professional AP publications prefer to avoid the *f*-word in connection with the T&Es. Every unauthorized extra dollar claimed on a reimbursement request is tax free income. Therefore, the T&E reporting standards must be strict while reasonable, detailed and properly explained, in order to fully account for all expenses; a personal expense report may at times present Accounts Payable specialist with the privacy issues. Few *rotten apples* have made the process electrified.

Yes, **there is an emotional component to the T&E processing**. You won't miss the component, if you process T&Es for one day. What solves the situation is clear, logical, industry-standardized and well promulgated within your company T&E guidelines.

All T&E reimbursements assume processing under the Accountable Plan concept. To comply with § 274 of the accountable plan, your employer's reimbursement or allowance arrangements must conform to all three of the following rules.

(a) The expenses must have a business connection — that is, paid or incurred as deductible expenses while performing services as an employee of your employer.

(b) Employee must adequately account to employer for the expenses within a reasonable period of time.

(c) Employee must return any excess reimbursement or allowance within a reasonable period of time.

**Unaccounted for expenses are not reimbursed and unaccounted-for advances are considered and reported to employee and the IRS as income.**

The travel guidelines must clearly communicate policies and guidelines regarding allowable expenses and restrictions to all prospective travelers. Failure to comply with the guidelines must result in denial of reimbursement for out-of-policy expenditures. The principle underlying travel expensc reimbursement is that travelers must be travelling on the pre-approved appropriate and necessary company business and should make all efforts to obtain the best available pricing for transportation and lodging, and, yes, should neither gain nor lose personal funds. A list of items allowed for reimbursement and dollar thresholds for each type must be establish internally and may exclude certain traveler's expenses such as alcohol, laundry and valet service.

All travelers must save their airline or train ticket stubs or e-tickets, boarding passes, detailed hotel bills, car rental bills, and receipts for all other expenses. Credit cards statements are not adequate documentation for travel expenses, proof of travel, business meals or other travel-related expenses. For all travel, including local travel, travelers must complete the travel reimbursement form and submit it within 10 days after the trip. Most of companies today use online travel processing tools such as SAP Concur, Workday, or Trinet. Travelers must retain paper or electronic copies of all receipts for their records and attach the originals to the reimbursement form. Today, one just snaps a picture of the receipt with a smartphone, through the receipt away, and find the image ready for processing in the travel application. SAP Concur is one such popular travel receipt imaging and OCR application (OCR stands for optical character recognition).

If an advance was received it should be subtracted from the total travel expense amount to arrive to the net reimbursement amount or refund payable by traveler back to the company if the advance exceeds the actual travel expenses.

It is important to have a set frequency of travel reports submission – once per month is my advice based on experience.

Supporting documentation for the purpose of business trip must be supplied with all travel reimbursement requests. In all cases, the traveler must (e)sign the reimbursement form to certify that the reported expenses are accurate and correct. Departments' heads or a company's officer next up in the hierarchy must approve all travel reimbursement requests. Some companies have 'no receipt' allowance per expense report. Some companies have a process of certifying a no-receipt situation to allow a reimbursement, usually as an one-off instance. Some companies may have an extended list of items that don't require receipts, based on the nature of industry and business assignment – I theorize here that a CIA agent in Iran may have other than 'mileage and tips' categories that don't require documented expenses for reimbursement.

Entertainment expenses take place most frequently in executive offices and sales departments. It must be established internally what is allowable and what is not. The spectrum of allowable expenses varies from practically close to nothing allowed for governmental and not-for-profit businesses to almost all-inclusive reimbursable entertainment expenses in the investment banking, entertainment, gambling or other less restrictive entrepreneurial, fashion, creative, and artistic types of businesses.

A few words about the *per diem* (per-day, from Latin) type of reimbursement and other standardized travel reimbursement rates policies used by governmental employees, but also adopted by many educational, not-for-profits, health care and other types of organizations. Current Federal *per diem* rates for lodging and meals and incidental expenses for locations throughout the continental US and non-continental US locations may be found at: http://www.gsa.gov/portal/category/100120

If actual or expected travel expenses exceed the above amounts, travelers may find it more advantageous to use the actual expenses up to allowed maximum for approved expense categories. The State Department sets the per diem rates for foreign travel; a web-link is found at:

http://aoprals.state.gov/web920/per_diem.asp

Authorized use of a personally-owned automobile is currently reimbursed at the rate of 58 cents per mile (2019), subject to review and change by the IRS once every year. Mileage reimbursement cannot be claimed in conjunction with car rental or reimbursement for gasoline. Read more about standard mileage rates on the following IRS' web-page:

http://www.irs.gov/uac/2013-Standard-Mileage-Rates-Up-1-Cent-per-Mile-for-Business,-Medical-and-Moving

I provide below an *old-school* sample travel reimbursement form request used by employees to claim to be reimbursed, if you still use the paper:

*-Name and address of Traveler*
*-Purpose of Trip*
*-Itinerary:*
> *Dates of Departure and Return*
> *Destination*
*Travel Expenses:*
*-Transportation*
*-Lodging*

*-Meals*
*-Local Travel:*
*-Personal Car Use: x miles at $0.xx per mile reimbursement*
*-Entertainment*
*-Other*
<u>*Total Expenses:*</u>
<u>*Less: Advance:*</u>
<u>**Net Reimbursement Due:**</u>
    *Signature of Traveler*
    *Department/Office*
    *Date of Request*
    *Travel Reimbursement Approved by*
*(Attach all relevant to the travel reimbursement request documentation)*

Some companies include T&E reimbursement payments with regular payroll payments (checks or direct deposits). It is a good and advisable practice, but its implementation depends on frequency of your company's payroll and level of patience of those people reimbursed, of course.

According to the IRS ***moving expenses*** that are deductible and those that are not, may be reimbursed to an individual. Those reimbursements that are not deductible must be treated as taxable wages, subject to FICA and income tax and reported on form W2 (non-taxable moving expenses must also be reported on form W2 in box 12). If the individual whom you reimburse for moving expenses is not employed by your company (when your company acts as a payment agent for another business), both taxable and non-taxable expenses may be reimbursed, but the taxable expenses must be reported on form 1099-MISC. Read the IRS Topic 455 – Moving Expenses, below:

*If you moved due to a change in your job or business location, or because you started a new job or business, you may be able to deduct your reasonable moving expenses but not any expenses for meals. To qualify for the moving expense deduction, you must satisfy two tests. Under the first test, the "**distance test**," your new workplace must be at least 50 miles farther from your old home than your old job location was from your old home. If you had no previous workplace, your new job location must be at least 50 miles from your old home.*

*The second test is the "**time test**." If you are an employee, you must work full-time for at least 39 weeks during the first 12 months immediately following your arrival in the general area of your new job location. If you are self-employed, you must work full time for at least 39 weeks during the first 12 months and for a total of at least 78 weeks during the first 24 months immediately following your arrival in the general area of your new work location. There are exceptions to the time test in case of death, disability and involuntary separation, among other things.*

*(http://www.irs.gov/taxtopics/tc455.html )*

Non-taxable moving expenses include: (a) cost of packing, crating and transportation of household goods and personal items, (b) shipping of car and household pets to new residence, (c) travel expenses to new residence, including car rental and gas, lodging (only *to* new residence). For the use of personal car an individual can claim actual gas cost *or* current mileage rate reimbursement, (d) storage and insurance of household goods for a period of up to 30 days, (e) expenses of shipping household goods to and from storage.

Taxable moving expenses include: (a) any portion of purchase price of new residence, (b) expenses of buying or selling of old/new residence, (c) expenses of getting into or "breaking" a lease, (d) home improvements to sell old residence, (e) loss on sale of old residence, (f) meal expenses, (g) new residence "house-hunting" expenses, (h) temporary living expenses, (i) repair, maintenance, insurance or depreciation of a car, (j) legal fees.

Request for reimbursement for moving expenses must be submitted within 60 days of relocation and incurring of such expenses.

I strongly advise to take advantage, if possible, of SAP Concur online expense reporting application. The following chapter is dedicated to SAP Concur processes. Concur allows users to report expenses and apply for reimbursements anywhere where there is internet connection. Making the process easier for the travelers, Concur also assures a greater fiscal control and audit tracking of the submitted payments. *https://www.concur.com/*

# Concur Processing

These days Concur is owned by the SAP and this relationship adds to Concur's weight, prestige, capabilities, and name – SAP Concur. I like Concur. It is a very robust and capable software. I attend Concur Fusion conferences any time I can, meaning, any time they happen to take place in New York City.

These are random notes about Concur use. I don't want to paraphrase the already available information on Concur's website at http://www.concurtraining.com/. I want to give you a real life and experience advice and share what I know about Concur.

Step One? Incorporate your company's travel procedures into Concur audit rules. Work with you Concur representative to adjust the audit rules, workflows, and GL accounts during the implementation phase. Establish a reporting frequency, which is "monthly reporting" for most of companies. Travelers tend to be more disciplined with monthly reports if they claim their own money back. Travelers tend to get tardy when they account for the transactions processed with a corporate card. There must be a requirement to process expenses on a required (set the time frame) basis.

The Concur process must reflect the Accounts Payable and HR rules for business-related 'out of pocket' reimbursement. There are numerous limits and allowances. A company may use per diem rates for meals and lodging, which is not recommended for a good control environment (people may not spend any money and get 'reimbursed'). I believe that per diem can be used as bench marks, but not as a basis for reimbursement – per diems tempt traveler to 'earn' tax free cash bonuses. Think about it: some people may well survive in Las Vegas on the McDonalds meals instead of the per diem allowed by the GSA's allowance (Meals and Incidental Expenses, M&IC) of $64 when breakfast and lunch are usually served by the hotel and conference organizer.

New user set up. Setting up a user involves entering name, email, employee ID, and default cost center information. Approving manager(s) is added. Users are able to charge expenses to other cost centers, allocate, or split expenses. In all such cases, a manager of the added cost center must be manually looped-in to the workflow. A new user must first provide her bank account information and get it confirmed (it takes two-three days) before the first expense report can be submitted. You can assign a delegate to a user's profile. A delegate is usually an administrative assistant to a person who is too busy to process his own reports. The bank account information field is not available for processing by the delegates – the account owner must set up the bank account information.

Concur has built-in custom work flows that are set up for your company's specifications by Concur specialists. Usually, a company does not get to program or change workflows (workflows are called *policies* in Concur lingo), while being able to do other 'programming' of Concur menus. A typical workflow includes the following: (1) traveler, (2 - optional) reviewer, (3) manager, (3a - optional) another cost center manager's review, (4 - optional) division head, based on dollar amount threshold or an added cost center, (5) AP review, (5a - optional) CFOs review, based on dollar amount threshold, (6) release for payment.

All fully approved payments are batched up at a certain, usually, 'after end of business' hour (cut-off time) and prepared for deposit a few days later with a selected frequency (weekly, monthly). You should be able to set up and control this process. Concur is capable of processing direct deposits by directly 'lump sum' debiting your business checking account and then distributing individuals' deposits to their bank accounts. Concur is currently in the process of outsourcing the payment processing function to Western Union. Another payment option is for fully processed reports is to be sent for payment as 'open bill' into your AP system, which will then distribute (pay) checks or direct deposits.

There is an option to release into payment additionally accumulated and fully approved reports: *Administration – Company – Tools – Monitor Batches, Reschedule Batch* (Close and Send date should be the same). A report can be paid outside of Concur: Client Pay is set up in Tools – Payment Manager – Monitor Payees, find the payee with a report fully approved but not swooped into a payment batch, select Client Pay – and, don't forget to pay it.

(Skip this paragraph is your accounting system is directly integrated with Concur.) The last step in the processing of Concur reports is a data upload process to the AP/GL legers. For data uploads Concur provides a SAE (standard accounting extract) text file in Administration-Company-Tools, Import/Extract Monitor which you need to transfer to excel (CSV-type file) and adjust the data before it becomes download-able into the accounting system. I have a master excel file prepared with a macro built into it. I copy-paste Concur's text file, run the macro and get the data in a format that allows download into the AP Ledger. When I prepare the download file, I group payments by vendor ID (traveler's payee account) and assign "invoice number" (I recommend for use the excel' Flash Fill for this purpose). In the end of this process I generate a number of payments to the reimbursed travelers which in total match the Concur's batch and direct debit to the company's checking account. The direct debit then distributes payments to individuals' checking accounts: Debit – expenses, Credit – cash (total by report). At the time of this writing I am working on directly integrating my SAP Concur with Intacct using software product called Wipfli.

This process does not include a corporate credit card's use, just the travelers' reimbursed personal funds. If you add a corporate card or cards to the process, the debit side of data upload remains to be expenses or pre-pays, while the credit side is a payable GL account (liability) which is cleared when you pay your credit card issuing bank on a monthly basis. CBCP, Central Bill Client Pay, in the Amex parlance.

It is important to develop a policy and discipline to have expense reports submitted on a pre-determined basis; monthly is the most logical and convenient to all frequency. You won't be asking yourself whether the person has already submitted a monthly reimbursement for cell phone or airfare two months ago if there is a process of the monthly reports submissions.

Watch out for pre-paid expenses; an airfare ticket purchased months in advance may be submitted right after the purchase, as it should be, and again, later-on, included with all travel receipts, unintentionally, most of times. An advance airfare can be reimbursed to traveler, and then refunded by airline if travel plans changed. There should be audit rules set up for all kinds of possible 'red flag' scenarios: duplicate amounts, airfare limit, meals limit, etc. The audit rules are set up by Concur consultants during the initial implementation, but can be adjusted and added if you know how to do it. An example of 'Airfare over $600' audit rule taxonomy is: *Entry – Expense Type – Equal – Value – Airfare AND Entry – Amount – Greater Than – Value – 600.00 USD.*

When reviewing a Concur report, sort transactions by date and go over them making sure that expenses make sense based on the 'timing of event to event level'. Second, re-sort the reviewed transactions by amount to find any possible duplications. The Audit Rules should flag any possible duplications, but manual review is still a good practice. Here's another taxonomy for the 'duplicate transaction' Audit Rule, which is found in Administration-Company-Company Administration, Audit Rules, Duplicate Transaction: *Entry-Expense Type, Value – [select all expense types that you use], AND, Entry – Duplicate Transaction Variance, Value – 0.01, Entry – Personal Expense, Value – No.*

During the review process the approver can only make a comment, attach additional document, approve, approve and forward, add workflow and reject a Concur report. An approver can also reject a single line of a report back to the traveler, while approving the rest of the report. Such returned to the user line, becomes a new report named 'Addendum: [original report's name]'.

My ongoing Concur struggle with the users is sketchy or missing documents attachments and payment to vendors and service providers. Missing attachments do not qualify a transaction to be reimbursed, unless it's something that your company does reimburse under the travel guidelines: personal car mileage, tips, etc. There may be a manager-approved certification about a missing attachment with the transaction's description and the amount. Such certifications acceptance may be allowed by your internal guidelines up to a certain dollar limit.

Individuals' personal payment to vendors for services is a bigger issue. It must be discouraged. Employees who do it may claim circumstances that prevented them the proper action of submitting a payment request to the Accounts Payable. Whatever the excuse may be, it does not relief you from the obligation to report to the IRS any service payment made by your company via Concur (see the 1099 section) even if such payment was first made by your employee with the personal funds, and then reimbursed to the employee (a third-party payment situation). Many users, usually higher up managers, are notorious for running their own AP operations with their credit cards, bypassing the rules for payables processing, to "make it simple" and generate rewards and points on their personal cards accounts.

Concur's customer service is good, I like it. Chat is available most of times. If Chat is not available, the link is not available as well. Right now, I am connected to Juvilyn C. from Concur's support team; I've asked her for a general advice to Concur users.

*The agent is typing: I suggest you to direct your employees to our Training Site with training videos available: www.concurtraining.com.* Great!

Concur Chat Support answers general questions, and refers you to a specialist (you must open a case or go through an additional fee SOF, sales order form) if your inquiry is more complicated, like changing the workflow, setting up new audit rule, or adding a new GL expense accounts to the existing list. I use the 'case' approach almost exclusively these days – there is no waiting to get connected and answers are always provided, if they are available.

The chat advisor will not provide advice on the more advanced topics such as workflows, list management, import or Canadian HST tax set up.

I will not go over the expense report creation process. You must know how to do it because you are a *Concur Expert*, and many times you will find yourself helping your company travelers creating and fixing their reports – it's not rocket science and it builds rapport.

Concur transactions are entered into a report with a couple of clicks if there are 'available expenses' processed with SAP Concur phone application, manually or available from transactions list that a traveler generates with a linked to Concur company credit card, uploaded by a third-party travel agent's website, or uploaded by an app (such as Egencia).    Personal business expenses are reimbursed to the traveler, while the company card-related expenses are paid by the company on the monthly basis. Avoid using a company-paid cards; it's a slippery slope to bad compliance. *SAP Concur* phone application is the best tool to work with: the receipts appear in *Available Expenses* and can be used to quickly initiate and 50-70% data system-populate a new report. Emailed-in documents appear in *Available Receipts*: they are available to be attached to already created transactions in a report – one must link/validate email account (up to three) to a Concur profile to simply forward all receipts to *receipts@concur.com.*

Concur workflow will bring you a travel report to review after it's been reviewed in the cost center (department). Departments often time do a very general 'business purpose' review and 'rubber stamp' reports because they have other things to do. Again, when you open a report to review, I suggest sorting by "date". Sorting by date will tell you a story: first, there was an airfare ticket purchase, then a taxi ride from home, then Hudson News Stand bottle of spring water, Wi-Fi on the fly, taxi to hotel, hotel bill, etc.… You get the picture. It must all make sense to you – the events and the associated dollar outlays.

The Expense tab must have all the relevant and required fields completed with meaningful information. I just had a report in review with 'business purpose' stated as *Joplin, MO.* Yes, the event was held in Joplin, MO, but the business purpose was something else. You can inquire with the traveler, and compete the business purpose upon hearing back information in the Comment section (the only section available to add information). Or you can take a hard-liner approach and 'reject' the report to the traveler with a request to complete the missing information. Rejecting or "send back to employee" process is a proper formal process that requires the traveler to correct and re-submit the travel report. The report will pop up on the traveler's boss screen for approval the second time. It is your call which route to take here – a simple inaccuracy that you are willing to fix for the traveler, or a more rigid approach to errors that you cannot fix in the report. I don't 'walk extra mile' adjusting someone's report if the errors are chronic and the person obviously does not want to follow the established process.

Keep in mind, you may add missing pieces to a report such as additional image attachments, expense type correction, or a comment. You must return a report that requires the dollar amount change.

Set up a frequency of Concur payout batch processing. My batch pay-cycle is weekly – fully approved reports are paid weekly. This is unrelated to the requirement that the reports are submitted on the monthly basis. Every pay-cycle triggers an expense data transfer from Concur to your accounting system. In case that Concur is not integrated with your ERP you need to export-import data to the AP system manually. If you use excel for data transfers, I suggest that you set up a Master Export File with a built-in macro, as I mentioned earlier. The macro should take Concur extract data and put it into a load-able to your system format. Otherwise you will be spending hours on end copying and pasting data. Manual data transfer is a very laborious process, no matter how much it's finetuned.

My advice to all new Concur users: download SAP Concur app on your phone and use it, link emails to your Concur account (up to three emails can be linked), read my *New Concur User Manual* (see Appendix).

Concur is a good fun to work with. I like the system. The SAP Concur folks are friendly and professional.

### Scholarship and Fellowship payments

If your Accounts Payable department is a part of college, university, research foundation or other educational organizations you are most likely to process numerous scholarship and fellowship payments. Although the terms appear to be simple, there are many common misconceptions and misunderstanding of what true, as defined by the IRS, scholarship and fellowship are. Read the Internal Revenue Code §117 below. This is a very useful document to get familiar with; I've had it taped to my documents board for many years.

*Internal Revenue Code § 1 1 7*

*Sec. 117 QUALIFIED SCHOLARSHIPS.*

*(a) GENERAL RULE.-- Gross income does not include any amount received as a qualified scholarship by an individual who is a candidate for a degree at an educational organization described in section 1 70(b)(1)(A)(ii).*

*(b) QUALIFIED SCHOLARSHIP.-- For purposes of this section--*

*(1) IN GENERAL--The term 'qualified scholarship means any amount received by an individual as a scholarship or fellowship grant to the extent the individual establishes that, in accordance with the conditions of the grant, such amount was used for qualified tuition and related expenses.*

*(2) QUALIFIED TUITION AND RELATED EXPENSES--*
*For purposes of paragraph (1), the term qualified tuition and related expenses" means--*

*(A) tuition and fees required for the enrollment or attendance of a student at an educational organization described in section 1 70(b)(1)(A)(ii), and*

*(B) fees, books, supplies, and equipment required for courses of instruction at such an educational organization.*

*(c) LIMITATION.-- Subsections (a) and (d) shall not apply to that portion of any amount received which represents payment for teaching, research, or other services by the student required as a condition for receiving the qualified scholarship or qualified tuition reduction.*

The scholarship/fellowship payments are <u>not</u> payments for services – they are awarded to students who are enrolled at educational institutions to help them pursue their studies and must not have any compensatory elements within.

This is a very important concept to understand: scholarship/fellowship payments must not be a form of compensation for work, teaching, participating or other kind of service. Often times you may see the words *non-service scholarship/fellowship*, which is an oxymoron, since scholarship/fellowship is by definition a non-service payments.

There are no reporting requirements (1099 or W2) for scholarship/fellowship payments made to the US students (the rule does not apply to scholarship/fellowship payments made to nonresident aliens), although it is required that scholarship/fellowship recipients include all or portion of the scholarship/fellowship receipts (non-qualified scholarship portion) in their gross income. This is a personal income tax issue and beyond the scope of this book.

Classifying service payments as scholarship/fellowship or scholarship/fellowship with service components as pure scholarship/fellowship allows for not reporting of income to the IRS and tax avoidance by the recipients. This may create huge liability for your organization; FICA, income, unemployment taxes in arrears, fees and penalties. Do not let this happen. Create a certification form to be completed by scholarship/fellowship granting office which will be used to document that scholarship/fellowship grants are indeed not payments for services.

There may be educational conditions attached to the scholarship/fellowship payments; full time college enrollment, certain GPA level, participating in research, discussions, seminars, and other non-service type academic activities. I will discuss scholarship/fellowship payments in greater details in the *nonresident alien* section of this book.

## Accounts Payable Data Entry

When a fully approved and coded invoice is on your desk it is time to input it in the system without delay. Depending on your AP volumes, you may be doing it less or more frequently or all the time. At this time, most of the invoices are input by Accounts Payable clerks or remotely, via web-AP services by the departments, offices or locations, which ordered goods or services and received invoices. Receiving *e-invoices* from vendors directly is gaining popularity where technical capabilities allow for it. Invoice feeds are generated by the vendors' billing departments and sent to your company.

There can be no invoice-related information error in case of the e-invoicing. Two popular platforms that support the e-invoicing are **GXS** *(http://www.gxs.com/ )* and **IBX**. **GHX**, Global Healthcare Exchange platform, is widely used by medical schools and hospitals. Read an excerpt from the *Capgemini's* website about the *IBX eInvoice* services that the company offers (Disclaimer: I have no relations with either company):

*IBX eInvoice is a full service offering from IBX including everything you need to receive up to 100 per cent of your invoices electronically through one single interface:*

- *Hosted application for document routing*
- *Implementation Program Management, including activation of your suppliers*
- *Technical integration of your invoice management system to IBX eInvoice platform*
- *Support & Maintenance of the entire solution*

*With eInvoice your invoice management process becomes highly efficient. Straight through invoice registration, easier authorization and improved document quality contribute to significant cost savings. Even archiving of invoices is improved since storing paper is superfluous, while the complete and original electronic invoice information will always be easily accessible.*

*With fully electronic invoices the quality of incoming invoices will improve, and reduce workload in exception management. Automatic format controls and content validations will filter and reject incomplete or unauthorized invoices.*

*IBX eInvoice allows suppliers to send 100 per cent of their invoices through the same channel, with only a limited technology investment. IBX eInvoice has multiple access alternatives to accommodate suppliers of all sizes and by utilizing already existing infrastructure one installation reaches many buyers.*

*IBX eInvoice enables a total and fully electronic process from procure to payment.*

*(Source:*
*http://www.ibxplatform.com/procurement_solutions/procure-to-pay_suite/ibx_einvoice/ )*

*In the report, "Electronic Invoice Management: Going with the Workflow", research firm PayStream Advisors revealed 2014 as a key year for e-invoicing. The firm surveyed more than 300 AP professionals in the US on their AP plans, including their current invoicing preferences and challenges ahead. A key result was that more firms turned to e-invoicing solutions, and more than 70 percent of those surveyed had either already adopted an initiative, or were working on one.*

*In this joint report, "Global Electronic Invoicing - The State of AP Automation Worldwide", PayStream Advisors and Purchasing Insight reveal that e-invoicing is a top priority for companies worldwide and that 2013 should prove to be a banner year in terms of automation adoptions globally. With over 200 responses from global companies, paper-based invoicing is identified as by far the most common system, with 60 percent of respondents receiving 90 percent of invoices by paper. Only 5 percent of AP departments currently receive over 75 percent of invoices electronically*

*(Source:*
*http://www.gxs.com/resources/strategic_b2b_tools/paystrea m-technology-insight-report-series )*

All uploaded into your Accounts Payable system e-invoices must have default "on hold" status; they must not be accidentally paid based on the invoice date and payment terms combination prior to the ordering departments and the AP's review. All e-invoices must also have a special category assigned to them, based on your system parameters: it may be payment voucher type, category, sub-category that clearly identifies all e-voices as such. You must also be able to run the AP reports or e-processing operations based on this criterion that separates all e-invoices from the rest of payment vouchers. Upon upload into the AP system all e-invoice do appear as open invoices with the assigned special e-category and "on hold" in the AP Ledger. You may decide not to post them to the General Ledger until completion of final review and release from "hold".

E-invoices may be routed to the ordering department based on the departmental mapping that your company must develop with vendors prior to the e-invoice process rollout.

Based on the ordering department's information that the vendor has as one of the processing e-invoice variables, all e-invoices (upon upload) are channeled directly to the ordering department, and not to the AP for sorting and forwarding. Another simplified e-processing requires initial preliminary review action on all e-invoices by the AP department before the e-invoices are forwarded to the approving department.

The department-approved invoices are channeled by the system's work-flow to the Accounts Payable department for final review and scheduling for payment. Exceptions can be made at any processing point and e-invoices forwarded for additional review to any department involved in the "procure to pay" process. E-invoices can be set up to be automatically released for payment when system-matched with a PO and Receiver without matching exception.

Every "reviewer-approver" must be able to add a comment about the performed e-invoice processing, if there is such need. Each e-invoice must have a processing status assigned to it; the status changes as the processing progresses. There must be *Audit Trail*, which shows every action taken on the e-invoice processing with the approvers' names and "time stamps". Run periodic reports on the average by reviewer processing times of the e-invoices to highlight possible points of delays in the processing. Your inquiry on any uploaded e-invoice must tell you at which processing stage such e-invoice is. The "due for payment" report of open invoices must flag all e-invoices that are not fully processed; you must take the necessary actions to have such invoices fully processed and scheduled for payment.

In case that there is a question to the vendor, email links and phone numbers of your company's customer representative are provided within the system; you may generate an email, which your system must pre-populate with all the relevant to the invoice under review information – invoice number, invoice amount, description and possibly have the image of the invoice attached to the email. The system must retain a record of your email and the vendor's response to it.

E-invoices may undergo two or three-way matching process in case that the POs and receiving documents are required for payment processing. After the final AP review, e-invoice is released from hold and assumes "normal" open payment voucher status to be paid based on the payment terms. All other "procure to pay" related documents, such as purchase requisitions, requests for quotes, purchase orders, receiving documents are generated within and managed by the ERP's workflow. They are available for two- or three-way matching when required as well as for other AP referencing purposes.

Manual AP data entry is still being performed to various degrees by most of US businesses; there are very few companies that are capable to fully transition to the e-invoicing. Even when the technical and funding aspects are not an issue, the variety of the AP types precludes a complete e-invoicing conversion. The manual data entry tasks may become somewhat monotonous if this is your main daily activity. Your primary concern, when processing such manual invoice data entries, is to select from your payees' data base the correct payee to pay. Be careful when selecting a payee to pay with the commonly used business names, such as "first", "American", "united", "general", "east coast", etc. If there are more than two payee names in your AP database, it may be a duplicate payee ID or two different businesses (e.g. First American Company). Compare the addresses to select the correct payee. There may be more than one remittance address for a payee. It is important to mail payment to the *Remit To* address on invoice and not mail payments to corporate or any addresses that may appear on vendor's invoice. Many companies have outsourced the accounts receivable operations and checks are often mailed to third party processors; you may recall seeing PO Box remittance address on Collection Drive, Remittance Drive (to the point, my favorite), Paysphere Circle, Network Place or Innovation Way in Chicago IL.

After the selection of the correct payee ID, the next item of importance is the dollar amount. Pay attention to any adjustments that the approving departments or signatories made to the invoice. Ideally, there should be no adjustments.

Invoice number is another crucial data entry item. It allows for proper accounts receivable application of payments (and eliminates payees inquiries) and highlights duplicate invoice entry attempt by your Accounts Payable department. Processing of duplicate invoices is one of the notorious blunders that the Accounts Payable department can make. How to avoid processing of duplicate invoices? One rule is to **always input the invoice numbers <u>exactly</u> as they appear on vendors' invoices**. Do not eliminate leading zeroes as some AP consultants suggest. Keep all symbols used by your vendors on their invoices: dashes, underscores, slashes, space. Some invoices have *"xxxx-INV", "INVxxxx, "INxxxx"* added – keep that too. This one is a much easier and effective single rule of capturing invoice numbers as shown on the invoices compared to developing and following uniformly a system (many rules) of simplifying and modifying invoice numbers (e.g. delete leading zeroes, eliminating *INV*). **Do not change the format of the invoice numbers presented on your vendors' invoices when entering them into the AP system.** Another bold font about the same in a single paragraph – it is worth knowing and following. Processing payments to payees that don't provide invoice numbers (utilities, payments to individuals, small businesses, independent contractors, etc.) is a challenge to the AP process sometimes resulting in duplicate payments.

Having duplicate payee IDs in the system must be avoided. Pay attention to the Tax Name and the DBA name, which may allow for duplicate payee ID creation under different names. Your system will not validate a duplicate invoice entry in case where an identical invoice was paid under a different payee ID for the same business. Before creating a new payee ID, thoroughly check to establish if there is no existing payee ID to use. Run periodic payees' tax ID reports, based on the tax ID numbers, to flag duplicate tax IDs for different payee IDs (and other tax payees' ID related issues (no tax ID, other than 9-digit tax IDs (not all system validate tax IDs)). The accounting system must disallow a duplicate tax ID entry for different payee IDs.

Invoice date is the next item of importance, since based on this date and the payment terms invoices are paid. Practically non-existent today discounts for early payments must be taken any time there is such opportunity. This is where timing is very important – the usual ten days to pay a *1.5%/10 NET30* invoice is a very short and rather unrealistic time frame for early paper invoice payment processing.

Inputting invoices includes coding to (a) cost center/department/college/other reporting unit and (b) expense or other account. The coding and accounts are provided by the approving departments or get transferred from the PO records, in case that PO matching is performed.

It must be established as a rule that after the AP data entry each invoice is marked with the system assigned transaction number (payment voucher number, AP voucher number, etc.), signed and dated by data entry Accounts Payable clerk. Input paper invoices then filed alphabetically in the *Open Invoice* files. One is inclined to think that all companies use the electronic work flow system of one brand or another and there is no paper filing of open invoices. Not true; the paper invoice is still a very much alive and used item in the Accounts Payable departments.

As I mentioned earlier, there is not data entry in the Accounts Payable department related to the processing of e-invoicing and remote web-AP invoices, but monitoring and resolving of processing exceptions.

With the remote web-AP systems, departments which ordered goods or services and receive invoices, input invoices (by a designated *de facto* Accounts Payable person(s)) into web-based AP system and route them to the central Accounts Payable department for review, correction and upload of invoices from remote web-AP into main AP system (imaged documents are attached to e-payments). This is not the ERP approach, where all processes are housed in one system. Many companies have added various modules, including remote web-AP, to their legacy systems to approximate the ERP capabilities. Under this scenario, system to system uploads, verifications, loss of data and duplication of efforts are unavoidable disadvantage of the "fractured databases" system architecture, but it is still superior to the mail-in paper documents processing.

## Two-, Three-, Four-way AP Matching

AP matching is a form of internal control to assure that the company gets the products that were properly requested, the best prices for products or services were negotiated, all goods invoiced for are indeed received, and invoices are based on the previously agreed upon prices, goods and quantities. The *three-way matching* involves documents from three different departments within a company in the procurement process. The matching process provides for (a) lesser likelihood of collusion between employees to order supplies or services from businesses that employees may have connections to, (b) best market prices for purchases (often through the competitive bidding), (c) receiving of no more (or less) than the quantities ordered, (d) control of goods or materials that vendors ship and bill for and (e) paying invoices with agreed upon prices and terms.

The *four-way matching* adds *inspection* of goods received as the fourth element (there is no fifth element in the AP matching process) in addition to the PO - Receiving Report - Invoice in the three-way matching process. The four-way matching is the most potent process that assures that the internal controls are strong, but more complicated that the others and suited more for merchandise/equipment buying rather than payments for services. The only businesses I know of that have the four-way matching process implemented for some transactions are the North-Shore Long Island Jewish Health System and New York University Medical Center, both utilizing the PeopleSoft ERP.

The buying process begins with the *Purchase Requisition* prepared by the department in need of additional supplies, equipment, materials or services. An approved requisition is sent to the purchasing department, which then finds the best market pricing for the requested supplies. There may be restrictions on where and from whom to buy or not buy. There may be official preferences or preferred businesses requirements, which I believe to be an impediment to the free market operations and fair competition. The Purchasing Department requests the quotes - vendors send them in. The Purchasing Department negotiates prices (or not) and then issues a Purchase Order (PO) that lists requested goods description, prices, quantities and shipping dates. The PO may quote a contract, in case there is related to purchase order contract, negotiated by the company's Legal Department.

The kind of sale where invoice follows delivery is called *Credit Sale*, since suppliers ship goods first and receive payments later. Vendors often request from buyers *Credit References* and other documents to establish the creditworthiness of the buyer, offer their terms of purchasing/selling process, negotiate, and sign procurement contract. In case that a seller refuses to give credit, the transaction is done on the C.O.D. (collect on delivery) basis, which is normally the case for smaller businesses, such as local convenience stores, diners and food- and news-stands.

Goods are shipped mostly under the *FOB destination* term, which means that the seller delivers the goods and this is where the title passes on to the buyer – at the buyer's loading dock. Other popular shipping term is *FOB shipping point* – a point where seller ships goods via shipping company to buyer. FOB means "free on board". Goods are only accepted if there's reference to the company's purchase order on the seller's *Bill of Lading*. Upon delivery, all goods are checked for correctness and counted. A copy of a PO with the quantities blacked out must be sent to the loading dock prior to the scheduled delivery date; the PO in receiving department authorizes the acceptance of the delivered goods, allows for description verification, and counting of the actually delivered quantities. The omitted quantities of ordered goods on the Purchase Order assure that the goods are actually counted and not just signed for (internal control). A receiving document is created by the *Receiving Department* and sent to the Accounts Payable department.

An invoice is mailed by the vendor to the company, approved internally and is ready to be input into Accounts Payable system. The invoice may also be transmitted through a data interchange platform (such as the GHX) and loaded into the Accounts Payable system with a data feed. At this point, there are two possible scenarios. Two-way match is described by most Accounts Payable books and publications as *receiving document* to *invoice* match. I have a different experience. I have myself processed countless two-way matching of invoices and it has always been *invoice-to-purchase order* match. But one way or the other, two documents must be matched for all listed items/terms – vendor name, quantities, prices, items. All discrepancies are referred to respective departments; purchasing department, ordering department or receiving department. Technical matching issues are solved within the Accounts Payable department before the invoice processing can continue.

Three-way is matching of purchase order, receiving document and invoice. The three-way matching is the most controlled and orderly procurement process; it provides assurance that the right goods were ordered (PO), received (receiving document) and properly billed for (invoice). A four-way matching adds the inspection document to the mix.

When a data exchange platform is used, your POs go out to vendors, vendors deliver, receipts are entered into the company's system, invoices are transferred through the same data exchange platform by vendors to the buyer (your company). In case that an invoice finds match with a noted on it PO, and a related receiving document, a three-way match happens without any human input. When the invoice becomes due, it gets paid. I love the system; it's not a perfect one either. I remember 'duplicate PO dispatch' being a big issue at a certain organization I worked for: vendors would get duplicate requests, deliver more than needed (deliveries were accepted based on the duplicate POs created in the GHX, but not in the accounting system), perishable goods would sit in a warehouse unused and unpaid because the system only listed one PO record and place the whole situation in the 'match-exception' area. Not perfect, but best of what's available.

During the process, it is most important to have smooth flow of documentation from department to department to avoid delayed deliveries, waiting delivery tracks at the loading dock, holding off on processing invoices due to missing documents. As it is true with all other Accounts Payable activities, the ERP and other paperless AP applications that our technologically advanced times offer to the Accounts Payable department are great improvements of the archaic and outdated paper-based work-flow process. The *Procure To Pay* workflow is managed within the ERP creating all required for efficient processing action alerts and documents, purchase requisition, request for quote, purchase order, receiving documents which are then matched with invoice sent electronically or via regular mail.

## Payment methods

### *Checks*

Now that you have a stack of freshly printed checks and *check file/white copies* printed (by a different data entry or checks reviewer employees) the *Positive Pay* file (listing of all issued checks) must be sent to your bank to be compared against checks to be presented to your bank for clearing by check recipients. You are ready to distribute payments (distribute checks only after *positive pay* is processed lest checks are returned to payees as invalid). Unless final review was performed, on the open payment vouchers before posting/paying them, which is my advice, the printed checks must be matched with supporting documents. The AP department must have the positive pay process in place if you want to be protected against the check-fraud.

There are paper documents (invoice, purchase orders, receiving documents, travel reimbursement requests etc.), which are compared to information on checks and attached to checks file/white copies (*checks file/white copy* is a copy of the check's remittance portion, but not the actual check. Some systems leave the "top portion" of a printed check with the AP – is has the check information). Any discrepancy between the payment documents and issued checks is reviewed and corrected. This is where problems begin. While you definitely must void a check made to a wrong payee, you will only correct the invoice number if incorrect on the remittance advice and thus leave incorrect information in the AP system. Voiding checks is also a nonproductive activity and this is why I advocate doing **the last AP review**

**not on processed payments, but on open payment vouchers, which are scheduled to be released for payment.** This makes for much more efficient and cleaner Accounts Payable work. I often joked with my staff when they used to bring me discrepancies on processed checks: *When in doubt – mail it out.* Never, never process or release a payment when you have doubts about it. **Err on the side of not releasing a payment, rather than believing that a missing piece of information or discrepancy was somehow accounted for by others who reviewed it before you**. I once returned requiring more information half a million dollars wire transfer to none other than the company president's secretary, who literally *went ballistic* when she learned of my inquiry (management override was in place, controls weren't followed). The invoice number was identical (slightly modified to "cheat" the system) than the one processed recently, and the amount was the same (a duplicate payment submission). All hell broke loose, but I held my ground firm. I required explanations, as a matter of fact, any time I am "in doubt", any time there is Accounts Payable *red flag*.

With the ERPs and other paperless web or intranet-based AP systems, open checks (or scheduled for posting payment vouchers) are compared to e-records randomly, based on payment voucher or other reference numbers. This paperless process is much more efficient during all processing stages, and at this final step it fully eliminates the issue of misplaced paper documents, which is a very embarrassing situation to any Accounts Payable department.

All printed checks must be postmarked with the same date as the issuance date to avoid possible arguments with the vendors' AR about the timing of payments. The mailing stamp is often used as an evidence to establish the timing of checks release.

All check file/white copies, or top 1/3 of the three-part check paper, with or without (if e-payments) payment documentation attached to them are stored in sequential order. I advise to store all checks for the current and last year on the company's premises, unless you have a system of imaging of processed paper-based checks into a document imaging system. All e-payments are available from the e-system(s) where they originated.

Maintain a check log to make sure that there is no gap in the sequence numbers of processed checks.

### Electronic Fund Transfers

The Electronic Funds Transfer payments (EFTs), also called ACH credits (Automated Clearing House credits) have gained popularity in the past decade. There are very good reasons for this transitioning from paying vendors by paper checks to the EFTs. I cannot think of one valid reason for not switching to the EFT method of payments with all payees that have bank accounts. And how many of your payees don't have bank accounts? This may be a valid question to ask if your company is a not-for-profit organization serving unemployed or population below the poverty line.

Other reason for issuing paper checks today may be a request for a check to present during a sales meeting, award ceremony or s specific request to pay by check (e.g. governmental agency's bill). I have heard vendors' statements like *my boss just likes seeing a pile of customers' checks on his desk*, as explanation of a vendor's reluctance to switch to EFT receipts. **Other than a few valid exceptions, all commercial vendors must be paid at this time by the Electronic Fund Transfers.**

EFTs have no expenses associated with the paper check such as blank checks, postage expense and banking services fees (positive pay, checks reconciliation, checks imaging fees) that adds up to close to $1.17 per check as of this writing in May 2019. Just think about it – it costs over a dollar to process one paper check (only the direct printing and processing expenses). While the EFT cost pennies to process, there is no possibility of an EFT to be lost or stolen (given the accurate and correct vendors' bank information data collection and entry). Additional advantages are next business day payment processing (if submitted before 10 p.m.), invoice information submission in the EFTs addenda records and EFT-related emails sent to the receiving vendors' accounts receivable departments, practical elimination of the cumbersome escheat process, simplified and less expensive archiving. **The benefits of switching from paper checks processing to the EFTs processing are huge and immediately realizable both in monetary terms, quality of Accounts Payable process and security of released payments.**

The first step in your department's transitioning to the EFT processing is to collect the banking information from your payees. It is good to know that most of your payees are more than willing to provide that information to you. All you need to do is contact your vendors' customer service representatives or their Accounts Receivable departments. A word of caution: you must be certain as to whom are you calling and from whom you are receiving that banking information. Another word of caution: once a payee is set up for the EFT processing, it may take some time to realize that the information used is not correct (upon vendor's AR inquiries), if misleading banking information was provided to you. In case of a banking data entry error, your EFT will be returned by your bank on the next business day). Many companies have official EFT/ACH enrollment forms where they state their business name and tax ID, remittance addresses and bank ABA number (also called the *routing number*), account number(s), account name, AR email address, telephone number and other information that vendors may find useful for the purpose. Vendors may also request that you follow certain EFT/EDI formats, such as CCD, CCD+ or CTX. You can see a sample EFT data file in the appendix and read more about ACH standards on this web site:

http://www.regaltek.com/docs/NACHA%20Format.pdf

The ABA stands for American Banking Association and serves as ID number for any American bank. One bank can have numerous ABA/Routing numbers for various locations. A bank can have different ABA numbers for ACH and Wires. A bank often has different ABA numbers for customers' deposits and outside credits (wires and ACHs). Always ask your vendor this specific question: What is your ABA for ACH? What is you ABA for wires? It is always a good idea to validate such number in the ABA database, access to which is available using the link below:

http://abanumberlookup.com/

In the case that a payee does not have a formal EFT information letter, the bank information should be provided and certified on your *New Payee Questionnaire*, which I mentioned earlier, to request along with a completed form W-9. It is advisable to obtain a copy of a payee's check marked *VOID*, to validate the information provided manually on the form. To pay vendors by the EFT method, the following questions must be answered and statements made:

*- Payee's Name*
*- Payee's "Remit To/Mail Payment to" address*

*We authorize (your company name) to submit payments to the bank account listed below:*

*- Account Name*
*- Type of account: checking or saving*
*- Accounts Number*
*- Depository Bank Name*
*- Routing Number (same as ABA number) for ACH*
*(ABA number must be nine digits and only used by the American banks)*
*-Email Address for Remittance information:*
*-Contact Name*
*-Telephone Number*
*-Name*
*-Signature*
*-Date*

There should be a legal statement as to the terms of the electronic deposit agreement:

*This authorization is to remain in full force and effect until (your company name) has received written notification from RHYOLITE TOWNSHIP INC. of its termination of this direct deposit authorization in such time and in such manner so as to afford (your company name) and the Depository Bank a reasonable opportunity to complete processing of all already schedules for processing through the ACH payments.*

The payee's bank information must be input only by a designated person and reviewed and approved by the AP manager. **It is of utmost importance to review the information on the EFT enrollment form carefully and enter it in the accounting system without any discrepancy from the information provided.** These two steps – obtaining banking information and correctly entering it into Accounts Payable system assure 90% of the future success and ease of use of the EFT payment method.

**For all due for payment EFT payment vouchers, the final review must be done prior to the posting/paying.** Your accounting system will create a data file (*b*-file/*flat* file or *XML*-type file), which must be "locked" and inaccessible for any change or adjustment. The bank file contains bank accounts, payees' names, amounts, invoices and addenda information, which is posted to your bank's website dedicated place where you process EFTs, wire transfers, direct debits, upload positive pay files and do all other related to online AP and cash management activities. A sample of the bank file, also called *ACH/NACHA* file is available in the appendix.

It is possible that the bank file is not uploaded automatically, but is saved by the AP system to a secure shared-drive; in this case the bank's website upload and release must be processed manually as two separate functions and performed by two separate manager's level persons.

A common procedure is to date, assign the *Effective Date* (deposit date) to your bank file two business days ahead of the submission date, to allow for a possible audit of the posted EFT payments. You can recall an ACH payment tomorrow if the effective date is a day after tomorrow (two business days ahead set up). Technically, all EFT files uploaded and submitted to the bank before 10 p.m. are deposited into the recipients' accounts on the next business day.

You should always print out *Bank Validator* (that lists exceptions, if there are failed EFT submissions) and *Batch Summary* (that lists all processed payments' information: names, ABA/Account numbers, bank trace numbers and bank deposit effective date) reports and attach them to the payment registers (that list all posted EFTs) and save both reports electronically. There is no "signed back of check" proof of the EFT payments; you are asked sometimes to provide proof of EFT payment made. I admit that the Batch Report only proves your transfer of funds and not the recipients' receipts of fund (which are confirmed by endorsing signature on checks). But most of the times your Batch Report is sufficient to confirm with your payees the processed EFT transfers and allows to find your EFT in the payees' bank records. Otherwise, you will need your bank's confirmation of deposit; the confirmation process may take several days.

Many of your payees' AR inquiries are avoided by having the *addenda records* within your bank's file, which lists all paid invoice numbers and amounts separately, although your total payment to a given payee groups all payments together into one payment deposit. To address a possible incompatibility between different banks processing systems, addenda transfer formats and possible loss of EFT addenda, separate emails are generated based on the processed EFTs. The process is handled automatically by the AP system if the technical functionality allows for it, or processed by a separate email generator that sends emails to all EFT-paid vendors.

Again, there is huge difference in quality and ease of payment distribution with the EFTs process compared to the outdated paper checks processing. There are big savings in checks processing expenses, which can be quite heavy for high volume payment processing Accounts Payable departments. There is much lesser possibility of fraud, no lost or damaged payments, no EFT (similar to check) reconciliation or stale-dated checks issues to worry about. Those rare reports of EFT non-receipts are most of times misapplication of EFT payments or payee's internal poor AR controls. All such complaints are handled with your bank representative's help, who can trace EFT payment to the exact recipient's account.

In very rare cases where fraudulent bank information was input into the AP system, it will take time to figure (based on real payee's AR inquiries) that payments have been sent to the wrong bank account. This is why it is so important to authenticate the banking information before it is input into your Accounts Payable system. I have also dealt with cases where funds were deposited into bank account that had different than the account name on file (due to business reorganization). It is, therefore, important to always require payees to provide the *account name* associated with ABA and account number as a part of the EFT information collection.

There are instances when the *DBA (Doing Business As...)* names may be identical for different businesses (franchisees), but different for all other purposes. This is why *business name, bank account name* and *tax ID* must be a part of your payee's bank information gathering (this is another way to confirm a business's tax ID for your other purposes).

Last, but not least, I clearly mark every processed with bank batch of EFT payments as "PAID", so it will eliminate the possibility of processing (uploading, validating and releasing) in the heat of the day, the same EFT batch via your bank's website again. Maintain EFT numbers log to make sure that all EFT numbers are sequential and there are no EFTs batches that were left not processed with your bank; "paid" in your accounting system, but not processed with the bank. This may be another EFT processing pitfall, although not as grave as the duplicate EFT batch processing.

It is very important to receive timely and accurate (name, amount, dates, other information) information about all returned EFTs from your partner-bank to analyze, correct and reprocess all returned EFTs promptly.

With all the great advantages that the ACH process has over the paper checks process, there is one minor inconvenience that you will undoubtedly encounter during the ACH credits processing (this effects the wires processing as well). Any time that a payee reports a non-receipt of an

EFT (or wire) or requests a proof of payment, there can only be a negative confirmation readily available to you – a transfer records with bank account and other information. There is no image of a signature on the back of a cashed check, which convincingly proves the receipt of funds. With the EFTs and wires there is only the processing information that you have in your accounting system and your bank system that relate to 'your' side of the processing (that along with the absence of the funds' return information proves the successful transfer – a negative confirmation), but not the payee's receipt of funds. You can request your bank confirming of an EFT or wire successful deposit to the beneficiary's account, which is again not as persuasive as seeing an endorsed copy of a cashed check. Many a time an EFT tracking number (obtained from your bank) can help to pinpoint the deposit in your payee's banking records. You can obtain the tracking number from your bank (it's not assigned at the time of ACH processing) and communicate the number to the requesting party.

## Wire transfers

Wire transfer is a bank transfer that cannot be set up in the automated fashion similar to the EFT processing. Wire transfer is a set of instructions, which are given to a bank to transfer funds from one bank account to another bank account. It can be done via facsimile request to your bank or through your bank's website. Wire transfer can be processed to domestic and foreign bank accounts. EFT payment cannot be sent via the Automated Clearing House (ACH) to a foreign bank account. Therefore, for any foreign bank transfer, the wire transfer method must be used (With the exception of the Canadian banks. They follow the AFT (not NACHA) direct deposit format). It is more labor intense and expensive than the EFT processing. All domestic bank transfers are processed as EFTs unless it is a company's policy to process large dollar amount bank transfers as wire transfers, so the process is not as automated (read, more controlled) as the EFT process.

The bank information verification must be given highest priority, since retrieving foreign bank transfers is a very difficult and laborious process. There are two types of bank information that you need to process a wire transfer: IBAN-based or BIC/Account numbers-based. The IBAN system is being used by the European Union banks (Israel and Turkey as well). The International Bank Account Number (IBAN) is an internationally agreed mean of identifying bank accounts across national borders with a reduced risk of propagating transcription errors. The IBAN consists of up to 34 alphanumeric characters (the IBAN length is different for different countries): the first two-letters are country code, followed by two check digits, bank and account number information. I suggest validating every IBAN that you plan to process payment with; I have seen incorrect IBAN on official companies' invoices and banking instructions. You can use the following website to validate the IBANs:

http://www.currencysolutions.co.uk/resources/iban-and-swift-codes/iban-checker

Using the IBAN requires no separate bank ID (SWIFT/BIC) or account number use, although both may be provided along with the IBAN. Also, processing just the IBAN is usually cheaper than processing SWIFT/BIC and account number combination. Remember, when processing bank transfers online, to enter the IBAN numbers with no spaces (the IBAN's are often shown with spaces to allow for easier reading of lengthy numbers) to avoid delays in bank processing and additional bank's verifications.

SWIFT stands for *Society for Worldwide Interbank Financial Telecommunications* and used to denote foreign bank ID code, which is BIC (bank identifier code). Note that SWIFT=BIC for your Accounts Payable purposes. You may see variations of bank ID codes – SWIFT, SWIFT/BIC or just BIC. This refers to the same bank ID code for any bank in the world. Let's analyze a few SWIFT/BIC codes:

*SCBLAFKA* or *SCBLAFKAXXX* (some banks request to leave out the X's at the end)
**SCBL – Standard Chartered Bank Limited**
**AF – Afghanistan, KA – Kabul**

*CITIUGKA*
**CITI – Citi Bank**
**UG – Uganda, KA – Kampala**

*RBOSGB2L*
**RBOS – Royal Bank of Scotland**
**GB – Great Britain, 2L - London**

I advise to validate every SWIFT/BIC code using the SWIFT's website:

http://www.swift.com/bsl/index.faces

As I mentioned before, retrieving a foreign wire transfers that was not deposited properly to the beneficiary's bank account is a difficult, sometimes impossible, task. You need your partner-bank full support in investigation of any pending or lost in transfer wire transfer. The retrieval process is more complicated if more than two banks (sending and receiving banks) are involved. It is not uncommon to see in the wire transfer instructions one or even two *intermediary* banks between your US bank and the beneficiary bank. There may be no direct relationship between your bank and the recipient bank – in such cases the intermediary banks are used. An intermediary bank is most often another bank in the United States that has banking relationships with the beneficiary bank (use ABA or SWIFT/BIC for US intermediary bank) or foreign bank has banking relationships with the beneficiary bank (use only SWIFT/BIC and account number). It is possible to have both ABA//SWIFT/BIC and Account Number for the intermediary bank to identify the beneficiary bank, or just ABA//SWIFT/BIC and no account number for the same purpose. On the wire transmittal forms that I have created and used, I always indicated *beneficiary bank name* for the intermediary bank instructions in line *"For Beneficiary Bank"*. Tracing of a *lost in transfer* wire transfer can be a tedious process, especially with those banks located in the countries with less developed baking systems.

Below is a sample wire transmittal form that should be prepared for all wire transfers, reviewed, used and signed by all involved in the wire transfer processing. Please note that bank's address and branch number are not required for the purpose of transferring funds.

**Beneficiary's Name\*:**

**Beneficiary's Bank Name\*:**

**Beneficiary's Bank Address:**

**Beneficiary's Bank SWIFT/BIC code\*\*:**

**Beneficiary's Bank IBAN or account number\*:**

**Amount in US Dollars\*: (or other currency, if your system and bank allows)**

**Reference\*:**

**First Intermediary Bank Name:**

**For Beneficiary Bank:**

**First Intermediary Bank SWIFT/BIC or ABA:**

**First Intermediary Bank Account Number for Beneficiary Bank:**

**Second Intermediary Bank Name:**

**For Beneficiary Bank:**

**Second Intermediary Bank SWIFT/BIC or ABA:**

**Second Intermediary Bank Account Number for Beneficiary Bank:**

**(\* required fields)**

**(\*\* No SWFIT/BIC is required if IBAN is used)**

A few words about the bank processing fees and currency conversion... Many foreign vendors require that all bank charges are paid by your company, so that the amount that the beneficiary receives equals the invoice amount. Even on the domestic bank transfers, I have seen a request to "add a 4.2% to recoup the recipient for the bank fees" (*verbatim*). I do not agree with such requests, since (first) I, as the payer, pay my bank's fees and (second) cannot know what the beneficiary bank charges for receiving of the wire transfer. This may become a point of contention; a separate clause in contract about the bank processing fees must be made whenever possible to avoid misunderstanding.

Another item that the parties must agree on is the *currency conversion rate*, that is, the parties must enter into *forward exchange contract*. I always advocate that the conversion rate should be agreed upon in writing when the prices for goods and services are reviewed and agreed upon by the buyer and seller. Using any other dates for conversion, based on various internal rules (such as invoice date, receipt date, processing date, etc.) and, subsequently, different rates, is subject to payment amount fluctuations, possibly manipulation and giving intended or unintended unfair advantage to the payer or payee. A commonly used website for currency conversion is www.oanda.com.

**Office of Foreign Assets Control Review**. *The Office of Foreign Assets Control* (OFAC) had started in the recent years to question more and more wire transfers sent to the (OFAC) targeted foreign countries.

*The Office of Foreign Assets Control administers and enforces economic sanctions programs primarily against countries and groups of individuals, such as terrorists and narcotics traffickers. The sanctions can be either comprehensive or selective, using the blocking of assets and trade restrictions to accomplish foreign policy and national security goals.*

*(http://www.treasury.gov/resource-center/faqs/Sanctions/Pages/answer.aspx)*

Any time that your partner-bank notifies you of a wire being held based on OFAC order, you should promptly provide all information that the OFAC seeks to obtain.

As is the case with the EFT transfers, it is very important to receive timely and accurate (name, amount, dates, other information) information from your partner-bank about all returns of wire transfers or other processing issues. Maintain wire transfers log to assure that all wire transfer numbers are sequential and all system-posted wire transfers are processed on your bank's website (that is, transferred out to recipients, one time).

Note that the routing numbers (ABA numbers) for wires are often different from the routing numbers for ACH/EFT transfers for the same (recipient's) bank account. Bank of America's ABA for wires is 026009593, while ACH/EFT ABA number for the same account is 011000013. When inquiring about the bank account, be specific for which purpose the routing number will be used, wire or ACH/EFT.

### Commercial Cards

This is not a chapter on the use of purchase cards – there will be a separate chapter on purchasing and travel cards the in hands of your employees. This chapter is about the Accounts Payable use of a commercial or corporate card (Visa, MasterCard, AmEx) as another payment method.

There must be a separate payment type in your accounting system for use with the commercial card that should reflect all transactions processed with the commercial card that most of times are initiated outside of the AP system through your partner bank.

I had a very negative experience using commercial cards to pay vendors. I still do; it makes your purchasing departments happy, your vendors very happy, the banks more than happy, and the AP clerks very unsettled. Giving away a sixteen-digit number is a *cart blanche*, a blank check.

I try to never use the commercial card account for any Accounts Payable invoice payment, other than possibly with a very limited number of high dollar volume and trusted payees to accumulate cash bonus points on the card's account. But, again, even those cash bonus points are not worth the risk you run when you communicate a commercial card authorization to charge your card's 16-digit account and provide the name on the card, expiration date and security code. Also, the bonus points are often end up being fool's gold since vendors up the price to recoup the bank fees or simply bill you for the loss in net receipt.

Credit card is a *carte blanche* kind of payment (unless a limited balance 'one-time charge' process is used). I had certain "proactive" accounts receivable individuals who would close their AR based on their own (aging) schedule and not my remittance advice. At times, the card account would be overcharged, since the balance was set high for other payees to dip into. Again, **do not use your commercial card accounts to pay vendors in the normal course of your AP activities**, unless you absolutely must. Or, if you have the virtual (one-time) card process available. The virtual card process entails a new card number issued for each payment, with a dollar limit being the payment amount, no plastic issued – just the number, CVV, name-address, and expiration date.

The commercial card AP accounting is different than the regular AP accounting since the cash is paid by your bank at the time of your monthly commercial cards bill payment, via the bank's direct debit or wire transfer in the next billing cycle. When you process a commercial card transaction, an expense account is debited and an intermediate payable account is credited.

*Commercial card AP payment system processing:*
**Expense                                          X**
**Intermediate Liability/Visa Payable                      X**

A credit card authorization is mailed to the vendor, or faxed, or communicated over the phone. The processed transactions are uploaded from your bank's web-site in real time or in batches, downloaded to excel (.csv) off bank website, or manually transferred off a paper statement into your general ledger. The liability account assigned to this commercial card account must be the intermediate liability account type, not the regular payables account. The expense (debit) side accumulates all the monthly expenses processed with the credit card. The intermediate liability (credit) side is accumulating the liability to the bank issuing the credit.

At the time of paying your bank, your total expense and intermediate liability for a given billing cycle must equal your bank's monthly statement amount. Work out any discrepancies there. Using a journal entry or AP voucher process, remove/debit the intermediate liability (zero it out) and create (credit) a liability balance that matches the bank's monthly statement. Now you have an AP balance (that is the sum-total of the credit card transaction for the billing cycle) that will be cleared when the issuing bank processes a direct debit or you initiate a payment to your issuing bank.

*Commercial cards sum-total IL reversal, AP liability set up:*
**Intermediate Liability/Visa Payable     X**
**Regular Payables                                          X**

*Commercial cards monthly bill payment:*
**Regular Payables                          X**
**Cash                                                              X**

As mentioned above, a monthly bill payment to the bank is initiated by the bank via pre-authorized by your company direct debit to your company's checking account or as a wire transfer payment initiated by the AP department. The direct debit is "booked" by a manual payment entry based on the bank's monthly commercial cards statement supported by the daily *cash log* information.

Again, do not use this payment type to pay vendors unless you absolutely must do so, and do it under a very close scrutiny. Reduce the number of daily transactions and set the available balance on the commercial card's account to

144

equal the approved/processed amount (s). Most of the times I used this payment method to process a single and very large dollar amount invoice transaction in pursuit of a single aim – to generate commercial card account cash bonus points. You should have one AP-operations designated commercial card but use it judiciously. Cash bonus points are often not worthy pursuing, since the bank is the only real beneficiary of the process. Credit card payment method is often favored when departments are late with processing of their invoices. I also use corporate Visa and Amex cards to auto-pay recurring utilities and telecom charges which are contract or usage determined charges and don't require close scrutiny.

*Virtual Cards.* The New York University Medical Center is widely using Visa cards to pay its vendors; a new 16-digit account is processed by JP Morgan Chase Bank for *each* payment and then recycled. There are no plastic cards issued, and, yes, a 16-digit card account number and a CVV are only used for one remittance processing (a remittance may have numerous invoices included within). The NYU can allow this luxury – a new account for each credit card invoice payment. I had spent six months with them – it was a great learning experience.

One word of wisdom repeated here: make sure your monthly credit card expenses match the bank's statement. These days I copy the bank's statement on the second or third of the next month, copy to an excel template, let my staff 'massage' it, adding vendor IDs, departments, codes, GL accounts. All this data entry is done based on departments-approved payment requests that triggered the processed credit card payments. Then I post it and make sure that my monthly credit card expenses posts match the bank's statements. Why bother doing it?

My clearing, intermediate liability, account is still not zero after I pay the bank on the '25th of the month" – there are transaction that were never captured in the AP years ago. It means the account was over-cleared with Cash which must tie-in to the actual bank charge, if you know what I mean. The cash is fine, always the amount of the monthly total. But my clearing account is out of balance – it has a debit balance, which means that some expenses (debits) are missing. I will write it off this year – there is no way to untangle the running balance which goes back years. Departments didn't welcome my own belated reconciliation of the clearing account when I would say – Bingo, found $2,000 of unprocessed expenses from year 2005, please approve. One doesn't make friends this way. An astute reader may ask – why a question was never raised about the clearing account being at the clear-zero point. Great point – but entries were done continuously (not matched to monthly statements), new ones already in, while the old ones were still there, there would always be 'logically' a balance. This is why I mirror my monthly 'wholesale' post with the bank statements and cash payments. Always.

P.S. Just saw this today on an invoice on my desk: 3% convenience fee will be added if credit card is used. There go the cash points.

### *Remotely Created Checks & Remote Capture*

Remotely created checks (RCC), which are also called *Telecheck*, *Demand Draft*, *Preauthorized Draft* are created by businesses or individuals other than paying banks and have no signature of issuer. It doesn't sound like a reliable method of payment and it is not. **RCC's should not be used except with your partner institutions**. This is where most payment fraud takes place. In the past, paying banks were responsible for reimbursing their customers for unauthorized RCC withdrawals; back in 2006 the liability was shifted by the Federal Reserve Board to depository banks to assure better control over the process.

The remote checks process was developed to allow telemarketers to close deals while having their customers on the phone. The idea obviously comes from before the credit cards commonplace use days. Presently, many insurance, credit card, utility and mobile phone companies use the remotely created checks process to collect payments and past due balances during collection calls to their customers.

For your business purposes, you should never authorize any remote check withdrawal and have a *direct deposit block* on your business checking account (unless, your business practice dictates to allow the direct deposits). If you need to allow direct deposits on your checking account, a separate account should be created and funded for the expected withdrawals (unless withdrawals are processed by your partner-bank with your permission for specific transactions).

In cases where you need to make an instant payment you should use your corporate card account where you can specify the card balance limit, number of daily transactions and have records about the merchants who use your corporate card account to get paid.

In contrast, the remote capture function is a widely used process, even by individual users snapping pictures of checks with the smart phones and 'depositing' the check this way. A physical or even a copy of an issued and signed check can be processed by a payee as soon as the payee gets hold of the check or image of it, signs/stamps and deposits it. This is how checks are deposited these day; a portable carousel-type scanner sends images to the bank and thus the deposit takes place. In July 2017, I had a very past-due check (not AP's fault) issued to the ADP, signed, imaged, emailed to the company, processed by the company, payment receipt sent back to me, all within one hour. If I sound excited about emailing checks images to companies, I am not. EFT is the way to process payments.

I still see these Remote Checks in my Positive Pay exception bank daily reports. Many 'over the phone' payments translate into Remote Check transaction (vs. ACH debit) with actual bank-generated 'check image'. Every time such check pops-up on Positive Pay exception, I check cash disbursement records of my remote offices to find a supporting record in the system. This is an exceptional payment method – try to avoid it.

### *EFTPS*

EFTPS stands for *Electronic Federal Taxes Payment System.* This payment method is required by the IRS to be used to pay federal taxes online. Taxes may originate in Accounts Payable (back up withholding and nonresident alien taxes), payroll or corporate tax departments. Processing of EFTPS payments are similar to processing of wire transfers: payment voucher with payment method (EFTPS or wire transfer) is entered with a debit to the federal tax liability account to clear the liability:

**Payroll deduction - Federal Tax    X**
**Accounts Payable                          X**

Then, the EFTPS is posted or "paid". The actual transfer is done after posting/paying of the EFTPS, but may take place before the EFTPS is processed in the Accounts Payable system to meet the IRS's deposit deadline. In either situation, just like it is the case with the EFTs and wire transfers, cash must be timely remitted (once) to the tax authorities to reflect the system-processed EFTPS payment.

https://www.eftps.com/eftps/

### Direct Debits

*Direct Debit* is a common place occurrence in most of the Accounts Payable departments, since it is an accepted practice to allow to debit your checking account without your explicit authorization. In case that your partner-bank is also the commercial cards issuing bank, you may allow your bank to debit your checking account for the amount of the commercial cards monthly bill (more about commercial cards in a later chapter). There may be other instances of recurring expenses (rents, leases) processing of which may be set up as direct debit on your account, or better, on a separate account funded for direct debits. Direct Debit is a reverse EFT/ACH credit – a vendor pays itself out of your company account once you authorize it. Direct Debit is similar to Remote Checks process in AP execution – although different banking method of transferring funds between accounts.

Any such debit should be immediately reported to the Accounts Payable department and processed with an appropriate payment method (CD, cash disbursement), or posted to proper accounts by a journal entry. If you process a journal entry for the direct debit it should be reviewed by another person before posting since you are crediting (reducing) your company's cash account. This is a very restricted operation and internal controls must limit its processing on exceptional occasions, reviewed and posted/released by someone from the management level.

## Tracking payments

It is not uncommon for a payment to get lost. No one in the Accounts Payable department likes these words, *lost check*. There are many reasons that may cause loss of a mailed payment. A check may be stolen from a mailbox, mailed to a wrong or old address, damaged in transit or just "disappear without a trace".

None of these problems happen with the EFTs, of course. With the EFTs, a *lost* payment may be a payment not properly applied by your vendor's accounts receivable and sitting in a clearing cash account waiting to be applied. Most accounts receivable departments are rather proactive: they immediately inquire on any unapplied payment sent by my Accounts Payable department. The rare inquiries result from invoice number errors and partial payments of invoices. Some EFT non-receipt complaints come from large companies – I resend bank transfer's remittance information to the other party; all lost payments are always eventually found. Again, you can't go wrong with the EFT payments once your vendors' records are accurately set up and secured form unauthorized or accidental change in your Accounts Payable system.

But since there is no Accounts Payable department which is 100% paperless, check payments are being made and those nagging *lost payments* issues present themselves ever so often. When you get a call from a payee about check non-receipt, the first step is to verify the address where a check was mailed to and approximate the delivery date. Make your best effort to help the payee locate the check. Placing "bank stop" on checks, voiding them in Accounts Payable system and reissuing checks is an expensive and time-consuming process, which may also have legal implications.

Do not void checks reported lost within ten days of issuance – make it a rule. If all reasonable terms to receive a check have elapsed, the check must be stopped with the bank and voided in the Accounts Payable system. There are many times when prematurely voided checks are found and deposited, which results in the NSF fees (*not sufficient funds* fees) and payee's request to reimburse for the bank's NSF fees. After ten days, notify the payee that check number (provide check number) is now void and should not be presented to the bank if found. Correct the error and reissue the payment. Communicating with the vendor about lost payment is a good opportunity to offer the EFT payment method (instead of check payment) and collect the required bank information.

If you have spent more than a year in Accounts Payable department you have probably encountered a situation where a stopped check was cashed. This scenario is more likely to happen when you pay individuals. Not only was a stopped check cashed, but there may have been a replacement check processed to substitute the (reported) lost original check, which was later found and cashed by the recipient, although properly stopped with the bank by your Accounts Payable department. How could this happen? Answer: one can clear a stopped with the bank check through the *Checks Cashing Place*. Check cashing points charge their customers, who most of times have no bank accounts, exorbitant fees for exchanging checks for cash and operate with no regard to the checks' status under the concept of *Holder in Due Course*. When presented to the checks cashing place, a stopped check still appears as a valid payment instrument, with no information available to the check cashing office of the check being stopped. Any time a voided check is cashed, the issuing bank (your bank) refuses to honor such a check when it is presented to your bank by the check cashing place for clearing. The check cashing company then sends you a claim to reimburse it for the face amount of check plus your bank's NSF fees after initial checks cashing company attempt to clear the check through the bank.

I provide the legal specs of the *Holder in Due Course* concept below.

*Section § 3-302 of the Uniform Commercial Code defines a holder in due course as "...the holder of an instrument if: (1) the instrument when issued or negotiated to the holder does not bear such apparent evidence of forgery or alteration or is not otherwise so irregular or incomplete as to call into question its authenticity; and (2) the holder took the instrument (i) for value, (ii) in good faith, (iii) without notice that the instrument...has been dishonored, (iv) without notice that the instrument contains an unauthorized signature or has been altered..." The UCC allows a holder in due course full transferability of rights to assure the*
*holder a free market for the instrument (§ 3-203). A holder in due course has three years from the date a check was dishonored or ten years from the date the check was issued,*
*whichever period expires first, to sue the maker for recoupment (§ 3-118).*

This is for all practical purposes an unavoidable situation and there are three lessons that must be learned here: (1) minimize checks stopping/voiding, (2) transition from issuing paper checks to EFT payments or (3) issue *payment cards* to payees with no bank account whenever possible. Payment Cards are similar to debit cards and are issued to repeating payees who have no back accounts (this situation primarily applies to governmental and not-for-profit organizations).

Tracking foreign wire transfers is difficult since there is no direct contact with the beneficiary bank. If there is a complaint of wire transfer non-receipt the following may happened: (1) the OFAC (Office of Foreign Assets Control) is holding the processing pending receiving additional information about the recipient, (2) wire transfer is held by your bank due to insufficient processing information, (3) wire transfer is held in the intermediary bank due to insufficient processing information, (4) wire transfer is held in the recipient bank due to insufficient account information. Issues on the US side of the processing must be communicated and resolved in a timely fashion to you by your servicing bank. Issues that arise outside of the US are often handled in a different way than is commonly accepted in the United States business practices and manners.

In any case, it is your duty to double check the bank account information used to process the transfer and inform the recipient about the exact bank account information used by your company to process the wire transfer. If information is confirmed as accurate, the recipient is asked to inquire with the receiving bank. Provide to the recipient the wire transfer's *trace* or *tracking number* that you can obtain from your bank (which, practically, is of little help to your foreign recipient).

Often times inquiries are triggered by the bank processing fees that the beneficiary bank subtracts from the wire transfer amount. Providing the recipient with processing dates may help find the wire transfer even if the amount had been reduced and was not recognized.

Bank processing fees may present similar problem to your Accounts Payable department as well when there is bank credit (wire transfer return) for the amount, which is not recognized as one of your processed payments. This may create a double issue – first, a wire transfer, which is considered fully processed did not, in fact, reach the beneficiary and, second, an open item may be sitting in your AR clearing account, not applied as payment and unrecognized as wire transfer returned due to the bank "returned wire" fees applied. It is important to have your servicing bank provide additional information (such as the payee's name) with all returned wire transfers and EFT payments.

## IWRP (Interactive Web Response Portals)

Any Accounts Payable professional knows that dealing with vendor inquiries about processed payments takes a substantial amount of the workday. Studies have shown that vendors inquiries with Accounts Payable departments by phone or via email takes up on average 12% of Accounts Payable staff work time. The questions are about payment status of open invoices. There are four stages that a vendor invoice can be at: invoice mailed and in transit or presumably lost, invoice just received, invoice in the system (open), invoice paid. In case that your company already uses the e-invoicing system, when vendors send invoices as batch files or upload them directly to your accounting system, open invoice stages one and two are eliminated, leaving 'open invoice' and 'paid invoice' as the only processing stages of AP invoices.

The Interactive Web Response Portal (IWRP) systems fully cover vendor inquiries for invoices in stage three and four – open and paid invoices. The IWRP cannot answer a vendor's concern about invoices lost in transit or not yet entered into the AP system – these situations still require AP personal interaction with vendors. The IWRP allows vendors to securely access your company's Accounts Payable environment to view, based on the assigned payee level, relevant Accounts Payable information – find invoices as 'open' or 'paid', find amounts of payments, dates of payments, remittance addresses used, and check numbers. The IWRP comes as a great help when you think of your workday as not being interrupted by routine requests for information – this is true for both your Accounts Payable and vendors' Accounts Receivable departments.

The company I work for uses an in-house built IWRP called "E-Vendor Desk"; I was behind the portal's idea and design, which was later developed by my IT department as a web-page of the company's website available to authorized users for access to a restricted segment of the AP information (i.e. a given vendors' access to the AP information of that vendor's AP records). The web page is simple and has three folders: 'open invoices', 'paid invoices', and 'inquiries'. The 'inquiries' section allows vendors to send messages to a shared AP inbox, which are answered by designated AP staff. Building a separate portal within the company's web-site was a logical choice (vs. buying IWRP in addition to your ERP system as a part of full suite, in case you use ERP) since all Accounts Payable information has already been fed for many years from the main ERP system to the company's website to populated web-based accounting reports. Your company's situation might be different, or you may already have an IWRP included with your ERP system, but not activated yet.

Communicate the availability of your IWRP to vendors; contact an AR representative to sell on the idea and arrange for user ID and password communication. This process of getting vendors 'on board' gives you another chance to offer the ACH process for those vendors who still receives paper checks.

The IWRP process greatly reduces the number of calls and email inquiries from your AR counterparts. It frees up the AP staff to actually process vendors' invoices. The process is available to vendors 24/7 and adds to the overall level of your vendors' satisfaction.

## Processing Form 1099-MISC and Form 1096

What is the busiest period in the Accounts Payable department? Without a doubt, it is the months of January through mid-April every year. This is the time when forms 1099s and 1042-S are processed by the AP departments and forms 1040 are filed by payees with the IRS. Also, if your fiscal year coincides with calendar year, this is the 'closing' and audit times.

The new IRS reporting rules require reporting by January 31 to both the recipients (complete information) and the Box 7 data to the IRS. The paper IRS reporting is due by end of February, and e-filing with the agency by end of March. I doubt any AP department will engage in a two-stage IRS reporting of Box 7 data first, by January 31st, and then other boxes' reporting at a later date. In all practical terms, with the most reportable values being in Box 7 (nonemployee compensation), the new IRS rules mean that the Accounts Payable must fully complete the 1099 reporting by January 31st. The busiest period just got a whole lot busier.

While it may depend on the types of payees and payments that your Accounts Payable department processed during the previous year, the 1099 review still presents a challenge to meet right after the New Year holidays. I have never experienced an easy "push of a button" kind of 1099 processing. I can imagine that the 1099 processing is probably fully automated in a bank processing forms 1099-INT, where all the information for the amounts paid and recipients of interest is in the bank's AP system – this is a straight-forward process. I can guess that your department's payees and payment types are much more diverse than interest recipients of a commercials bank. Correct processing of forms 1099-MISC is a time consuming and tedious task for most of medium to large businesses.

First, make sure that you have forms W-9 for all payees, new or existing, on file. Have the payees' AP records populated with the tax ID numbers and the form of business ownership information. Then report the totals for a given reported calendar year for rents, services, prizes and awards, other income payments, medical and health care payments, gross proceeds paid to an attorney of $600 or more and at least $10 in royalties. I cannot elaborate about "fishing boat proceeds" or "crop insurance proceeds" 1099 process – I don't know it and I don't know anyone who has ever processed any amounts to boxes 5 or 10 on form 1099-MISC.

One may ask, why bother doing the 1099 reporting at all? Don't people keep track of their earnings and report on their own? Some people do, some people don't. Some people don't because they honestly forget, some people don't want, when possible, to report their income and incur tax liability. Yes, some people in the United States are ready and willing, if presented with the opportunity, to conceal their income! And we know that reporting of income and tax collecting are important administrative functions that help to keep our country "going" and assure its continuous well-being. Fairness of the tax laws is a topic beyond the scope of this book; it can be addressed with the elected officials, if one feels strongly about making a change.

The accounts payable department's part in the process is to follow the tax law of the land, which simply requests to *report to recipients and the IRS (Nonemployee Compensation – Box 7) by January 31 payments of (1) $600 or more made during calendar year to all non-corporate income recipients, (2) medical/health and legal payments made to all business entities, (3) gross royalty payments of $10 or more paid to non-corporate recipients for patents, copyrights, trade names and trademarks and (4) file electronically with the IRS by March 31 (or by the end of February, if filed on paper) all payment types except the Nonemployee Compensation.* ***Note that 1099 reporting for year 2016 and after requires to furnish information to <u>both</u> recipients (All 1099 boxes) and the IRS (Box 7, Nonemployee compensation, filed with the IRS either on paper or electronically) by January 31st.***

Now, I will talk the "taxpayer conscience and moral responsibility" aspect of the reporting process. I don't assume that many people under-report their income – it is the truth and statistics. People desire to increase their discretionary income by reducing their taxes, often by not reporting income. Speak for myself? I will go as far as to state, that I will probably conveniently forget to include a piece of income if it is not reported to me and the IRS. Fair enough. If it's not a total black-out case, I admit that I may convincingly excuse myself for leaving a figure out of my 1040 form. It's just that I have never had a chance to. It's mostly been a few W-2s and 1099s duly mailed to my age-old residence in Bay Ridge NY.

As a fallible human being, who none the less understands the importance of fair tax laws supported and followed by all citizens of the country, I still humbly admit the possibility of my stumbling on the path of righteousness.

160

There is an ancient wisdom of not letting people come close to a desirable but forbidden thing, the wisdom not to test an individual's moral strength by placing him in the proximity to the sinful opportunities. That's what we do here. *Amen.*

We are, with our AP payments data and a stock of blank 1099-MISC forms, are the guardian angels in this case; we help assure honest dealings between the taxpayers and the tax authorities of our country. Form 1099-MISC reminds the recipients of the incomes received and alerts the IRS to expect that income to be included on individuals' forms 1040. Therefore, beware, the 1099 processing and customer service will at times become more adversarial than informational engagement.

Back to the 1099 processing business. Rents of $600 and over go to Box 1. Often rent is paid by your employee, during travel, to a non-corporate recipient. In the old days, I demanded that all third party reportable payments are made through the AP and not via the reimbursement process. While it may appear as a sound practice, it is impractical. I consulted the competent authorities and was told that the third-party *Reporting* is an acceptable practice if the information-gathering rules are followed. The process has less control indeed; you rely on someone else to make an inquiry with the rent collecting party (collecting the W-9 information) and have the information documented and provided to you. Good luck!

Royalty payments of at least $10 made to non-corporate intellectual property rights holders are reported in Box 2.

Other Income, reported in Box 3, must not be confused and used interchangeably with Nonemployee compensation of Box 7. Income in Box 7 is a service-type income (subject to self-employment tax) which reported on line 12 of *Form 1040* (US Individual Income Tax Return, see Appendix) and requires completing and attaching of *Schedule C (Profit and Loss From Business)*. The "Box 7" 1040 reporting process is more complicated for the income recipient than the "Box 3" 1040 reporting. There is of course no picking and choosing of what box to fill based on any preferences, you must follow the rules; but you need to be cognizant of what your reporting entails for the recipients. The 1099 is definitely not the "just report income in whatever box" approach and process.

Other Income (Box 3) may be prizes, awards, participant's fees, attendance fees, and other *passive* types of income. Other Income is thus very appropriately called 'passive income'.

Keep in mind, that non-service scholarship or fellowship, which must be truly *non-service*, by definition, are not reported to the IRS and the recipients. This may sound really odd as such scholarship and fellowship payments often amount to tens of thousands of dollars per year per student. But, the truth is, they are not required to be reported to the US persons. Students, on their own, must include the "non-qualifying" portion of scholarship or fellowship payments (for more information read Internal Revenue Section 117 in the Appendix) in their gross income. I was asked many times by the recipients about the process of scholarship or fellowship reporting and always surprised them by advising to merely include the *non-qualifying portion of scholarship or fellowship* (funds paid to a student at a qualified educational organization and not used for tuition, fees, books, supplies and equipment required for attendance, IRC § 117) on line 21 of the US individual income tax return (form 1040).

Be mindful that all scholarship or fellowship grants paid to a nonresident alien, [including non-*Accountable Plan* travel reimbursements, which are considered additional scholarship or fellowship], regardless of the amounts paid (there is no minimum reporting threshold), is reported on form 1042-S. Term *Scholarship* is mostly used for undergraduate grants payments. Term *Fellowship* is used for graduate and post-graduate grants payments. Avoid using term *Stipend* – it is vague and often all-inclusive.

The most used on form 1099-MISC Box 7, where payments for independent services are reported, may at times present you with a dilemma; service payments, when combined with travel reimbursements, can makes the total combined amount 1099-reportable (equal or more $600). A learned accountant knows that business expenses are accounted for on *Schedule C* and deducted from business income. The service fees amount taken separately, excluding the *Accountable Plan* business reimbursement that your company may have paid to a service provider, may alone not arise to the reporting threshold.

*To report or not to report – that is the question.* You will be correct following either approach. Practically, it is easier and less burdensome to separate service fees from *Accountable Plan* reimbursements payments and determine the report-ability solely on the total amount of service fees payments made to a contractor during calendar year. There will be no phone calls from the service providers complaining about your reporting practices and demands for cancellation of processed form 1099. There are two possible reasons why the recipients complain about this kind of borderline "service fees plus business expenses combined" reporting practice: filing of the tax return and Schedule C becomes a bit more cumbersome or, second, those desiring to "optimize taxes" (i.e. conceal income) are put on the IRS's radar by the issued form 1099 and now the income must be accounted for. Practically, there will be fewer 1099 forms to file and angry phone calls to answer if you do not include business reimbursements in your 1099 calculations; it makes sense to me not to do it – I have not been doing it. It should be decided as your company's policy to choose the *gross* or the *net* approach; once selected, the approach must be followed across the board uniformly for all payees. You should report payments for medical and health care services to all business entities, including corporations, in Box 6.

A special case in 1099 process: reporting federal income taxes withheld in Box 4. I haven't ever had any amount reported in Box 4. For accounts payable purposes, the 1099-MISC Box 4 shows back-up withholdings made from payments to the persons who have not furnished their W-9s to you. Remember an easy way out of the "No W-9 on file" situation – set up the 24% back-up tax withholding for the non-complying payees. Use it as a matter of fact tool – *I don't have your W-9 - I take 24% from your payments.* Practically speaking, the situation must not escalate to actually withholding the 24%. It is your leverage. And you only have the leverage before the payment is made.

With all the good advices provided hitherto, I know full well that there are situations when there is so much pressure to make a payment promptly, ASAP. And your boss wants this payment made with no W-9 on file – it's called 'management override'. But, in the end, *you* will be responsible for properly reporting this payment. True, you often find yourself between the rock and the hard place. I know it firsthand.

There *are* ways to find tax IDs online. Not all tax IDs – some of them. Use as the key words the company's tax name and *401 filing, SEC filing, state filing, form 990*. Many times, you will find the tax ID is some obscure pdf document filing with a pensions fund or state tax authorities.

Use this website to find out a corporation's EIN - https://opencorporates.com/info/about.

Match the number using the IRS ITIN Matching system. You will ask me: but how about the form of business ownership, what if it's a corporation? I'll tell you this – *forgetaboutit*. Report the payments made to the guy who refused to provide the W-9, but you were able to find the EIN for. If he doesn't like it – he will send over the W-9 after receiving the 1099.

The IRS alerts you [see Notice CP-2100 information] of prior year's 1099 names and tax IDs discrepancies; this is when you send out demands to your payees for updated forms W-9 (B-Notice or Back Up Withholding Warning Notice). It has never occurred in my practice that I demanded a corrected form W-9 from an active payee and was refused the information. You must begin 24% back-up tax withholding from all payments to non-compliant payees after certain actions and deadlines described in Notice CP-2100. If this tax withholding doesn't sound realistic, it is not. You will probably never have a case of back-up taxes reported in Box 4. For the payees, the trouble is not worth it.

Now you have your 1099 data ready for filing. Complete the forms. Let your system do it, of course. Your business address, your business tax ID, recipient's tax ID, recipient's name, address, account number (your internal payee account number – it comes in handy when/if the IRS communicates payee's information to you), reported amount or amounts (one form may show more than one amount, this rarely happens).

What's new on form 1099-MISC? Again, for year 2019, the tax ID number of the recipient may be "truncated", that is, shortened, for security purposes on paper forms (see proposed regulation §§1.6042-4(b) and 301.6109-4 (REG-148873-09)). Copy B, For Recipient, must be postmarked no later than January 31st. Box 7 payment data is reported to the IRS by January 31st as well. Again, this new process really amounts to a major change in the processing when the complete 1099 reporting must be finished by the end of January.

Paper returns to the IRS, Copy A, and summary form 1096 ('other than Box 7 amounts') must be postmarked no later than February 28th (or 29th). Electronic filing with the IRS ('other than Box 7 amounts') is due March 31st [no filing of form 1096 is required if filing with the IRS electronically]; the extra month is a very welcome extension since there are errors and discrepancies that will be reported to you by the 1099 recipients (the error rate depends on quality of the previous year W-9 data processing, complexity and variety of the payments your accounts payable department has made).

*If any of your Forms 1099-MISC reporting NEC will be filed after January 31, 2019, file them in a separate transmission from your Forms 1099-MISC without NEC (due April 1, 2019). Filers should anticipate that if transmissions sent after January 31, 2019, include both Forms 1099-MISC reporting NEC and Forms 1099-MISC that do not report NEC in a single transmission (on paper with a single Form 1096 or electronically through FIRE with a single payer "A" record), the IRS will treat every form in the single transmission as if it is subject to the section 6721 penalty for failure to file by January 31, 2019.*

Any correction on individual forms 1099 should ideally be made before you report the 1099 information to the IRS: first, the recipient does not get on the IRS' radar for "no good reason" (your erroneous reporting) and, second, the correction will be included in your original reporting to the IRS and will not require a separate correcting form 1099-MISC accompanied by summary form 1096 sent to the IRS on paper after the reporting deadline.

Unless your 1099 process is simple, transparent and flawless, do not rush getting individual forms mailed too early before January 31st. But watch the calendar! Don't be late with your filing!

Simple errors with your 1099 reporting (name and tax ID discrepancies) are reported to you by the IRS [via IRS Notice CP-2100, the *B-Notice*] in September-October, approximately nine months after your filing with the IRS.

That's all there is to keep in mind when processing the 1099-MISC forms; the following paragraphs are mere icing on the cake, the details. But, as you know, the devil is in the details. Remember that the IRS and the Treasure Department are tightening the individuals' tax reporting and compliance monitoring and requirements.

**Form W-9.** An efficient and tax compliant 1099 processing begins with requesting from all new payees and processing forms W-9. You must have current form W-9 for all your payees with no exception to the business ownership or tax exemption status. This does not mean that the most recent IRS version of the W-9 (October 2018) must be completed by all: only changes in the existing on file information, or additional FATCA requirements must be obtained from the vendors. You must receive a properly completed form W-9 (with some exception) from every new payee that you make payments to (I frequently use the word *payee* and not *vendor* since it is an all-inclusive, businesses and individuals, AP term).

Next is the proper new payee set up in the AP system. This is the time to ensure that there will be less hassle down the road. Pay attention to the DBA (*Doing Business As...*) name and the legal name. Tax ID numbers are assigned to legal names and not DBA names. Having DBA names on forms 1099 triggers a voluminous B-notice letter from the IRS.

Reading and understanding form W-9 and transferring the W-9 information into accounts payable system must be done by a trained person, who comprehends well the concepts of legal name, DBA, and related tax ID rules, forms of business ownership and rules of the US tax IDs structure. If there is a person's name in the "name, as shown on your income tax return" field and no social security number provided (but the employer ID) – ask for clarifications (individual's name, being the legal name, requires social security number to be provided, not employer identification number, unless a business is registered under the individual's name).

I want to emphasize – **an efficient and quality 1099 year-end processing never ends – tend to it at all time by maintaining the integrity of the accounts payable system payees' records.** New form W-9, revised by the IRS in October 2018, requires FATCA related codes entered in the 'exempt' section of the W-9. By the way, the 'not-for-profit' coding is '1' and 'A' for most 501(c) (3) companies.

Having repeated the importance of requesting the W-9 many times, can every new payee furnish form W-9 to you? No. A US business or person must supply form W-9. *A foreign payee cannot sign form W-9* and the most recent version of form W-9 has an important clarification about the W-9 filing requirement asking to certify that the person or business, named on the W-9, is a "US citizen or other US person" and requiring a "Signature of US person". Further in the W-9 instructions you can find the following: "If you are a foreign person, do not use Form W-9".

Why can't a foreign person who possesses a valid US social security or other tax ID number sign the W-9? Paying foreign payees requires a statutory 30% tax withholding, unless one of the IRS tax exemption codes can be applied (more about paying a foreign businesses or persons in later chapters). Not determining a proper residency status may cause tax liability, which adds up close to half of the payment amount processed improperly under the US residency assumption. *Example:*

*Payment of $100 was made, with an assumption of the US tax residency based on completed form W-9. 30% tax was not applied. Gross up the amount to what it should have* *been in order to issue a net $100 check after withholding 30% tax. $100 / 70% (100/0.7) = 143. <u>Back-tax owed to the IRS is $43 plus fees and penalties.</u>*

Keep in mind that many times form W-9 is completed by foreign individuals that have valid US tax IDs. This is improper unless you can establish that such individual is a *US tax resident*. Prior to about 2001 temporary visitors in the US were able to obtain a US social security number. I know because I was one of them way back.

For all domestic businesses and persons, form W-9 has two options for the name – *Name* (as shown on your income tax return) and *Business name* (that is, DBA – *Doing Business As*, not the tax name). This may be confusing for many; *Business name/DBA* may be the same as the *Tax Name*. But many times, *Business name/DBA* is not the *Tax Name* and since there is no tax ID for *Business name/DBA*, you will end up supplying technically incorrect information (if 1099 filing is required) to the IRS. The IRS will ask you to correct this discrepancy by mailing to you Notice CP-2100A (also called the B-Notice, but the two are different documents of the same process).

It is very important to understand, based on the completed form W-9, what form of business ownership the payee is formed under. The appropriate box must be checked. If the *Individual/sole proprietor* box is checked, a person's name must appear in the *Name* box and a social security number provided. For all other forms of business ownership, the *EIN* (employer identification number) must be provided. A *Limited Liability Company (LLC)* may be treated for tax purposes as a (1) *disregarded entity*, (2) *corporation* or (3) *partnership.* This is an important distinction to keep in mind, since the corporate treatment does not require you to file form 1099; corporate exemption does not apply to medical and legal LLC-corporations and corporations (Inc.).

Partnership form of business ownership does require the 1099 filing. This is a fine point to understand and apply. I believe that given the importance of practical W-9/1099 corporation-partnership classification it is worth a more in-depth analysis. Nathan M. Bisk, JD, CPA provides an excellent description of this partnership-corporation selection in his books "CPA Review: Regulations":

*Under the 'check-the-box' regulations, an eligible entity may elect its classification for federal tax purposes. An eligible entity is an entity that does not meet the definition of a corporation under the regulations, and is not a single owner entity, trust, or otherwise subject to special treatment under the IRC. If the entity fails to elect a classification, the regulations provide a default classification. The use is broader than the common law meaning and may include groups not commonly called partnerships. (a) A partnership is a syndicate, group, pool, joint venture, or other unincorporated entity through which a business is carried on, and which is not a corporation, trust, or estate. (b) Mere co-ownership of property is not a partnership. However, if the entity provides services in conjunction with the use of the property by the lessee or licensee, the entity may be characterized as a partnership. (c) Limited partnerships are subject to the same rules as general partnerships. (d) Limited liability entities may be classified for federal tax purposes as either corporations or partnerships. Limited liability companies (LLC), limited liability partnerships (LLP), professional limited liability companies, etc. are frequently designed to take advantage of the pass-through tax status of partnerships and limited legal liability of corporations, but the partnership tax status is not automatic. Unless a limited liability entity meets conditions that require it to be taxed as a corporation or it elects to be so treated, it is treated as a partnership for tax purposes.*

Governmental, not-for-profit and other tax-exempt businesses and organizations must enter the *Exempt Payee Code* if one is available from the list of codes found in the instructions for form W-9 revised in October 2018. [Note that 501(c)(3) not-for-profit organizations fall within IRC Section 501(a), Exemption Payee "1", Exempt from FATCA "A".]

The following codes identify payees that are exempt from backup withholding: 1 - An organization exempt from tax under section 501(a), any IRA, or a custodial account under section 403(b)(7) if the account satisfies the requirements of section 401(f)(2). 2 - The United States or any of its agencies or instrumentalities. 3 - A state, the District of Columbia, a possession of the United States, or any of their political subdivisions or instrumentalities. 4 - A foreign government or any of its political subdivisions, agencies, or instrumentalities. 5 – A corporation. 6 – A dealer in securities or commodities required to register in the United States, the District of Columbia, or a possession of the United States. 7 - A futures commission merchant registered with the Commodity Futures Trading Commission. 8 - A real estate investment trust. 9 - An entity registered at all times during the tax year under the

Investment Company Act of 1940. 10 - A common trust fund operated by a bank under section 584(a). 11 - A financial institution. 12 - A middleman known in the investment community as a nominee or custodian. 13 - A trust exempt from tax under section 664 or described in section 4947.

There are boxes on form W-9 for address, account number and signature. Having properly completed form W-9 on file fulfills your responsibility to collect payees' tax ID and business ownership status information. You may find it useful to register with *Dan & Bradstreet* services (http://www.dnb.com) to validate companies' names and receive other relevant for your accounts payable purposes information.

Another form required by your company (not the IRS) to be completed by all new payees should be your internally-created *New Payee Questionnaire*. This form should have additional payee's information, such as contact names, phone numbers, fax numbers, email addresses, company website, remittance address(s), bank account information (ABA/routing number, account number, account name, accounts receivable contact information and email address). Bank account information may be provided on the payee's dedicated form and supported by a copy of vendor's check usually marked "void". Your *New Payee Questionnaire* must require immigration status, tax residency and foreign business or individual's US tax ID information and certification, something that form W-9 is not designed to do.

Failure to furnish form W-9 to you must trigger back-up withholding at the rate of 24%. The back-up withholding is reported to the IRS on form *945* and to the payee on form

1099-MISC. I have not processed one such 24% withholding in my career, although had set up many payees for back-up tax withholding. All payees comply with your W-9 requirement once you explain what the noncompliance may trigger: back-up taxes and, possibly, IRS audit. So, remember that "no W-9 on file" is not a stalemate – take the tax and move on (by now you should be able to discern that this last advice is more theoretical than practical).

Did I say that the foreign persons cannot by IRS regulation sign form W-9? What form do the temporary residents sign to certify their possession of a US tax ID number? Many times, you hear the advice to "sign the appropriate form W-8". This is wrong. First, there may be no appropriate form for a temporary visitor to sign, and second, those forms W-8xxx (W-8BEN, W-8ECI, W-8EXP, W-8IMY) are not used for the purpose of collection nonresident alien tax IDs. Those forms serve other purposes: W-8BEN to certify foreign status of beneficial owner for United States tax withholding, W-ECI to certify foreign person's claim that income is effectively connected with the conduct of a trade or business in the United States. The bottom line is that any form W-8xxx (W-8 has been out of use for more than ten years) cannot be used with the temporary residents instead of form W-9. The AP professionals who suggest the W-8's use just do not know enough about the nonresident alien taxation. Also, allowing the foreign persons to use forms W-8xxx may give them a false impression that they may eligible to certain US tax benefits when, in fact, they are not. You can read more about forms W-8xxx on the following IRS web-page:

http://www.irs.gov/uac/Form-W-8,-Certificate-of-Foreign-Status

If you need to collect a US tax ID from a temporary US visitor, use your internally developed New Payee Questionnaire, on which you should also ask about the visa status and other nonresident alien-related questions (history of priory US visits, copies of various immigration forms (visa, I94, DS2019, I20, etc.).

The most recent updates to form W-9 were officiated in October 2018 to reflect the final amendment to the Income Tax Regulations commonly known as the Foreign Tax Compliance Act, or FATCA. The FATCA reporting requires a participating foreign financial institution to report all US account holders that are specified US persons. The FATCA is designed to better track worldwide income of US persons by requiring much greater information sharing by the US and foreign financial institutions. Certain payees are exempt from FATCA reporting. There is a list of codes (A through M) provided in the instructions to form W-9.

The new W-9 form has the former "Exempt Payee" section, which was used on all previous forms W-9 by not-for-profit organizations, United States agencies, etc., renamed "Exemptions" and separated into two sub-sections: the familiar "Exempt payee code" and the new *Exemption from FATCA reporting code*". The completion of the FATCA exemption code section does not affect your company's new payees or 1099 processing unless your company makes payments to financial institutions which are required to report income payments to account holders who are US persons under the FATCA regulations.

*(Form W-9, revised in October 2018)*

Document the 1099 processing in the department's policies and procedures. The 1099 policies and procedures must be approved and updated every time the process changes and reviewed once a year. The policies describe your tax treatment and coding of the AP payments. The procedures describe how your department is processing the 1099s. The 1099 processing includes the AP activities that begin with collecting of form W-9, setting up new payee ID correctly with the proper 1099 "flags", processing invoices and payment requests of your payees. Every action of the

1099 process must be outlined in your policies and procedures for you to refer to, for others who will one day replace you, or as a basis and justifications of the actions that you take in relation to the 1099 processing.

When form W-9 is submitted by a payee, your next step is creating a payee ID, which is the next crucial step in the 1099 compliance process. To create a new payee, you need to submit *New Payee Setup* requisition form to a person who, according to the segregation of duties concept, has no other accounts payable function, but new payees' creation. You must have an established payee IDs creating system which is logical, understood and consistent. I believe that using letters and numbers combination is the best system to unitize, where technically feasible. Using letters gives you more room to create new payees in the years to come, since there are 26 letters and (only) 10 numbers (0 to 9) to use in each place. Sequential payee ID generation is widely used in many AP systems.

There may be certain 1099 reports, depending on the system that your company is using, where only vendor IDs are showing against other AP data. It is impossible, using the "numbers only" payee IDs, to have a quick understanding of the payees' names without translating the payees' IDs into the names first. It does save time during AP data entry as well, to understand which payee is being processed by just seeing payee's ID.

If the business name is different from the legal name, use the name under which the business normally operates, shows on the invoices and represents itself under. Add a different tax name, if necessary, in the *Legal Name* field in the payee set up. The legal name may be very unfamiliar to people involved in the accounts payable process – making the legal name main search criteria may delay the search process or, worse, lead to an assumption that payee is a new payee, which results in (attempt of) duplicate payee creation. Duplicate payee's creation is one of the big *No-no's* in the accounts payable. One way to avoid this is to run duplicate payees' tax ID or 'duplicate address' reports or "flag and stop" new payee tax IDs entry (upon new payee creation) as a duplication of the existing one.

A payee may have many "remit-to" addresses. Usually, these multiple-remittance addresses payees are large corporations, such as AT&T, Verizon or various IRS's processing centers. Large companies process different locations' invoice at their different offices around the US.

What is more critical is to realize, in some cases, that "a new remittance address" for identically sounding business name is not a new remittance address at all, but a remittance address for a different business altogether, possibly a *franchise* which operates under the same brand name, but a different tax name and tax ID. Franchise is a right to operation under a well-known business name, such as McDonald's, with each franchisee being a separate business for all other purposes: "*McDonald's continues to be recognized as a premier franchising company around the world. More than 80% of our restaurants worldwide are owned and operated by our Franchisees*" (quoted from the McDonald Co. website, below):

http://www.aboutmcdonalds.com/mcd/franchising.html

Again, form W-9 provides the information about all the critical data in this less than clear situation, such as Business Name and tax ID number.

New payees' initial setup information and supporting documents (form W-9, New Payee Questionnaire) must be imaged and accessible from the *Payee* general informational menu for future 1099 references and verifications.

**Independent Contractor: How, When & Where.** One of the most important 1099-related determinations that is made in the Accounts Payable is the proper classification of the independent contractors and coding all such payee accordingly for 1099 reporting. Who is considered an independent contractor? Can one choose to be an independent contractor if it is more beneficial for the individual's tax purposes rather than becoming a company's employee?

*Who is an employee and who is independent contractors?*

The following is the IRS's approach to this crucial determination, which is made in the Accounts Payable department and cannot be decided by any other than the IRS mandated method:

*The general rule is that an individual is an independent contractor if the payer has the right to control or direct only the result of the work and not what will be done and how it will be done. The earnings of a person who is working as an independent contractor are subject to Self-Employment Tax.*

*It is critical that business owners correctly determine whether the individuals providing services are employees or independent contractors. Generally, you must withhold income taxes, withhold and pay Social Security and Medicare taxes, and pay unemployment tax on wages paid to an employee. You do not generally have to withhold or pay any taxes on payments to independent contractors.*

An independent contractor is an individual or business providing services free from direction and control of performance including the means and methods used. Independent contractors fall into two categories: a company or firm providing service or individuals who are clearly in business for themselves such as doctors, computer programmers, accountants, lawyers, construction contractors, electricians, and other. It is the responsibility of the department that hires independent contractors to make *initial* determination as to whether to classify an individual as an employee or an independent contractor.

The IRS has issued general guidelines rather than more specific regulations on the employee vs. independent contractor distinction. Each contract with independent contractor must be evaluated very carefully. There is no single criterion which determines classification one way or another. Extra caution must be taken before signing contracts with individuals (1) not ordinarily in consulting business or (2) with past company's employees.

The general IRS rule is: if an individual is subject to the control or direction of another merely as to the result to be accomplished by the work and not as to the means and methods for accomplishing the results, such individual is an independent contractor, rather than an employee. Most of the IRS's criteria for determining the status of a service provider hinge on the idea of *the degree of control the employer exercises over the individual.* Keep in mind that for the IRS, it doesn't matter whether or not this control is actually exercised, just that a relationship of control exists. In each case, it is very important to consider all the facts - no single fact provides the answer.

**Moving Expenses and 1099 Reporting.** According to the IRS moving expenses that are deductible and those that are not, may be reimbursed to an individual. Those reimbursements that are not deductible must be treated as taxable wages, subject to FICA and income tax and reported on form W2 (non-taxable moving expenses must also be reported on form W2 in box 12). If the individual whom you reimburse for moving expenses is not employed by your company (when your company acts as a payment agent for another business), both taxable and non-taxable expenses may be reimbursed, but the taxable expenses must be reported on form 1099-MISC. Read the IRS Topic 455 – Moving Expenses, below:

*If you moved due to a change in your job or business location, or because you started a new job or business, you may be able to deduct your reasonable moving expenses but not any expenses for meals. To qualify for the moving expense deduction, you must satisfy two tests. Under the first test, the "**distance test**," your new workplace must be at least 50 miles farther from your old home than your old job location was from your old home. If you had no previous workplace, your new job location must be at least 50 miles from your old home.*

*The second test is the "**time test**." If you are an employee, you must work full-time for at least 39 weeks during the first 12 months immediately following your arrival in the general* *area of your new job location. If you are self-employed, you must work full time for at least 39 weeks during the first 12 months and for a total of at least 78 weeks during the first 24 months immediately following your arrival in the general area of your new work location. There are exceptions to the time test in case of death, disability and involuntary separation, among other things.*

Non-taxable moving expenses include: (a) cost of packing, crating and transportation of household goods and personal items, (b) shipping of car and household pets to new residence, (c) travel expenses to new residence, including car rental and gas, lodging (only *to* new residence). For the use of personal car an individual can claim actual gas cost *or* current mileage rate reimbursement, (d) storage and insurance of household goods for a period of up to 30 days, (e) expenses of shipping household goods to and from storage.

Taxable moving expenses include: (a) any portion of purchase price of new residence, (b) expenses of buying or selling of old/new residence, (c) expenses of getting into or "breaking" a lease, (d) home improvements to sell old residence, (e) loss on sale of old residence, (f) meal expenses, (g) new residence "house-hunting" expenses, (h) temporary living expenses, (i) repair, maintenance, insurance or depreciation of a car, (j) legal fees.

Request for reimbursement for moving expenses must be submitted within 60 days of relocation and incurring of such expenses.

**Processing forms 1099-MISC and 1096.** Start the 1099 review on December 1st for the preceding eleven months of the year. Complete the 11/12 or the review job in December and review the month of December in January.

This will leave plenty of time in January to better review and structure the process and not be pressed too much by the January 31st deadline. Another important consideration for starting it all in December; if there are any AP and payroll unjustifiable overlaps they should be 'moved' to payroll and W2 forms. The best time to do it is before the year end in December.

There are important 1099-related deadlines to keep in mind. Just like the W2's, *copy B* (For recipient) of form 1099 must be postmarked no later than January 31st. Box 7 1099 reporting to the IRS is due January 31st, as well. Paper 1099 reporting to the IRS along with the summary form 1096 is due February 28 (except Nonemployee compensation information, Box 7 information). You will have more time to hear back from your 1099 recipients, and possibly make corrections on your 1099, if you file 1099s with the IRS electronically. The due date for filing the 1099 online is March 31st (except Nonemployee compensation, Box 7 information).

It is a good idea to set up a calendar with the internal 1099 processing deadlines and IRS filing due dates and monitor the 1099 process based on the target dates. *Note that 1099 reporting for year 2016 and after requires to furnish information to both recipients (All 1099 boxes) and the IRS (Box 7 1099 information, filed with the IRS either on paper form 1096 or electronically) by January 31st.*

You will need a *Transmitter Control Code* (TCC) to submit the 1099 to the IRS electronically. Read *IRS Publication 1220* to learn how to apply for the transmitter control code (TCC) and process forms 1099 online. The extra month (March) before your 1099 electronic reporting is due to the IRS allows extra time to correct any discrepancy reported to you by the 1099 recipients.

Any 1099 corrections done before submitting files to the IRS is a much easier process, since correcting 1099s after the IRS reporting requires correcting of both *Copy B* (for recipient) and *copy A* (for the IRS) along with form 1096, which (1099 copy A and form 1096) are then mailed to the IRS.

The correction process brings about another issue – mailing addresses on forms 1099. You must have a verification process in place that assures that all forms 1099 are mailed to the most recent and valid addresses. You can base this review on the last remittance address used to mail payments to. With the EFT's payment method becoming more and more dominant, it is possible to have old physical address information on file, while maintaining correct banking information. Therefore, pay attention to all returned to you by the USPS forms 1099 and re-address them promptly.

Make sure all your 1099 recipients to receive the forms not only to allow them a timely tax reporting, but to give them an opportunity to provide feedback on any possible errors or discrepancies on forms 1099 that you have mailed out. It is a very difficult situation to find yourself in when a misaddressed form is lost in transit, the intended recipient does not include the 1099 income on the tax return and is later contacted by the IRS about the under-reported income, resulting in additional taxes, penalties, and fees. To make the matter worse, the information on lost forms 1099 may be incorrect as reported to the IRS.

The order and ease of the 1099 review depends on quality of your accounts payable processing during the previous year. I admit that with large-scale distributed AP operations you cannot always control the AP quality 100%; you cannot review all payments processed during the year, cannot review correctness of payments coding by other departments or changes made to the vendors' tax reporting flags on the transaction level.

The accounts payable data entry may be also partially outsourced to remote offices and locations while your central-office Accounts Payable department only reviews the AP data entry, but does not originate them. There is a higher probability of AP tax reporting input errors in larger Accounts Payable departments, with high volume payment activity, numerous payments types made, and constant pressure to keep the AP payments processing flow. Even with the best internal controls and policies and procedures it is possible to have errors in the AP system that generates the 1099 data.

The quantity of errors is also affected by the AP system that you use; the ERP's capturing all information and having more built-in intelligence is far superior to the "fractured databases" scenario with independent processing systems used for various business purposes (AP, payroll, nonresident alien, imaging databases). For example:

*A payment was made to a nonresident alien in the US and reported on form 1042-S, but during the last year the person became US permanent resident and now his service payments are reported on form 1099. Unless the information was transferred from the nonresident alien database to the*

*AP database, the change in status will not be reflected automatically in the AP database.*

There are many other 1099 pitfalls that one may get into – let's review one more:

*An independent contractor, who had received reportable service payments in the prior to the reporting year, visited your company last year and only asked to be reimbursed for travel. A 1099 form was issued with the travel reimbursement payment amount on it, based on previous tax reporting classification.*

There may be reimbursements to your company's employees for service payments to third parties; this should be avoided and all such service payments are made directly to the service providers who are required to furnish forms W-9 and be set up properly as separate payees.

I recall a few instances where payments were made to individuals, but the 1099 tax names were corporate and non-reportable, *Inc.*-type names. This is incorrect and the trace of it goes back to receiving, reading, understanding and entering the W-9 information properly into AP system. A payment should not be made to an individual who has a W-9 form submitted for a non-reportable, corporate-type business (e.g. payments made to Bob Miles, while the W-9 (non-medical/legal service type) name on file is B Miles Corporation).

When I think and write about how *things should be done* in the accounts payable department, I wonder how errors can ever sneak into the accounts payable process undetected. But you and I know that in the real world the imperfections do enter into your department's work for a variety of objective, subjective, staff-related, mood-related, valid, silly, and many other reasons.

Remember that your company's employees must not be paid any kind of 1099-reportable compensation. All services performed by your company's employees must be processed through the Payroll Department. Ideally, even the out-of-pocket and travel reimbursements should be included with payroll payments. Processing a service payment from the Accounts Payable will result first in issuing of a 1099 form and subsequent voiding of the 1099 form and adjusting of the employee's W-2 form (W-2C). This will trigger your company's additional FICA and unemployment taxes liability and correction of the W-2 information already processed with the IRS; this is a very undesirable situation that can also invite an unwanted IRS's attention to your processing. Processing of form 1099 and W-2 for the same individual for the same year is possible when the individual initially had been an independent contractor and has later become employed by the company.

One 'classic' example of someone justifiably receiving both forms W2 and 1099 from the same business for the same period is often provided during the 1099 trainings seminars: an IT programmer cleans company's restrooms at night time, thus being employed as an IT specialist and contracted with for independent servicing of the company's premises as a janitor, providing different kinds of services and thus correctly receiving both forms 1099 and W-2. The restless IT Programmer gets picked on all the time.

Another 'suspect' W2 and 1099 recipient situation may come about when a former employee now provides independent consultant's 1099 services for the same business. The tax authorities may reasonably infer an illegal 'tax optimization' scheme in the same employment circumstances. It is a prudent and desired goal of an Accounts Payable (in team with payroll) department to avoid overlapping of names on forms W2 and 1099. It's best to have both Accounts Payable and Payroll records within one system to assure a better and system-based checking on any employee payment processed through the accounts payable process vs. payroll records. A good practice is to include any proper AP payments to employees (such as travel, out of pocket, tuition reimbursements) with employees' payroll payments or via Concur or similar reimbursement systems.

**Every Accounts Payable department must have all processed payments documents saved in the electronic format - indexed and readily available for reviews.**

Requesting paper documents for review from your in-house storage or, worse, outside storage location, waiting for documents to be delivered to your desk, is long and frustrating. Costs savings related to elimination of paper storage and document retrieval will quickly offset your investment in imaging systems and greatly improve the quality of all of your accounts payable work, not only your 1099 review.

90% of accounts payable 1099 process deals with generating forms **1099-MISC**; the form reports payments (total payments made in a calendar year) of $600 and more made to non-corporate businesses (exclude limited liability companies (LLC) treated as corporations for tax purposes) for rents, services (including parts and materials), prizes and awards, other income payments, medical and healthcare payments and royalties of $10 and more. The exemption from reporting payments made to corporations does not apply to payments for legal and medical/health care payments to corporations. Do not report on form 1099-MISC wages paid to employees, payments for merchandise, telephone, freight, storage or payment to tax-exempt organization.

A unique reporting item on form 1099-MISC is the deceased employee's wages. You must report the accrued wages and other compensation paid after the date of death to the estate of beneficiary (in box 3). This information can be found in the instructions for processing Form 1099-MISC on the following website:

http://www.irs.gov/uac/Form-1099-MISC,-Miscellaneous-Income-

The AP department may also process forms 1099-DIV, 1099-INT, 1099-B and 1099-C. Refer to the following IRS website for more information on other forms 1099:

http://apps.irs.gov/app/picklist/list/formsInstructions.html?value=1099&criteria=formNumber

Take your time during the months of December and January – do not rush the 1099 review unless the last year's AP payments were straight-forward one type of payment (e.g. interest on deposits reported by bank), or low volume AP payments, which allow a quick 1099 review. When you believe that your 1099 file has tax IDs for all generated forms 1099 which are nine digits in length, in proper xxx-xx-xxxx (SSN) or xx-xxxxxxx (EIN) format (b) correct business names for the respective tax IDs (c) correct reported amounts (d) in correct income types boxes selected, and, finally (e) correct mailing address, you can print and mail 1099s out to recipients (no later than January 31st). By the way, the IRS, while requesting a correct format for the SSNs and EINs, accepts a tax number provided as one nine-digit number. But for your processing purposes it is advisable to be able to differentiate between the SSNs and EINs to better monitor the tax ID relation to the tax name.

The online 1099 IRS submission is by all means a far superior process compared to the archaic filing of paper forms with the IRS. The FIRE System new account set up is found at this web-address: https://fire.irs.gov/firev1r/Register.aspx

The 1099 text data file, posted on the IRS website, if not formatted properly (the file should be a plain text file) will have a "BAD" status. All *bad* files must be corrected through the 'Replace' process. The old bad file's result status will change to 'replaced' and a new corrected file submission will have 'GOOD, Not Released' status assigned to it. It will remain in this status for ten days after which the IRS will have the file accepted. Keep in mind, that during the ten days while the file is in 'Good, Not Released' status, you can call the IRS to have its processing stopped. The IRS will advise you to wait until the 'Good, Not Released' status changes to 'BAD', after which you can process another file using the 'replace' process.

All corrections of individual forms 1099 after filing them with the IRS are done on paper; corrected paper forms sent to the IRS (Copy A) must be accompanied by summary form 1096. File the summary form 1096 just for the attached to the form 1096 form(s) 1099, nothing else.

It is very important, while correcting forms 1099s based on the recipients' feedback and before reporting 1099 data to the IRS, in case there is time between your January reporting to the recipients and January 31st reporting to the IRS to correct both *Copy B* (for recipient) and your 1099 IRS data file, which is later transmitted to the IRS. You do not want to have any discrepancy between what is reported to the recipients and the IRS – this is a very important consideration to keep in mind.

My last *1099 advice* is rather unusual. Being an accounts payable manager with many other responsibilities that fill my busy day in the office, I still stuff all processed forms 1099s in the envelopes *myself*. This tedious procedure allows for one last looks at each processed form, now printed on paper; it is a very laborious process of handling close to 2,000 forms, but I do it nonetheless and always find few issues during this process. I am a perfectionist and a controlling person – a mixed blessing.

The 1099 review is a time-consuming project for which there is no easy "system" solution. I was reassured early in year 2018 that this last manual 1099 review does make sense. When processing year 2017 forms 1099, I noticed during my mailing of the forms that some amounts on the 1099s looked wrong, being much larger than what I remembered they should be. I was baffled to say the least; this has happened after a thorough review of the 1099 forms and necessary adjustments to them – the 1099 forms were supposed to be flawless. It later transpired, after my emergency investigation of the situation, that my company's new ERP system (Kuali) was doubling the reported amounts for payees who received wire transfers (Fedwires) 1099 reportable payments every time I updated the 1099 totals during the review and correction process. The reason is still being investigated, but the damage could have been done if I'd trusted the system completely.

Another check point for this situation is of course a comparison of the '1099 boxes totals' of the manual file to the system records; that, again, is possible if one keeps a tally of the 1099 amounts in a separate file and doesn't rely on the system alone to keep accurate records, the old school approach.

Here is one more practical advice: err on the side of over-reporting and not the other way around. *A Big Corporation* that sells you "merchandise" and receives form 1099 from you will not bother to call to have the 1099 cancelled. An individual who finds discrepancy on form 1099 will definitely contact you (remember to use the most current and verified address). You don't want the IRS auditors to find reportable payments processed by your Accounts Payable department and not reported. Remember, *when in doubt – mail it out –* well, yes, in this situation, do.

**Correct and reissue the 1099 forms based on the 1099 recipients' feedback and adjust the IRS data file accordingly. Re-mail promptly all returned by the USPS (as undeliverable) forms 1099 to corrected addresses – leave no form undelivered and returned.**

The 1099 reporting process is often an adversarial process that receives little appreciation by the recipients or your company top managers; the reporting informs many recipients of additional tax liability and your company management may be contacted by complaining 1099 recipients who didn't receive relief from the tax reporting after their initial contacting and pleading with you. Many individuals are under the impression, falsely given to them by the departments and branches that initiated the contracts, that the payments are not reportable and will not be reported. This is especially true for companies that make a variety of diverse payments. Processing of 1099 often requires a degree of personal and professional character fortitude, thorough understanding of the process, ability to communicate, and knowing that your actions contribute to a better compliance and fiscal health of your company.

During the reporting period, besieged by the 1099 recipients who provide all kinds of reasons why the 1099 reporting must be reversed, quoting the IRS regulations, reminding of verbal promises of non-reporting made to them, or their tax accountants sending technical 'tricks' to zero the reported amounts I often jokingly say to myself: *The Pledge of Allegiance in the morning, a pint of beer at night – it'll be alright.*

*Commercial cards and 1099 reporting.* The IRS's section 6050W requires merchant banks to report to the IRS 1099 data processed through their networks. It is no longer your department's responsibility to issue forms 1099 for reportable payments made with commercial credit cards. The 6050W regulation came as great relief to the AP world; it was very difficult to properly report on commercial cards merchants over which accounts payable departments had no processing controls.

## IRS Notice CP-2100A and Backup Withholding

*We're notifying you that payee information may be incorrect. You may need to begin backup withholding.* This is the beginning of Notice CP-2100A. The language "may be incorrect" means that the **tax IDs** information or, note this, **tax names,** as provided on forms 1099-MISC, which you had filed earlier in the year, is incorrect. Some tax IDs and tax names do not match the IRS records. It is important to understand that notice CP-2100A does not tell you to assume (although it may be the case) that listed on the notice tax IDs are incorrect. It tells you that the IRS could not match the reported tax IDs with the reported tax names on your submitted forms 1099 and, as a result, could not track and compare reported by you (on from 1099) income to the income reported by the individuals and businesses who received your forms 1099. Therefore, your will be looking for errors in two places: tax IDs and/or respective tax names.

Why should I be investigating this and not merely request a new form W-9 completed? For two reasons; after reviewing the documents on file you may realize that some tax IDs or tax ID-associated names are not those reported to you by the payee on form W-9s. It was your internal clerical error and must be resolved internally. It can be fixed on the spot. Examples: misinterpreting handwritten on the W9s Tax ID numbers with 1s, 4s, and 7s, having DBAs in (tax) Name, etc.

If the IRS reports to you as incorrect the information as it appears on forms W-9s submitted to you, you must send out *First B-notice (Back-Up withholding notice)* within 15 business days from your receipt of the Notice CP-2100A.

The B-notice informs payee(s) that you are required to begin a backup withholding at a rate of 24% (the withheld tax is remitted to the IRS using the EFTPS processing and reported to the IRS on form 945). Ordered by the IRS action requires you to withhold the backup tax. But earlier the notice says that "you may need to update your records or begin backup withholding." This means that in case that you have your records corrected by mean of internal review or updated W-9 submission, there will be no need to withhold the 24% tax.

The payees to whom you mail the B-Notice must send you updated forms W-9. Note that the B-Notice is the Back-Up Withholding Notice that you send out to your payees with tax ID-name discrepancies. A payee is more likely to respond if you have ongoing payment relationships. There may be one-time payees, whom you had paid in the past and whose names appeared on the Notice CP-2100A who may never reply to you, because they do not want to provide you correct W9 information or just don't care to reply. On the other hand, there are many business and individuals who will immediately send you the required information. Keep in mind that you cannot update the tax ID information over the phone, according to the IRS' instructions.

As soon as you receive Notice CP-2100A, you should put all listed thereon payees *on AP-hold*. That means that from that day on you should not inadvertently make another payment to any payee on the list without first correcting their tax information (or withhold the 24% tax). And payees, understandingly, are much more willing to provide you the requested information if there are held, pending updated form W-9 receipt, payments.

Before I send a second B-notice out, I add the backup withholding percentage (24%) to those payees who did not respond to me, release the payees' ID from hold and make a note of the IRS notice in the payees' ID reference field. By this time, you have all those who responded released from hold and non-responders off hold with the tax rate assigned.

The *B-Notice* is supposed to be a straight-forward process, but like many other seemingly simple processes in the accounts payable it can become complicated where you least expect it. I had a person on the IRS notice CP-2100A with whom we had an ongoing business relationship, that is, he was billing for services and we were paying. I sent him a letter asking for update on the W-9 information. The W-9 was returned with the same information as before. I contacted the person again – same results. I then asked to send me a copy of the social security card. Why did I do it and not just keep the signed W-9 on file? The new reportable amount was quite substantial and I did not want to report it again with the same SSN, flagged by the IRS as erroneous. There were many payments made after the October 24th notice date – I could not use an excuse that the payments were made before the notice was received. And you don't want to be questioned by the IRS even if you have done it all right. I received a copy of the person's SSN. Lo and behold there was another name between first and last names used by the person. This is where the TIN matching system comes in so handy – I could only figure this situation with the help of the IRS's matching tool. The middle name, never used by the person, was the first part of the person's last name, according to the IRS records. How was he doing his person tax reporting all his life – I know not.

Correction of tax IDs, being the first "action", the second one is "requesting the TIN", if payee's TIN is missing from your records all together. This should not be the case for any orderly accounts payable operation. You must have tax IDs on file for all payees. At this time, most of the AP systems "flag" the missing or incorrectly structured tax IDs and don't allow for 1099 processing if a tax ID is missing or formatted incorrectly. I have suggested to my IT team to add functionality to our ERP system when each tax ID is checked against the tax name, based on my access to the IRS TIN-matching system. I do not know of any ERP that currently does this kind of IRS-linked matching within the system.

Keep track of all B-Notices that you mail out and payees' responses. Update the AP records and assign the 24% tax to the non-responders. Make sure that the assigned tax is not removed by another AP system' authorized user.

In year 2016 the IRS made the B-Notice process a little easier for an unlikely situation that are you paying a vendor with a B-Notice, still have no correct EIN on file, and collecting the 24% back up withholding. The rule is called "2nd Tin not." – see a quote from the 2016 1099-MISC Instructions on it:

*You may enter an "X" in this box if you were notified by the IRS twice within 3 calendar years that the payee provided an incorrect taxpayer identification number (TIN). If you mark this box, the IRS will not send you any further notices about this account.*

Will IRS show at your door to check on all those X'd accounts, and other things? You don't want to find out.

# Nonresident alien tax compliance in Accounts Payable operations

With our business world becoming more and more international, mobile and interdependent you may have noticed the increased number of payments made to nonresident alien (NRA) payees. Nonresident alien, also called *temporary resident*, is a person who is in the United States on a non-immigrant visa (see listing of visas in the appendix). Depending on your company specifics, those nonresident aliens may be *E, H1B, J, O, TN* visa employees, *F, J, M, Q* visa students, religious worker (*R* visa), diplomats or international organization employees (*A, G, NATO* visas).

There is one simple *Internal Revenue Code* rule that applies to all payments to nonresident aliens. The rule orders to "*deduct and withhold from such items a tax equal to 30 percent thereof*" (Internal Revenue Code §1441 – see the appendix). A 30% statutory tax is applicable to all payments to nonresident aliens (unless they can be exempt). If the tax is not withheld from a $100 payment, your company is liable for $43 back taxes, fees and penalties, not $30 tax. You need to *gross up* the amount paid; ask what the gross amount would have been to arrive at net $100 payment after withholding 30% tax? 100 / (100%-30%), that is, 100/0.7=143. The grossed-up tax amount, paid to the IRS by your company, may be claimed back by the recipient and thus become additional income to the nonresident alien recipient.

Your company may be liable for huge amount of back taxes, fees and penalties on payments made to non-US businesses and individuals in case that you had classified them in your Accounts Payable system as US-businesses or individuals based on forms W-9 submitted and accepted by your company. Form W-9 is designed solely for use by the US businesses or individuals, or US resident aliens for tax purposes. This is the situation where you internally created *New Payee Questionnaire* form (besides the form W-9) come in so handy – you must ask a question on the form about residency status of businesses or individuals. **Do not use the invalid since year 2001 form W8 or any of the currently used forms W8xxx for the purpose of inquiring about residency status and US tax ID information**. You must know whom do you pay and, if need be, apply the rules that regulate the nonresident alien Accounts Payable tax compliance.

## US Tax Residency

Let us start off with a somewhat confusing concept of the *US tax residency*. A nonimmigrant visa visitor (temporary resident) may be considered **Nonresident Alien** *(NRA)* for tax purposes or **Resident Alien** *for Tax Purposes (RA)*. We treat as US-persons all US citizens and US permanent residents (those residents with the Green Card (form I-551)). There is also a very substantial number of individuals residing in the United States who are classified as Resident Aliens for Tax Purposes and who are treated in the same manner as the US persons. How do we know that someone is a US resident for tax purposes? There is one important idea to keep in mind when discussing this topic: there are tax laws and immigration laws.

Therefore, when I say that a person who came to the US in the year 2014 on B2 visa (tourist visa), has overstayed the usual six months of B2 visa terms and became an illegal immigrant from the immigration laws standpoint, this person is now considered a *resident alien* for tax purposes (no, he doesn't get a green card just yet). Do not be surprised and accept this as a tax law treatment. There may be instances where an illegal immigrant who is considered resident alien for tax purposes receives a "better" tax treatment than a lawful F1 visa student who is a nonresident alien for both tax and immigration purposes. This situation may feel uncomfortable and unfair to you, but this is the tax law and I will explain how it works in the following chapters.

## Substantial Presence Test

To be considered *resident alien for tax purposes* in immigrant status other than US Permanent Resident (Green Card/I-551) or limited refugee or asylum cases, a person must pass the *Substantial Presence Test*. The test has two parts: (1) *31-day test* and (2) *183-day test*. A temporary visitor must be present in the US for at least 31 days during the current year to allow further calculations of substantial presence test for tax residency status. The second part tests the person's presence in the US in the current (besides the 31 days) and two prior years, unless the years counted are *exempt (from calculation) years* (discussed later in this chapter).

To figure Part Two of the test, count all days of US presence in the current year, 1/3 of days of previous year and 1/6 of days in the year preceding the last year (if applies, based on the visitor's presence in the US). The idea is to accumulate 183 days (including 31 days in a current year); 183 days may be accumulated all in the current year, in the current and last year or in the current and last two years – but not in any year further back. Let us say it is February 1 and a B-2 visa tourist has been in the United States for the past four years (the person is likely to be "out of status" from the immigration stand point). The first part of the test is satisfied, since the person has accumulated at least 31 days in the current year. Last year's 1/3 of days gives us 121 days (365/3) and the preceding year gives 61 days (365/6). The result of the substantial presence test is 214 days (more than 183 days with 31 days in the current year) and thus the person is considered *resident alien for tax purposes*. Payments to individuals who are "out of status" from the immigration stand-point are not uncommon for educational or not-for-profit institutions.

The rule is not universal to all visa types. Those non-student visitors on J-1 or Q-1 visa cannot use two years (*exempt years*) of US presence for the substantial present test calculations. The two years are the current year and any one year of non-student J-1 or Q-1 visa presence in the previous six years. There is a total of seven years to consider for exempt years when counting days for non-student J-1 or Q-1 visitor. A "year" to consider for the substantial present test is not a full 365 days term; any number of days of US presence in the considered year marks one year of US presence (the visa status must remain unchanged during those years).

*Example: A J-1 Research Scholar comes to the US in the year 2016; he has visited the US once in year 2011 as a J-1 professor and again in 2014 as J-1 international visitor. The two exempt years are years 2011 and 2014 (being within the six "past years" range) and the 31 and 183-day tests can possibly be satisfied in the current year 2016 rendering the person a US tax resident status.*

Students on F/J/M/Q-1 visas cannot use the first five years of their presence in the US (under the current F/J/M/Q-1 visa) for the calculation of the substantial presence test. These are five e*xempt years*. The 'five years' is a once-in-lifetime event for a student; there is no second counting of exempt five years in the unlikely scenario that someone comes to the US to be an F/J/M/Q-1 student for a second time.

*Example: An F-1 student from Italy, who came to the US in 2013 has Duration of Study marked as "DOS" on the Arrival/Departure Form I-94 (see image of I-94 on page*

*167, or online I-94 form if arrival date is after April 25, 2016) and legal permission to remain in the US until 06/01/2024 (this date appears on the student's school form I-20). The student's exempt years will be 2016, 2017, 2018, 2019, and 2020. On July 3rd in 2021 (the sixth year) the student will have satisfied both the 31-day rule and the 183-day tests. Remember that this year's 31 day is not added to this year's 183 days – it is 31 days in the current year and the total of 183 days accumulated in current and last two years (based on 100%, 1/3 and 1/6 rule). Be aware that a visitor's residency status may change back and forth many times during a prolonged visit to the US, based on the substantial presence test (the same student from Italy will revert to non-resident for tax purposes status in January of year 2019 since the '31-day' test will not be satisfied until February 1, 2022).*

A few practical examples: 02/01/x1 US entry H-1B visa employee technically becomes resident alien for tax purposes on 08/03/x1 (31 days and total of 183 days in the current year), but is considered resident alien for [payroll] tax purposes from day one, given the visa-holder's ostensible intent to stay in the US for at least three years. A J-1 teacher who comes together with the H-1B visitor on 02/01/x1 does not count year x1 and year x2 days (two exempt years) and becomes a resident alien for tax purposes on 08/03/x3. Once a person accumulates 183 days during the year, US tax residency status is assigned retroactively back to the beginning of the year, January 1st.

Why is it important to know? The residency calculation may appear to be burdensome, superfluous and impractical knowledge. Keep in mind that the substantial presence test is a very important tax concept to understand and use, especially in the light of the general 30% withholding requirement on payments to all nonresident for tax purposes aliens. Payments to nonresident for tax purposes aliens, whose payments are not eligible for any of the three IRS code exemptions (which will be discussed next) and taxed 30%; the taxed individuals are only too eager to become or claim the resident alien for tax purposes status to forgo the tax liability at the time of payment - you must know when they qualify to become such US tax residents.

To complete this somewhat elaborate explanation, I will add that resident aliens for tax purposes are taxed on their worldwide income, just like the US persons. This is a personal matter that may arise between a foreigner who is US tax resident and the IRS, but never a concern for your Accounts Payable department.

## IRS Exemption Codes

There are three most used IRS exemption codes applicable to payments to nonresident alien. Keep in mind that those individuals who have become resident aliens for tax purposes are taxed in the same manner as US persons. The IRS codes are:

- IRS Code Exclusion

- Foreign Source Income Exclusion

- Income Tax Treaty Exclusion

### *IRS Code Exclusion (IRS exemption code 02): Sec. 117 / Qualified Scholarship*

This is one of the most applied IRS codes exclusions. It is called Section 117 "Qualified Scholarship". It applies to all students in the US (both nonresident alien and US students). The code defines the student's income for federal income tax purposes, which is not subject to federal income tax withholding. For a payment to be considered "qualified," a student must use scholarship/fellowship payments for:

*a. tuition and fees required for enrollment or attendance, or*

*b. fees, books, supplies, and equipment required for courses of instruction.*

Scholarship/fellowship payments paid in excess of the qualified scholarships (i.e. room and board, travel, dorm charges, etc.) are includable in the student's gross income.

Section 117 also establishes a reduced tax rate of 14% on non-qualified portion of the scholarship/fellowship paid to F/J/M/Q (1) visa students.

*Subject to the provisions of applicable income tax treaties, such excess payments are subject to withholding under the following rules: Federal income tax at a rate of 14% (Internal Revenue Code § 1441(b)), provided that:*

> *a. the recipient is temporarily present in the US*

> *b. the recipient is in F, J, M, or Q immigration status, and*

> *c. the recipient must be a "Candidate for a Degree" - present to pursue study, training, or research.*

If a student does not meet the above requirements for application of the 14% withholding rate, withhold federal income tax from the scholarship/fellowship payment at the rate of 30%. Before you get any more confused, let us define the terms. The student may be either an undergraduate or graduate student, enrolled at an educational institution. Terms scholarship and fellowship are often used interchangeably. The IRS *Topic 421*, defines scholarship and fellowship grants as the following: *a scholarship is generally an amount paid or allowed to a student at an educational institution for the purpose of study. A fellowship is generally an amount paid to an individual for the purpose of research.* Keep in mind that the term "stipend" has no independent meaning and mostly used to denote scholarship or fellowship. A crucial characteristic of scholarship or fellowship is that either cannot represent payments for performance of any past, present, or future teaching, research, or other services that benefit the grantor.

I had difficulties earlier in my career understanding how a fellowship paid to a graduate student (future professor) is required to be void of any teaching element, which may be a part of the educational training process. Later, an additional term was developed that helped to clarify the "teaching and research" component (graduate students do non-service kind of research all the time). The term "that benefits the grantor" was added to establish when the true service element is present in the students' activities.

We have progressed as far as establishing that US-based non-service scholarship/fellowship payments made to F/J/M/Q (1) visa students *in excess* of tuition and fees required for enrollment or attendance, or fees, books, supplies, and equipment required for courses of instruction is taxed at the reduced 14% tax rate. If requested for payment scholarship/fellowship grants are intended for tuition, fees and book payments (not taxable), to avoid investigating and stipulating of how the scholarship/fellowship funds paid to students will be used by students, it is best to pay such *qualified scholarship* directly to the bursar's office or college book store on the students' behalf, especially for those students whose payments must be taxed otherwise.

As an Accounts Payable manager, you may be challenged at times on your tax withholdings on scholarship/fellowship grants by students, faculty and other educational administrators as to the fairness of such taxation. There are three reasons this taxing is fair and logical. The truth is that the same tax rules apply to the US students as well: Section 117 advises that any scholarship/fellowship non-service payments in excess of tuition, books, and fees made to any student, regardless of the residency status, is includable in the students' gross income. The tax is collected from payments to nonresident alien at the time of payment, since there is no assurance of their voluntary tax reconciliation and tax remittance in the next year (given their international mobility), when tax returns are submitted to the IRS. There is no tax collection made at the time of payment to US students, because the IRS allows the US students to do their tax reconciliation when they prepare their returns.

Second, the tax on the non-qualified portion of the scholarship/fellowship is collected because taxes are generally due on income (US-based income for nonresident aliens and worldwide income for US citizens, US permanent residents and resident aliens for tax purposes (based on the substantial presence test)).

And last, many a nonresident alien student is able to claim all or a portion of the withheld taxes back, upon filing tax return form 1040NR. The filing is based on generated by your accounting department forms 1042-S that must be sent to the nonresident aliens by March 15th and depends on the scholarship/fellowship amounts paid and personal exemption and standard deduction rates for the year.

I believe that in many instances the nonresident alien students receive a better tax treatment compared to the US students (US citizen, US permanent residents and non-immigrant visa students who have become resident alien for tax purposes). The tax treaties, which we will discuss later, allow in many cases unlimited amounts of scholarship/fellowship to be exempt from tax, based on the students' article in the tax treaty (one good example is a tax treaty with China, which supplies close to half of all non-immigrant visa students to the US colleges and universities).

## IRS Code Exclusion (IRS exemption code 02): Sec. 274 / The Accountable Plan

Another very used (and, sometimes, abused) IRS code exclusion is *Section 274 - Accountable Plan*. The IRS defines the Accountable Plans as follows:

*Expense reimbursement or allowance arrangements are not considered taxable income if they are made under an accountable plan as defined by the Internal Revenue Service (IRS). Under these rules, three tests must be met.*

*1. Expenses must have a business connection to the employer.*

*2. Expenses must be substantiated to the employer within a reasonable period of time.*

*3. Any excess reimbursement or allowance must be returned within a reasonable time.*

Under the IRS Code Section 274(d), substantiation requires an employee to establish with adequate record such as receipts, account book, etc.

*1. The amount of the expense*

*2. The time and place of the expense.*

*3. The business purpose of the expense*

*4. The business relationship of the employee to the persons receiving a gift, being entertained or utilizing a facility or property.*

A request for reimbursement must be made within reasonable period of time. The IRS considers reasonable period when expenses are properly accounted for within 60 days after they were incurred. Any excess amounts paid in advance must be returned within 120 days after the expenses were paid or incurred. The un-refunded excess of advance over expenses becomes taxable income to employees.

What is important to establish when making a travel reimbursement payment to a nonresident alien is *business connection* or *service component* of travel. Business purpose or service component is present in travel reimbursements to your H-1B employees (which are treated as resident aliens for tax purposes, given their visa rules), a J visa researcher (who came to the US to collaborate on research), a scholar (who is in the US to make a presentation), a teacher, a TN visa employee (both employed by US businesses), O, WB or B1 business visa visitors (who give speeches, attend seminars or conferences as mediators or guests of honor). ***There must be no <u>payment for services</u> component in such travel reimbursement.*** The possibility of including service payment is precluded by submission of the required receipts, hotel bills, boarding passes, etc. But it is not impossible to find a request for a *per diem* based living expense reimbursement, which requires no receipts submission; living expenses of the requestor may be already covered by another institution, and your payment of the *per diem* based request is, in fact, a *de facto* non-reportable service payment. You cannot detect this kind of schemes and you are not responsible to investigate payment requests based on the possibility of misrepresentation of facts, having performed the necessary AP review.

Travel reimbursements paid to nonresident alien students on F/J/M/Q (1) visa are taxed at the reduced student's rate of 14%. This may come as a surprise, but this is what the law requires. Travel reimbursement paid to nonresident alien students (on F/J/Q/M (1)) visa is considered an additional scholarship/fellowship payment, unless such student is employed (if permitted) and travelled on the employer's business assignment.

This may become a contentious point – many foreign students and their mentors had fierce arguments with me on the issue. But the truth is, if a student is not being sent by an employer to perform job duties while "on the road", the travel benefits the student only, and no one else. Why should the US-sourced funds should be paid free and clear from any tax consideration to nonresident alien students who will leave the US after completing their studying and use gained in the US knowledge someplace else?! I was once presented with a puzzle by one student whose travel payment was taxed. He challenged me on the 14% tax withholding on his travel reimbursement: "I have spent my already taxed fellowship money for this travel. Why do you tax me again on the same funds?" (I will provide my answer at the end of the nonresident alien chapter of this book).

## Foreign Source Income Exclusion (IRS Exemption Code 03)

This exclusion is probably the easiest to comprehend and apply. The US tax law classifies all payments as either *US source* or *Foreign Source*. Foreign source actually does not imply the source from which a payment is issued (it is always the US for our purposes), but *a place where services were performed*. Such foreign source income (of non US persons) is not taxed in the US, not reported to recipients and not reported to the IRS or the foreign country tax authorities by you. The business or the individual, who is getting paid, must be a foreign resident – not incorporated in the US, not US citizen or US permanent resident, since those are considered US persons or businesses and are taxed on the worldwide income. Again, <u>the location where services are performed determines whether those services qualify for foreign source income exclusion</u>. I do not call foreign residents who perform such services "nonresident aliens", as many Accounts Payable and NRA specialists do. Foreign service-providers or businesses remain in their home countries, being citizens or other types of residents outside of the US, and they are not US nonresident aliens.

I advise that you do not accept a brief sentence on invoice or in email informing you of the residency status of a payee. Create a form using which foreign persons or businesses will certify their non-US status, place of service performance outside of the US, and the amount that is being paid or billed for. I also require a confirmation of my company's legal department and the department, which had contracted the payee that the information submitted to me by the payee, is true and correct. You may use a sample below as a starting point to develop your own internal form and may adjust the form for payments made to foreign source business or other purposes.

*I, (name), hereby certify, under the penalties of perjury, that the personal services that I performed (or will perform), for ABC Company were performed (or will be performed) outside of the United States of America, in the following country or countries: _____ .*
*No part of the compensation that I received (or will have received) under my current collaboration with ABC*

*Company is for personal services rendered within the United States of America. As such, my compensation in the amount of $_____from ABC Company constitutes gross income from sources outside the United States under Section 862 (a) of the Internal Revenue Code.*

*I certify that the above statements are true and correct*

*Contractor's signature      &      Date*

Why so much legality? Consider this: a payment may be in thousands of dollars and it is not reportable to the payee, the IRS, or another country's tax authority. You want to have the assurance and positive confirmation that it is not a US citizen who lives and works in a foreign country and submits invoices to you for work done in that country.

Given the recent rise in the cross-border telecommuting, the foreign source income exclusion is a very advantageous tax situation to the foreign source service provider that reminds me of the pre-income tax days in the United States. The situation is being reviewed by the IRS and the lawmakers to reassess the foreign source nature of the telecommuting and possibly regulate that a part of foreign telecommuting (to US) services may be considered US sourced.

Remember that currently, the service provider cannot come to the US to perform any part of services to fully qualify for the foreign source income exclusion. If that happens, a percentage of total contract payment must be recalculated and reclassified as the US source income and possibly taxed 30%.

### Income Tax Treaties Exclusion (IRS exemption code 04)

Now we will review the most difficult topic of the non-resident alien Accounts Payable tax compliance – the United States income tax treaties. We currently have over sixty income tax treaties in order to reciprocally avoid double taxation of the same income by the treaty countries. Tax treaties describe various payment codes and agreed upon treatments of such payment codes. The language of a tax treaty may be confusing and unclear in the beginning – you should familiarize yourself with it, as it becomes necessary to bring to the discussion table the exact language of a treaty. Read Article 8 of US – Trinidad & Tobago tax treaty about business profits next:

*1. Industrial or commercial profits of a resident of one of the Contracting States shall be taxable only in that Contracting State unless such resident is engaged in industrial or commercial activity through a permanent establishment in the other Contracting State. If such a resident of one of the Contracting States is so engaged, tax may be imposed by that other Contracting State on the industrial or commercial profits of that resident but only on so much of such profits as are attributable to the permanent establishment in that other Contracting State.*
*2. Where a resident of one of the Contracting States engages in industrial or commercial activity in the other Contracting State through a permanent establishment situated therein, there shall be attributed to that permanent establishment the industrial or commercial profits which it*
*might be expected to derive in that other Contracting State if it were an independent entity engaged in the same or similar activities under the same or similar conditions and dealing*

*at arm's length with the resident of which it is a permanent establishment.*

A link to all current tax treaties is provided below:

http://www.irs.gov/Businesses/International-Businesses/United-States-Income-Tax-Treaties---A-to-Z)

Refer to the tables in this book's appendix to find the Current Tax Treaties Articles (IRS Pub. 901) which are available at this web address:

(http://www.irs.gov/pub/irs-pdf/p901.pdf)

It becomes much clearer from looking at the tables that the US-Trinidad has five income codes that include: 15 – scholarship or fellowship grant, 16 – independent personal services, 17 – dependent personal services, 18 – teaching and 19 – compensation during studying and training and 50 – other income. Any independent contractor, resident of Trinidad & Tobago and non-resident alien in the US, is relieved from tax with no dollar limit for 183 days of maximum annual presence in the US. I hope that number 183 reminds about the Substantial Presence Test and the *31-183 days rule.* A person becomes US resident alien for tax purposes after spending 183 days in the US. The 183 days threshold marks the beginning of the *saving clause* process, which "saves" the right of each country to tax its own residents as if no tax treaty existed. Therefore, if you become a resident alien for tax purposes in the USA, you generally lose any tax treaty benefits. The related treaty article number is 17, which will be needed to complete form **8233** - *Exemption from withholding on compensation for independent (and certain dependent) personal services of a non-resident alien individual.* I will discuss this and other tax treaty forms later in this chapter.

I want to present a few more examples of treaties applications, explain new concepts as they enter the discussion, and hope that your will gain understanding of how to read and apply the tax treaties.

A scientist from Madagascar makes a presentation at a US college, during his short (less than 183 days) visit to the US. There is no tax treaty with Madagascar and the payment is taxed at 30% rate, reported to the individual and the IRS, regardless of payment amount.

A J-1 visa trainee from Norway came to the US to work for company ABC Inc. in its training program. Article 16 of the US - Norway tax treaty (Students and Trainees) is:

*(a) An individual who is a resident of one of the Contracting States at the time he becomes temporarily present in the other Contracting State and who is temporarily present in that other Contracting State for the primary purpose of-*

*(i) Studying at a university or other recognized educational institution in*
*that other Contracting State, or*
*(ii) Securing training required to qualify him to practice a profession or professional specialty, or*
*(iii) Studying or doing research as a recipient of a grant, allowance, or award from a governmental, religious, charitable, scientific, literary, or educational organization, shall be exempt from tax by that other Contracting State with respect to amounts described in subparagraph (b) for a period not exceeding five taxable years from the date of his arrival in that other Contracting State.*
*(b) The amounts referred to in subparagraph (a) are-*
*(i) Gifts from abroad for the purpose of his maintenance, education, study, research, or training;*
*(ii) The grant, allowance, or award; and*

*(iii) Income from personal services performed in that other Contracting State in an amount not in excess of 2,000 United States dollars or its equivalent in Norwegian kroner for any taxable year.*

Again, it is much easier to refer to the tax treaty tables from the IRS publications 901, which are located in the appendix of this book. You can easily find that Code 19 (Studying and training) of the US-Norway treaty has *compensation during training* type of income, which is valid for five years with a $2000 annual cap on the amount to which federal tax is not applied. (As a non-resident alien and J-1 trainee, the person is also exempt from FICA). The amount covered by the tax treaty (maximum of $2000) is reported on form 1042-S and any amount paid in excess of $2000 is reported on form W2. In order to apply for the tax treaty exemption, the person should submit form 8233 (treaty article 16(1)) to the employer (more about forms, tax reporting and payroll in later chapters). Keep in mind that you, as a payment agent, do not grant the tax treaty treatment; you only facilitate not-withholding of tax at the time of payment. The person claims the treaty benefits when he or she submits personal or business tax return to the IRS.

An H-1B (or TN (Trade NAFTA)) visa employee from Canada comes to the US to work. Refer to the table in the appendix of this book – Canada does have a tax treaty with the US. IRS Income Code 17 (dependent personal services) lists two scenarios: a person is in the US for less than 183 days (remains a non-resident alien) – there is no limit on the treaty amount that is exempt from federal tax in this case. If the person is in the US for more than 183 days, the treaty amount limit is $10,000. The person should sign form 8233 to claim the tax treaty benefits. When processing the year-end tax reporting, the treaty amount is reported on form 1042-S and any excess of the treaty limit, with resulting payroll taxes, is reported on form W2.

A student from Italy comes to your office; she brings a signed form W-8BEN and informs you that there should be no federal tax withholding on her fellowship payments, because there is a treaty between the US and Italy. Look at the treaty tables in the appendix (always do it before engaging in readying of the treaty text and technical explanations). There is a tax treaty between the US and Italy indeed. But the tax treaty does not have the students' article, there is no IRS Income Code 15 in it – the student is not eligible for tax treaty treatment. The student's fellowship payments must be taxed at a reduced 14% tax rate.

We have already discussed a concept of *Saving Clause*. A person may only be eligible for treaty benefits for a limited period of time – usually for 183 days in the first year until the person becomes a resident alien for tax purposes. The "saving" indicates saving from non-collecting of taxes by the tax authorities and it limits the span of time when tax savings can be enjoyed. There is *Exemption to the Saving Clause* concept, which allows continued use of tax treaty even if a person has become a resident alien for tax purposes. You can refer to a treaty with China to see that there are limits on three types of income and "no specific limit" on maximum presence in the US for three other types of income listed in the treaty.

By the way, the income tax treaty with China is one of the most "generous" of all 68 current income tax treaties.

Some income tax treaties contain the *Once in a Lifetime Clause* (US-France Income Tax Treaty). The treaty language is the following: *exemption does not apply if the individual previously claimed the benefit of this Article.* If an

| | |
|---|---|
| Scholarship or fellowship grant[6] . . . . . . . . . . . . | No specific limit |
| Independent personal services[7] . . . . . . . . . . . . . | 183 days . . . . . |
| Dependent personal services[8] [17] . . . . . . . . . . . . | 183 days . . . . . |
| Public entertainment[39] . . . . . . . . . . . . . . . . . . . | |
| Teaching[4] . . . . . . . . . . . . . . . . . . . . . . . . . . . . | 3 years . . . . . . |
| Studying and training: | |
|   Remittances or allowances . . . . . . . . . . . . . . | No specific limit |
|   Compensation during training or while gaining | |
|     experience . . . . . . . . . . . . . . . . . . . . . . . | No specific limit |

individual has ever claimed an exemption from tax for compensation, salary, or wages as a professor or researcher, such individual may not claim another exemption for the same type of income.

We will review one more tax treaty example with the United Kingdom, which has a concept of *Retroactive Clause*. There are times when you do need to read a tax treaty's technical explanation, which is a separate document, in order to fully understand a treaty. In this example, the tax treaty does not mention the retroactive clause, but the technical explanation does.

*Paragraph (1) provides that a professor or teacher who visits one of the Contracting States for a period not exceeding two years, for the purpose of teaching or engaging in research at a university, college, or other recognized educational institution in that Contracting State, and who was immediately before that visit a resident of that other Contracting State, will be exempted from tax by the first-mentioned Contracting State on any remuneration for such teaching or research for a period not exceeding two years from the date he first visits that State for the purpose of teaching or engaging in research. Since this two-year period is determined from the date he first visits the Contracting State, periodic vacations outside the first-mentioned Contracting State, or a brief return to the other Contracting State will not toll the running of the two-year period. Unlike the existing Convention, if the two-year period beginning from the date of his arrival is exceeded, the exemption will be lost* **retroactively.**

Look at the income tax treaty table with the UK in the appendix. IRS Income Code 18 (teaching or research) has a two-year limit with no limit on dollar amount (reference "4" clarifies that the treaty does not apply to compensation for research work primarily for private

220

benefit). A teacher from the UK plans to work in the US for 20 months. To claim the treaty benefits, the person must be a non-resident alien for tax purposes. The exempt years (years that are not counted for the substantial present test calculation) are the first two years, regardless of the number of days of a person's presence in the US during those two years (visa status must be the same). You must obtain information about the length of this teaching assignment, since in case that the person overstays the two-year limit, the tax treaty benefit will be lost retroactively, going back to day one. The back-taxes will be owed to the IRS by both the teacher and your company. The person must sign form 8233 (more about form 8233 in the following chapter). You must notify the person about the retroactive clause and its implication.

The tax treaty application may be a cumbersome task, even for an experienced Accounts Payable professional. If the need to read technical explanations as well as tax treaties appears to be too much of a burden and your payments to non-resident alien are numerous, you may think of signing up with an outside non-resident alien consulting company. They will guide you on all tax-related issues, based on the information that you receive from your non-resident alien payees. One such service can be contracted with *Arctic International LLC* – the company charges reasonable fees, provides excellent NRA consulting and database maintenance services, and conducts semiannual conferences in Las Vegas, NV (a link to the website is provided below. Disclaimer: I have known the president of the company, Donna Kepley, for many years).
(https://www.arcticintl.com/index.asp)

Do not accept your payees' claims for tax treaties and signed tax treaties forms before you review facts and documents relevant to the situation. To properly establish the residency status for the Substantial Presence Test calculations, you must obtain from all temporary visitors the arrival-departure form, which used to be called *white card*, or form I-94, which has been replaced in April 2013 by Admission I-94 Number Retrieval available from the Department of Homeland Security's web-site. Obtain form I-20 for F1 visa students or form DSDS-2019 for J visa

holders. Ask all non-resident aliens to complete the New Payee Questionnaire, where they will answer question about their US tax ID among other things.

*(Sample Arrival/Departure Form I-94 used prior to April 2013; date of US entry is June 25, 2006 and permission to remain in the US is until April 23, 2009)*

Effective April 26, 2013, the DHS (Department of Homeland Security) began automating the I-94 admission process. An alien lawfully admitted or paroled into the U.S. is no longer required to be in possession of a preprinted and hand-filled form I-94. A record of admission printed from the CBP (Customs and Border Protection) website (the document's exact name is "Admission (I-94) Number Retrieval") constitutes a lawful record of admission. See 8 CFR §1.4(d). The I-94 process (that is, establishing of the arrival and (scheduled) departure dates and visa type) has been made much more secure by the new procedure; it is no longer possible to alter the paper form I-94, since the arrival-departure records are now accessible online from the DHS database based on entered on https://i94.cbp.dhs.gov/I94/request.html *Family Name, First Name, Birth Date, Passport Number, Country of Issuance, Most Recent Date of Entry, Class of Admission* (*visa type*).

Another improvement to the process of tracking temporary visitors in the US, introduced by the Department of Homeland Security in year 2013, was an F, M or J visa stamp above the visa sticker in the visitors' passports. The stamp requires all F, M and J visa holders to be in possession of both a valid visa and form I-20 (for F and M visa holders) or form DS-DS-2019 (for J visa holders). [See a rather poor sample of the stamp available to me on the next page.] The oval stamp that has been used remains in use; it shows the date of entry and the limit of permitted US presence. For F, M, and J visitors, the actual limit is never noted in that stamp, but shows a handwritten *DOS or D/S* (duration of status) abbreviation instead. I believe that this uncertain term many times concealed the "out of status" immigration status for some F, M or J visitors who overstayed their form I-20 or DS-2019 visa terms. The text alerts all those not very familiar with F, M and J visa regulations to request the forms to fully establish a temporary visitor's visa terms.

To reiterate, nonresident aliens often times become *resident aliens for tax purposes* in the United States. The determination is made based on the Substantial Presence Test calculations. The dates on form I-94 or I-20 / DS-DS-2019 are required to properly establish a visitor's tax residency status. Most of the treaties or tax treaties' articles do not apply to the US tax residents even though those tax residents are nonresident alien for immigration purposes.

Always read the tax treaty text and the technical explanations, look for previously processed similar cases, and contact colleagues in your non-resident alien taxation professional circles for advice or guidance. There may be important caveats to otherwise clear instructions in the treaties. One example is a US-Pakistan Income Tax Treaty

Article XIII (1) concerning scholarship and fellowship grants. While appearing applicable with no maximum US presence (exemption to the savings clause concept) and no maximum limit on the amount of payment, the article only applies to employees of Pakistani nonprofit organizations ostensibly undergoing studying or training in the US.

**Tax Treaties Forms 8233 and W-8BEN** (including Year 2014 FATCA-related Changes)

There are two main forms used when processing tax treaty exempt payments to non-resident aliens: **8233** - *Exemption From Withholding on Compensation for Independent (and Certain Dependent) Personal Services of a Non-resident Alien Individual*, and form **W-8BEN** - *Certificate of Foreign Status of Beneficial Owner for United States Tax Withholding*. Form W8, with no extension, was put out of use by the IRS many years ago. <u>Do not use it to collect a non-resident alien payee's US tax ID information</u> – use you internal New Payee Questionnaire form. Instead of the discontinued since 2001 form W8, the IRS established five other W-8xxx forms – W-8BEN, W-8BEN-E, W-8ECI, W-8EXP and W-8IMY. (form **W-8ECI** - *Certificate of Foreign Person's Claim That Income Is Effectively Connected with the Conduct of a Trade or Business in the United States*, is sometimes used by the Accounts Payable department to establish that a foreign business is *connected* to US trade or business; has a US tax ID, pays taxes in the US and files US tax returns and thus is treated as a domestic company for tax withholding and reporting purposes).

Form 8233 is used by non-resident alien employees, contractors, speakers, researchers, and teachers, whose payments may be exempt from the federal tax withholding based on a tax treaty between the US and an individual's country of residence. You must check the correctness of the submitted by the non-resident alien to you tax treaty form before accepting it. But for practical purposes, do not waste your time waiting for forms to be submitted to you – there are always errors and missed pieces of information. Prepare the form, let the person sign it and send it to the IRS. The form must be sent to the IRS for their review and acceptance. You will get a negative confirmation of the IRS's accepting the form, i.e. the IRS will not contact you if the form is accepted (give the agency 10 days to do it (i.e. wait ten days before processing payments with no tax applied). I have never had a case where a form 8233 was not accepted by the IRS. A signed form is faxed to the IRS (IRS' fax number is included in my sample 8233 fax transmittal letter).

*To: Internal Revenue Service*
*International Section*
*Facsimile: 267-941-1365*
*October 18, 201x*
*Dear Sir or Madam,*
*Please review the attached form 8233 for J. Chen from the UK.*
*Sincerely,*
*Costa Levi (phone and fax numbers, email address)*

The form itself can be found at this web address:
http://www.irs.gov/pub/irs-pdf/f8233.pdf )

Form 8233 is valid for one year – the year of filing. File another form 8233 in the next year to continue the tax treaty coverage, if applicable. Form 8233 can also be used by students who receive non-service scholarship/fellowship payments, but form W-8BEN is an easier process to claim students' tax treaty-related scholarship benefits.

Note that effective July 2014, formW-8BEN is required to be completed (in addition to form 8233 if applying for tax treaty) for independent contractors, speakers, research collaborators, and royalty recipients' payments to all non-resident aliens, regardless of income tax treaty application.

Use form W-8BEN (Certificate of Foreign Status of Beneficial Owner for United States Tax Withholding - http://www.irs.gov/pub/irs-pdf/fw8ben.pdf) for all non-service scholarship/fellowship payments to non-resident aliens. I advise to complete form W-8BEN based on the documents submitted to you by non-resident alien students (copies of visa, form I-94, form I-20 (for F1 visa holders) or form DS-2019 (for J1 visa holders)). There are three reasons why I advise that you complete the form: first, a non-resident alien may not be eligible to claim a tax treaty; second, a non-resident alien does not know how to complete it properly; third, given the volume of information related to foreign residency address, names, tax IDs, tax treaty description, tax treaty article citation – the often handwritten information is illegible and is most of the times reprocessed by you anyway. Collect the information (copies of the visa-related documents and information of the prior visits to properly calculate the Substantial Presence Test) and prepare W-8BEN form for non-resident alien to sign. Do not mail the form to the IRS – there is no such requirement. Keep it on file together with other non-resident alien visa-related documents. The form is valid for the current and three subsequent to the filing years.

Until the recent FATCA-related changes, a non-resident alien had to possess a US tax ID (social security number/SSN or individual taxpayer ID number/ITIN) to claim a tax treaty. Any payment to a non-resident alien who did not have a US tax ID number, whether there is a tax treaty or not, was taxed at 30% rate (reduced 14% rated for students on F/J/Q/M(1) visa). This is no longer the case – a foreign tax ID can be used for the purposes of tax treaty application.

Advise any non-resident alien desiring to apply for a tax ID number to file form W7 with the IRS to apply for an ITIN; the form is long and the IRS review process exceeds six weeks. An easier and quicker way to obtain a US tax ID is to apply for social security number. Only eligible non-resident aliens (those who can prove to the Social Security Administration that they intend to work in the US) can do so by going directly to a local social security administration office (office locator link is provided below).

http://www.ssa.gov/ny/services-fo.htm

A note about the new form W-8BEN-E (*Certificate of Status of Beneficial Owner for United States Tax Withholding and Reporting (Entities)*; the form is used by non-resident alien businesses. If the business is eligible to submit form W-8ECI or W-8EXP, form W-8BEN-E is not required. The purpose of the form W-8BEN-E is to establish foreign tax residency status and, if applicable, claim a tax treaty exemption on tax withholding. The form is valid for four calendar years including the year of completion. The form is expected to be mostly used by foreign financial institutions for reporting their status under the Internal Revenue Code as related to FATCA. Foreign financial institutions that do not verify their status using form W-BEN-E will be subject to 30% withholding on US-source income, as per FATCA regulation. The 30% withholding is not a new procedure dictated by FATCA; it's been in force for many years described in IRC section 1441 (see Sec. 1441 in this book's appendix).

## Processing forms 1042 and 1042-S

Form 1042 is a federal tax return form filed by your Accounts Payable department to summarize the gross amounts paid for scholarship/fellowships, independent or dependent compensation, royalties and other US-sourced income of nonresident alien payees. The form also shows the tax liability related to the gross income reported on the form and total amount of taxes withheld and remitted to the IRS. Note that as of August 2014, the IRS has provided the new versions of form 1042, changed to suit FATCA reporting requirements, for informational purposes only.

The form requires your entry of the quarter-monthly tax liability, which is the total nonresident alien taxes, withheld for each "quarter" of the month – by the 7th, 15th, 22nd and 31st of each month. The liability is then compared by the IRS to the timing of your remittance of the nonresident alien taxes (via the EFTPS) to assess whether or not your company complied with the payment requirements, which are based on the amount of taxed withheld in each quarter-monthly period. Remember to remit taxes within three days when they exceed $2000 amount for a quarter-monthly period, $200-$2000 by the 15th of the following month, less than $200 in a year – by March 15th. March 15th is the reporting deadline for both forms 1042 and 1042-S filing (1042-S is individual information return to report US source income paid to a nonresident alien).

You need to have your payees categorized as nonresident aliens for tax purposes appropriately marked in your accounting system and those, with no applicable exemptions, set up for appropriate tax rates withholding. The "behind the screen" journal entries for taxed AP payments are the following, assuming the 30% tax rate:

*Payment voucher input:*

| | | |
|---|---|---|
| **Expense** | **100** | |
| **Accounts Payable** | | **100** |

*Payment voucher payment:*

| | | |
|---|---|---|
| **Accounts Payable** | **100** | |
| **Cash** | | **70** |
| **Due to the IRS/NRA Taxes collected** | | **30** |

*(On the day of payment, when the 30% tax amount is posted to payable (to the IRS) account, a quarter-monthly liability is created)*

*Remittance of taxes to the IRS:*

| | | |
|---|---|---|
| **Due to the IRS/NRA Taxes Collected** | **30** | |
| **Cash** | | **30** |

*(Note that the payment is done via the EFTPS (electronic federal tax payment system). It is a separate from your accounting system function. Therefore, you should first pay/post NRA taxes due, based on the combined tax amount and remittance requirements, and then transfer the posted amount via the EFTPS to the IRS)*

Form 1042 shows the total number of forms 1042-S processed (electronically or/and on paper). There may be over or under-remittance (to the IRS) of taxes withheld from the payments to the nonresident aliens. Ideally, the tax amount withheld should match the tax liability. If the tax remittances were made in accordance with the deposit rules, there will be no IRS penalty for late deposits. Practically, there is often some balance due to the IRS after you complete the 1042 form reconciliation, stemming from grossing up of "missed" taxes and other issues. You may intentionally overpay the IRS to have a "cushion" of paid NRA taxes to allow for any contingency liabilities. If there is overpayment to the IRS, do not ask for credit, because such credit is often posted to your company's payroll federal income tax 941 account; ask for a refund payment to your company.

You must mail forms 1042 to the IRS by March 15th. If you withheld taxes from individuals with no US tax numbers, you must supply an affidavit that states the following:

*Pursuant to Treasury Regulations under section 301.6109-1(c) of the Internal Revenue Code, we submit this Affidavit as an attachment to our 20xx Annual Withholding Tax Return for US Source Income of Foreign Persons. We hereby declare that as required by law we have requested an US tax ID numbers from each of the listed below individuals and each individual has failed to provide such number. Therefore, we have submitted 20xx forms 1042x for these individuals without US tax ID numbers.*

File forms 1042-S electronically using the same IRS web-service that I suggested earlier in the book for 1099 submission. The web-address is http://fire.irs.gov. The 1042 tax return (with Affidavit if necessary) is mailed to the IRS office in Ogden Service Center, POBOX 409101, Ogden UT 84409, no matter how you filed the 1042-S, on paper or electronically.

Individual information return form 1042-S reports the US-sourced income paid to nonresident aliens. The form reports scholarship/fellowship (IRS code 15): both exempt under tax treaty and not exempt (i.e. taxed), independent personal services (IRS Income Code 16), dependent personal services (IRS Income Code 17), compensation for teaching (IRS Income Code18), compensation while studying or training (IRS Income Code 19) or code 50 (other income)). For dependent personal services or teaching, which is part of payroll reporting, forms 1042-S only report the tax treaty amount. In cases where total gross payroll payments exceeded the tax treaty amount, the excess of the tax treaty amount is reported on form W2. Each form 1042-S can show only one type of income per individual; if there were more than one type of income paid to an individual in a calendar year (fellowship payments first, then dependent personal services) two forms 1042-S are issued for the same individual. The two forms will show different IRS income codes and their respective amounts.

1042-S is a simple form that has six basic items besides your institution's information: type of income paid, gross amount, applicable tax rate (10, 14 or 30%) or tax exemption code (02 – IRS code exclusion, 03 – Foreign Source income, 04 – Income Tax Treaty Exclusion), total amount of income tax withheld, country of recipient's residence, recipient's personal information.

All exempt from tax forms 1042-S must show one of the exemptions codes (one code per form). All tax dollar amounts must be 10%, 14% or 30% of the gross amount. The reduced 14% tax rate is only applicable to IRS income code 15 – scholarship or fellowship grants, the rate of 14% cannot be applied to any other type of income. If a nonresident alien has no US tax ID number, the withholding tax rate and corresponding tax dollar amount must be 30%, except for F/J/M/Q (1) students with no US tax IDs where the reduced rate is 14%, no matter whether there is a tax treaty with their home countries or not.

There is no reporting threshold limit for individual forms 1042-S. To avoid complications with the IRS, always double check that the total gross income on distributed forms 1042-S and total taxes withheld add-up to the gross income reported on nonresident income tax return form 1042 and the total taxes reported on form 1042 and remitted to the IRS during the calendar year (the tax remittance amount may be adjusted in a form of additional payment or refund claim upon completion of form 1042).

Although both forms 1042 and 1042-S are due by March 15th, I advise to mail forms 1042-S by January 31st (the 1099 and W2 deadline), if possible under your tax reporting schedule. This will allow nonresident aliens more time to review the forms and communicate back to you any discrepancies to make necessary adjustments before your filing of form 1042. Form 1042 and paper forms 1042-S (if you file 1042-S on paper or submit late original forms 1042-S) must be filed with the IRS separately, although the mailing address is the same. All paper forms 1042-S must be accompanied by form 1042-T. File form 1042 before March 15 deadline – do not "rush" the filing, unless your nonresident alien reporting is simple and low in volume. I advise to wait as long as possible to account for all possible 1042-S forms information corrections to avoid filing of an amended form 1042.

***My answer to the question about tax on travel reimbursement, for which the already taxed fellowship funds were allegedly used, was: If your fellowship funds were earmarked for travel, you should not have applied for travel reimbursement. The [ineligible for Accountable Plan treatment] travel expenses reimbursement is a new fellowship grant when requested to be reimbursed for non-service related travel expenses. (The case is more obvious if the travel expenses were paid for with a credit card).*

# Purchasing Cards Operations

## Purchasing Cards' Purpose

Purchasing cards operations have been gaining popularity in the past decade. The advantages to the card holders are obvious: world-wide acceptance of major payment card systems gives the flexibility of use at millions of locations wherever a particular type of your p-card is accepted, immediate access to the company's funds for purchases, reduced Accounts Payable processing costs and overall administrative burden, paperwork reduction and online access to make business-related purchases.

The main purpose of p-cards is to make "out of pocket", T&E, office supplies and incidental expenses type of purchases that do not require a Purchase Order. Purchasing cards eliminate the need to apply for a credit line or prepay for minor expenses which greatly relive the administrative burden and relieve employees of the need to use their own funds or credit cards. Purchasing cards often generate rebates if the usage volumes exceed set by the issuing bank dollar benchmarks, which is an additional revenue source to your company... often billed back by vendors to make up for lost revenue (bank fees).

A purchasing card system may be revolving credit or debit type. The credit limit returns on the monthly basis to the established amount upon your company's payment or bank's direct withdrawal of funds due for the prior month. The debit type works like debit card with a fixed dollar amount assigned to the purchasing card account, which is reduced by the amount of purchases. The advantage of the debit type of commercial credit card is better fiscal control of purchases made with p-cards. The dollar limit is increased upon fiscal administrator's periodical review of user's purchases. All card holders are required to submit monthly statements to account for the purchases made. The monthly reconciliations, besides fiscal monitoring, also enable the purchasing cards fiscal administrators to re-allocate all posted transactions form a temporary clearing account to "normal" expense accounts. Again, only when fiscal administrator has the assurance that the purchasing card is used in accordance within the established guidelines, additional funds are added to the card if requested by the user.

With the revolving credit type the limit is reset automatically which may allow for additional unchecked and improper spending by p-card user before misuse comes to the attention of fiscal administrator. Since it is decided at the onset of purchasing card project, you must thoroughly weigh all pros and cons of each type of purchasing card, your fiscal controls' requirements and internal users' fiscal discipline to make the right decision as to what type of purchasing card to choose.

A purchasing card project may be a stand-alone endeavor, such as JP Morgan's Payment Net application. Or it can me tied into a T&Es processing system such as Concur; AmEx coupled with Concur allows for purchasing operations, receipts imaging capabilities, and modifiable workflows that carry a card account review from a manager to an accountant before transactions are approved and downloaded into your accounting system. I have a number of Amex CBCP (central bill central pay) accounts under my control. Given that the users are not finance people, it takes ongoing reminding to keep the reporting follow the spending.

In the past years I have come to like the purchasing card process less and less. These is an underlying problem from the AP with the cards' use: I call it "swipe first – account later" problem. Once a purchase is made the buying departments (sales, marketing, IT, executive) have naturally moved on and are not interested to account for the purchases made. Yes, they are required to do so. And, yes, they drag their feet while deadlines approach and are missed again. Credit card fraud or unauthorized use is another ongoing problem with the process. Credit card is the hotels and transportation industries preferred method of payment – who doesn't like getting a signed 'blank check' issued – this is what the credit card often ends up being. Use the ACH deposits, avoid credit card use.

## Purchasing Cards accounting

The following journal entries illustrate how purchasing cards work from the accounting standpoint. All p-cards have a set of records in the bank's database which are linked to your internal accounting system. Besides the usual names, SSN, address, date of birth and other users' information, a purchasing card account must be linked to one of your cost centers, departments or other reporting units' account. Depending on the set up that is technically available to you, transactions processed with purchasing cards are posted form the bank's database into your accounting system in real time, ever so often (every three hours, at midnight, etc.) or require periodic manual uploads form bank's database into your accounting system.

All individual purchasing cards transactions are posted to the assigned cost centers and to assigned p-card clearing advance-type accounts. Any p-card transaction is considered to be an advance to the card holder before it is accounted for. Your Chart of Accounts must have a range (there are often more than one purchasing card per cost center) of p-cards clearing accounts in the expense accounts category. The purchasing card advance accounts must be "cleared", that is, accounted for and journalized to regular expense accounts before the fiscal period closing date.

Some businesses allow the p-cards users to assign the accounting codes within the bank's system and attach explanations for expense and supporting documents. The transactions are posted directly to the respective P&L accounts and the clearing account process is not used.

Let us assume that your expense codes are in the 5xxx range (1xxx-assets, 2xxx-liabilities, 3xxx-equity, 4xxx-revenues). You many have accounts 5690 through 5699 reserved for the p-cards use. Cost centers (departments, colleges, other reporting units) may be denoted as 10000 (Main Office), 20000 (Warehouse), 3000 (Sales). The 16-

digits p-card account in the bank's data base must be assigned to *Cost Center – Clearing Account* combination, let us say *10000 - 5690*. Any time a transaction is processed, it is uploaded into that 10000-5690 clearing account. Clearing account is a temporary account that must be periodically "cleared" – older transactions are journalized out to normal, most often, expense accounts. The clearing is performed based on the users' periodic accounting for purchases made with purchasing cards. Keep in mind that all p-card's purchases must be approved by a budget owner, just like any other payment.

The fiscal administrator receives users' accounting for purchases made, reviews the completeness and appropriateness of all such purchases and then processes journal entries that transfer transactions from clearing account to actual expense accounts. It is not possible, given the number and variety of merchants and merchandises, to pre-assign your internal expense codes in the bank's database based on various criteria (vendor type, purchase type, merchandise category).

Also, having all new transaction in one account for a given user allows for better fiscal monitoring of purchasing card usage. Example:

*Purchase transaction upload into Accounts Payable system:*

CostCenterA__ **CommCardClearingAcc** **xxx**
DueToBank_ **CommCards** **xxx**

*A special payable account is credited. The account is reversed manually (by a journal entry) upon monthly payment of your company's p-card bill.*

Manual clearing by a journal entry of purchasing card clearing account to expense account, transaction by transaction, based on users' accounting for purchases:

CostCenterA_ **Office Supplies**       **xxx**
CostCenterA__**CommCardClearingAcc**       **xxx**

When all monthly transactions are tallied on a monthly statement and your bank initiates a direct debit for the amount. The total debit should equal the balance (for fiscal period / month) in the *Due to Bank/P-Cards* account. A manual entry clears the liability account and reduces cash balance to account for monthly bill payment.

DuetoBank_**CommCards**     **xxx,xxx**
Cash           **xxx,xxx**

In case you do not allow your bank direct withdrawal of monthly p-cards' bill amount, you should process an Accounts Payable payment (direct bank transfer, wire transfer) with a debit to account *Due to Bank/P-Cards* and a credit to regular *Accounts Payable account:*

Due to Bank_**CommCards**    **xxx,xxx**
**Accounts Payable**        **xxx,xxx**
*(This entry clears Due to Bank/P-Cards balance for the previous month)*

**Accounts Payable**        **xxx,xxx**
**Cash**         **xxx,xxx**
*(Payment to bank is made)*

It is possible to have the purchasing cards users to code the processed transactions themselves by logging in to your bank's web site designated p-cards environment. The coding is based on the type of expenses and the expense codes used in your financial system are assigned by users to individual transactions. Transactions are submitted by users, reviewed and posted by AP directly to the "normal" expense accounts. This bypasses the clearing account's review process. The transactions are still required to be reviewed for compliance with policies and approval by an authorized manager. All such posted transactions must have a separate "purchasing card" origin flag to be "collected" for review in a report, or posted to a designated General Ledger Journal, for example, Purchase Card Journal (note that sending cc transactions in the GL directly bypasses the AP journals). Users are often required to attach image or pdf file (various phone apps are available) to individual transactions to substantiate the business purpose of their use of p-cards.

Very frequently still in these days a manual upload of the credit card transactions is performed by the AP clerk, from the bank's statement to the AP Ledger, directly into the expense accounts. What is important during this manual process is the completeness of the monthly transactions transfer. When transferring monthly credit card transactions to the accounting system I copy the monthly statement off a bank's web site, post the data, which mirrors the bank statement, into an excel .csv type template and let my AP administrator complete the file with departments, GL codes, and other attributes before the template file is loaded into the system. Again, your file's total must match the bank's monthly statement total to avoid transactions 'falling through the cracks'.

## Purchasing Cards Use

P-cards must only be used to make business-related purchases and any unauthorized purchase should lead to personal liability for the account holder. P-cards cannot be used to make purchases from regular suppliers and vendors who normally invoice/bill your company directly (there is a possibility to pay for the same item both with purchasing card and through the Accounts Payable department on the same invoice presented by the supplier). There must be a limit on a single purchase transaction (depending on the user's authorization and credibility level) and a limit on the number of daily transactions. You don't want your company's departments' card holders to become little independent AP departments within the company with no rules and policies.

A purchasing card user must sign an official purchasing cardholder agreement where all conditions of the account's use are spelled out. An account is applied for and a plastic card is sent to your Accounts Payable department. The cost center is notified of the card's arrival (the cost center had previously authorized the issuance of the purchasing card account). The user begins to use the cards, expenses are uploaded into clearing account, the user submits the receipts and explanations for purchases made, the clearing account's charges are re-classified, that is, cleared (via journal entries to normal expense accounts).

As the balance of the purchasing card's account goes down (debit type), the user may request an increase, which is reviewed by cost center's fiscal manager and, if approved, communicated to the purchasing cards administrator for another account balance increase. The available balance information, purchase history and other related to purchasing card activity information should be available on servicing bank's monthly statements, website and in your accounting system's financial reports. Often times all company cards share in the total Company-level spend limit, let's say $1M, which makes for a possibility of a single account great spend or fraud.

The purchasing card is a great tool to simplify small scale and travel-related purchasing; it greatly relives the Account Payable department from processing petty and numerous invoices, allows the company's executives, salesmen, office administrators, and frequent travelers to make instantaneous business purchases and not use their own personal payment instruments (which translates to less T&E processing for the Accounts Payable department).

There may be pitfalls, too. The p-card system allows for the so- called *preauthorization* of transactions: let's say, a debit-type card account has a $5 balance and $1 preauthorization is successfully validated against the $5 balance. The problem is that the real transaction amount can be $100 and it will be posted to the account, based on the preauthorization, thus creating a negative $95 balance in the account (the negative balance is allowed based on the historic/cumulative purchasing card's balance). I had fought with Chase bank for years on this issue, which was described to me as "the industry-standard" procedure. This is why purchasing cards users must monitor their card accounts balances and be fiscally responsible. Easier said than done? My vast experience confirms that personal responsibility for card transactions and payments on account provides much better compliance than 'central bill, central pay' type of set up, no matter where you work.

It is commonplace to use a payment processing platform, like Concur Invoice, to link the card issuing bank with the accounting system. Concur receives bank's e-receipts, provides for efficient receipts uploads and OCR reading, provides strong internal-control workflows, and audit trails.

The benefits of purchasing cards without a doubt greatly outweigh a few related issues. Purchasing card program is a "must have" financial payment instrument for any business; with proper fiscal controls, fiscal spending discipline and timely accounting for purchases, the program is a win-win for all: you – the Accounts Payable professional and your company purchasing cards' users. However, the process can become a major AP headache if the users consider the AP p-card requirements obnoxious, which is not unusual.

Below are links to various banks' purchasing cards programs description:

www.pexcards.com

www.cardflexprepaid.com

http://corporate.americanexpress.com/forms/corporate-card-program?extlink=ps-us-corp-landing-2

http://www.citigroup.com/transactionservices/home/card_sol utions/commercial_cards/index.jsp

https://prepaid.bankofamerica.com/commercialprepaidcard/personal/pages/home.aspx

http://www.tdbank.com/business/treasury-management-commercial-card.html

I still face an ongoing 'blank check' aspect of the credit card payment nature; some vendors pay themselves using the card information saved, caterers add unauthorized tips, direct debits are not account for by the departments who requested them. As I said earlier, the vendor is happy, the department is very happy, the bank is more than happy, but the AP Clerk is in the bind – so many transactions on the monthly statement, so few approved payment requests. The credit card payment process does help running of business – the AP should accept the reality and bite the bullet.

# Other Accounts Payable Concepts and Processes

## Escheat – Unclaimed Property

*Unclaimed Property*, also commonly referred to as *Abandoned Property*, is defined as tangible or intangible property held by an organization that has not had contact with the rightful owner for a specific period of time. The abandoned property that the Accounts Payable is concerned with is unclaimed checks. The total dollar balance of the unclaimed checks is not your company's money – that is the bottom line. Who owns that money? The payee, or the state of the payee's last known residence. But you cannot simply void a check and reverse the underlying expense. No.

Checks usually revert to unclaimed category after 180 days. A separate process is run to void/reverse all *stale-dated* checks (expired and no longer accepted by banks): the cash account is increased (as normal) and a special "unclaimed checks" liability account is credited. Payments are made (again) either to the rightful owners of funds (if located) or the state (after the statutory deadline) from the "unclaimed checks" liability account, not regular Accounts Payable account. The "unclaimed checks" liability account is a temporary holding account for the unclaimed checks. Voided in such fashion checks must have a separate void status. *Original expenses associated with such stale-dated checks are never reversed (unless there is an applicable exception, very few in number, such as 'the 13 states' business-to-business rule).*

I provide below a sample letter to a property owner with a special "California header" on the letter. Each state has its own requirement as to how contact the check owners – read the instruction available through the NAUPA (The National Association of Unclaimed Property Administrators) web site: www.unclaimed.org. You well often see the "not earlier than 120 days, nor later than 60 days" requirement to contact the owners before dormancy end day. My advice is to try as hard as possible to locate the owners during the dormancy period to spare you the state reporting pains.

**THE STATE OF CALIFORNIA REQUIRES US TO NOTIFY YOU THAT YOUR UNCLAIMED PROPERTY MAY BE TRANSFERRED TO THE STATE IF YOU DO NOT CONTACT US**

**Costa Levi P., CPA [212-xxx-xxxx]
email: CLEVI@HolderCompany.up**

Dear Rochelle:

Our records indicate that you or your company may be the owner of funds represented by the item(s) listed below.

No transaction or other activity has occurred for a significant period of time. If you have an interest in the funds and wish to prevent the funds from being reported and remitted as unclaimed property to the State of California, please indicate the disposition of the item(s) listed below.

After you complete the form, please mail it to me immediately. Thank you

Please reply by September 30, 2016

Nature of Funds: AP Check

Date Issued: 11/21/2015

Amount / Name of Payee: **USD / Rochelle Riley**

Description: Travel Reimbursement – October 2014

Original check # 0013015978

**Disposition of Items (Check next to one of the following and mail or email the form to the Holder / C Levi):**

_____*This check was not received and our records indicate the amount is still due. Please issue another check.*

_____ *Check was received but not cashed/applied. (If you still possess the check (s) / credit memo please return it/them along with this letter indicating if you are still entitled to these funds.)*

_____ *Check is no longer required. There are no outstanding invoices for this amount and the obligation has been satisfied.*

_____ *Other:* _____

Name: _____ Signature: _____

**Address (if different from the one used to mail this notice):**

Date: _____

As a holder of unclaimed property, your business is required by law to report and remit any property that is considered abandoned, pursuant to the unclaimed property laws and regulations of the state of the owner's last known address, through a process known as *Escheat*. The process is very complicated. Every state has its own dormancy periods, reporting dates and requirements.

The Accounts Payable department must do its best to find the owners of the income and remit the unclaimed funds. The best time to do it is ASAP, as soon as a check is flagged as 'staledated', usually after 180 days after issuance.

To find the rightful funds owners I use Intelius' database. Intelius is a public records business company. $21buys me a 24-hour access to the database – there is no need to pay thousands of dollars for annual subscription. I use First, Last name and State criteria. Ideally, I find a person with the same as my system's address (the last known place/state of residence) in the person's records and a different, current (top position) address. Bingo! I send a letter to the current address and hope to hear back. There are also phone numbers listed by Intelius – you can call to validate the person's whereabouts. Make sure you 'connect the dots' and establish that the person is indeed you company's payee. I often ask a potential 'rightful owner' – you used to live on Monroe Street in Ithaca, NY, what was the house number there? Mind you – you must establish your identity first to not sound like a con artist.

Finding the rightful owners does two big things: it relieves you from the state reporting and gives your company a good PR.

Pursuant to jurisdictional regulations, Accounts Payable should mail out notices to property owners informing them of property in their name held by your business. Usually, there are usually three years (less often, five) of the Dormancy Period after which unclaimed checks must be remitted to the state of "last known residency" of the check owner. During the dormancy period, as already mentioned, your company should make a good faith effort to find the recipients of the checks. The sooner you begin searching for the unclaimed checks owner, the higher the chances that they will be found.

*Example: In New York state the Dormancy Period is three years. A check issued on May 2 2013 and not cashed should be processed by (1) contacting the payee first, at the address last known, (2) considered an escheat item as of December 31 2016, and (3) remitted to NYS Office of the Comptroller with the required information by March 10 2017.*

All checks that are being stopped due to the validity time expiration (180 days) do not cause the expenses or other original charges related to the issuance of checks to be reversed. There are a few, strictly-conditioned exception that allow the expense reversal as the end of the stale-dated check processing. *Business-to-business* is the most used one; payor and payee must be located/incorporated in one of the 13 participating states. It is presumed that businesses reconcile their fiscal claims in one way or another (think about the presumed perpetual life-span of a corporation). A stale-dated check is allowed to be reversed to decrease the current expense - no escheatment process follows. Reversing a capital account charge presents its own challenges.

During the escheat process stale-dated checks voiding, a special liability account is credited and cash is debited. All subsequent payments to the located rightful owners of the payments, or the state, if no rightful owners found, are made out of the unclaimed checks liability accounts (one unclaimed liability account for Accounts Payable and one for the payroll). Below is a journal entry that shows the effect of check stopping and later remittance of the payment to the rightful owner or the state:


**Cash**                    **xxx**
**Unclaimed Checks – A/P**                    **xxx**
*(Note that in case of "unclaimed" check stopping, the credit goes to special "holding" payables account.)*

**Unclaimed Checks – A/P**  **xxx**
**Cash**                    **xxx**
*(A payment is made to either the income owner, if one is located; or the state of last known owner's residence.)*


Property that remains unclaimed is escheated (remitted) to the state of the owner's last known address in accordance with the laws of that jurisdiction. The rightful owner retains his rights to the property without a limit and may contact the appropriate jurisdictional agency to file a claim for escheated property at any time. All checks not claimed prior to deadline are escheated to the state of the owner's last known address. It is very important, to prevent the possibility of fraudulent claims, to relay to the states accurate recipients' information. Each individual state requirement will force you to provide as detailed information as the state deems necessary.

You can take a break here and find any state's unclaimed property website, type in your name, and, bingo –

find out that some distant uncle left you $10M inheritance some time ago (read – he wrote a check which never found you; the check is 'unclaimed property'). I checked all 50 states – no such luck for me.

Many states require online filing when the number of properties exceed a certain number, or online is the only option to report (e.g. NV). You must able to create a NAUPA-compliance reports, which you cannot do with your own smarts. I suggest that you download a free version of the HRS Pro software at this website and use it: https://www.wagers.net/hrs/downloads.php.

The *HRS Pro* application not only allows to create NAUPA-compliant reports, but also provides 'submission requirements' by state and other helpful reporting information.

Claims for the escheated funds should be directed to the state listed on the notice that you sent out. You are protected by the law and absolved of any further liability related to the remittances escheated to the state.

My Unclaimed Property Master File has the following information for each state: Dormancy Period (mostly 3 years), Abandoned by Date (mostly June 1st), Report by Date (very often November 1st), Aggregate Under ($50, $25), Property Type (e.g. MS08 – Accounts Payable). Don't save the instructions and the forms as the rules always change – use the NAUPA website as your unclaimed property informational data bank.

Notice how I always use the word "checks" and never "EFT" or "wire transfer". The issue of unclaimed property, along with many other Accounts Payable checks-processing related "pains" does not apply to the electronic bank transfers (EFTs) since all transfers find their ways into recipients' banks accounts or return within a few days if the banking information is incorrect and the returned transfer gets verified, adjusted, and resent.

The issue of unclaimed property is most poignant for those companies, colleges and universities, health care organizations, and royalty and interest paying companies that make numerous checks payments to individuals. If your Accounts Payable department is working with a stable base of institutional vendors, the issue may be non-existent. I recently got a phone call from MN unclaimed property department about my $0.16 remittance and report that was sent in. Some codes were off – we figured things out, 10 minutes and $0.16 was placed in the right category in the state's coffers. No price too high for good compliance, I learned.

## Bank Reconciliation

Bank reconciliation synchronizes your books cash balance to the bank's balance. Usually, you bank sends you a monthly checks status file as an upload in an encrypted message; it will update the AP checks status in your system as "paid" and may highlight various AP-to-bank discrepancies (such as check voided in AP system in error, but cleared by the bank). Deposits in transit are added to your bank account balance, checks outstanding subtracted, bank fees recorded as expense, nonsufficient check deposits (NSF) are reversed and researched, any accounting errors that resurface are corrected as well. It may be the Accounts Payable department's responsibility to do bank reconciliation, but most likely, it is not. There are two reasons – you may be fully engaged in other AP activities, and second, for the purpose of better internal controls and better cash monitoring, the bank reconciliation is done by a different group than the AP team.

What concerns you regarding the bank reconciliation is most likely communicated to you by the "bank team" on a monthly basis. The reconciling items may involve the following:

- Checks stopped but not voided (void them)
- Checks voided in the system, but cleared by bank (investigate; reinstate voided checks)
- EFTs booked, but not transmitted (transmit EFTs)
- EFTs voided in the system, but transmitted (investigate; reinstate voided EFTs)
- Wire transfer booked, but not transferred (process wire transfers)

- Wire transfer voided in the system, but transmitted (investigate; reinstate wire transfers)
- Wire transfer amount booked differs from the amount transferred (correct the booking or remit the difference)
- Timing issues related to dates of booking and transmitting of wire transfers (inform bank reconciliation persons of the transfers' dates and other debits to the company's bank account – taxes, recurring payments, Concur and pension plan transactions)
- Application of incorrect cash accounts to close indirect payment invoices (wires, online payments)
- Nickels and dimes discrepancies due to rounding of pension, health, and other employee percentage withholdings and remittances.
- Unauthorized debits

Ideally, all the discrepancies listed above should never occur, but they do from time to time. Most of them are caused by not following rules and procedures, which are supposed to prevent all "adjusted bank to book" discrepancies other than occasional human data entry errors. Review your procedures for processing and voiding of checks, EFTs or wire transfers – they may need to be updated if they periodically allow for payments processing errors. The modern accounting processes that we are using are only so good – there is still much of human input, sudden surges of activities, meeting and seasonal differences in your Accounts Payable workloads (think of times when you are reviewing and processing 1099s and 1042's in addition to your normal AP work-load) also contribute to the time and attention one can allocate to daily activities. The approach with the bank reconciliation error items must be immediate and proactive – address the issues by all means available, review and update your procedures if need be, discuss the issues with higher management if you need higher-level cooperation in dealing with the cause of errors or in case that other departments contributed to the problem. Having bank discrepancies originating in the Accounts Payable department is not a good record to have - make sure that the Accounts Payable-related bank activities are immaculate, or next to immaculate.

Only once in my career I received a monthly bank reconciliation report with no AP items on it (it was a $250M business). So, such thing is possible.

## Cash Operations

Cash operations must be avoided. No matter what form they have - petty cash, lock box, cash payroll, C.O.D. payments or cash prizes – cash operations must be eliminated. Eliminate all cash operations as much as you can from your department's operations. There is no need to use cash in our days; any vendor or store accepts payment cards. There should be one purchasing card issued for your Accounts Payable office needs instead of the petty cash box. I remember how back in my early Accounts Payable days I was reconciling the petty cash box: quarters – so many, dimes, nickels, pennies – so many, and I would often get a difference between the accounting balances. It was maddening! Spending a dollar (work time) chasing a dime! And this is a minor issue compared to other cash-related internal controls. I know that I don't need to sell you on this.

If your cash box operation is a legacy issue and you have no purchasing cards in use, select a few vendors from whom you make frequent cash purchases. Who are those vendors? Local stationary store, pizza or bagel shop, a limousine company, you name it. Talk to their owners or store managers – inform them that if they issue a line of monthly credit, you will use their services exclusively (provided that you are getting the best deals on the market). Ask them to bill your company on a monthly basis, providing all related details – items ordered and delivered, dates, names of people ordering services, amounts. You must have a few designated employees who are given the right to authorize purchases from the local vendors based on internal requests. But, don't use the cash.

I remember working as a consultant for a very busy automobile exporting company in New York City. The overseas customers were raving about getting used US automobiles from dealers in Virginia, North and South Carolinas – there were non-stop incoming bank transfers to the company's bank account. Buyers were running about with wads of cash, buying cars, transporting cars from the auctions and dealerships, shipping cars to ports, paying for most of those operations in cash. Well, they knew not to pay more than $10,000 at a time.

I was brought in to fix this "cash feast" – the owners felt that something isn't right. With so many orders and solid mark ups, the (cash) net income was much less than what a successful business rakes in. I said to the owners: You must control your cash operations – it makes a huge hole in your revenue. I had set up new Accounts Payable payments policies; check payments to the auctions, transporting companies, shipping companies and local repair shops. I introduced petty cash accounting, travel reimbursement request and out of pocket expense reimbursement request forms, which made the company buyers very hostile and resentful to my cash control actions. But the situation changed for better.

I believe, I have said enough – it is hard to monitor and track cash, it has warping and corruptive qualities - let it not enter or remain in the AP operations and come into contact with your employees.

# Accounts Payable Reports and Performance Metrics

I begin my day with Accounts Payable reports and end my day with Accounts Payable reports. There are two major types of Accounts Payable reports: financial data reports and performance metrics. The financial data reports are those reports that provide information on fiscal operations of the department: open payment vouchers reports (based on various criteria), check register, general ledger reports, payee history reports, statements of disbursements, payees reports (duplicate tax ID reports, foreign payees, governmental entities reports), voided payments or voided payment vouchers reports, audit reports (changes made to payees set up, bank information), 1099 and 1042 data reports and any other kind of custom reports made to suit your accounting department particular needs.

If the system allows and you know how, you can tweak your query data yourself to get the desired results. Many times you need the system administrator's support to create a particular kind of report. It goes without saying that a thorough knowledge of your Accounts Payable system (be it a legacy system or an ERP) allows for quickest finding of necessary data and information from the system and allows you to concentrate your efforts on analytical, process development and problem-solving aspects of the Accounts Payable work and avoid getting mired in tedious data mining work. If you realize that you lack in knowledge of the accounting system used by your company, insist on being enrolled in training classes or attend a conference offered by your system provider. Present the benefits of the improved quality of your work when you are able to fully use the potential of the accounting system. It only makes good sense for any company that is paying top dollars to buy and maintain financial system application to use its full potential and capabilities.

Performance metrics reports are used to monitor and manage various aspects of the Accounts Payable department's performance to access the effectiveness of the AP operations and insure that best practices are in place. Performance metrics analyze the human factor in the Accounts Payable process rather than financial data. Peter Drucker, an author and expert of business management, once said: "If you are not measuring it, how can you manage it?" You may use metrics reports to find out a problem in Accounts Payable process or, if aware of the problem, present it in a quantifiable format that highlights the issue and presents it in impersonal and matter-of-fact format to be reported and acted on. You may have your metrics reports run periodically or on a need basis. Running of periodic metrics reports must be included in your policies and procedures as periodical processes; these metrics may include and not limited to AP Processing Timelines, AP Processing Quality, Correction Rate, Individual Performance, AP Errors and Payees' Satisfaction reports. An example of a need-based metrics report may be Payment Transition Report, which uses the volumes of transitioning from paper checks payment to the EFT payments, during your company's transition to the ACH processing. The reports are compared to the set goals.

You need to know what is to be measured and why, how to measure and how frequently to do it, how to report the results and what action to take, based on the reported data. You may find out that it takes on average 50% of overall processing times of invoices electronically submitted into your ERP system (mailing and data entry is not a factor) to be approved by a certain department's manager who requested goods or services, which causes delays in processing of payments for goods ordered by that department. Or you may realize that 10% of payees, who have banking information on file, are still receiving paper checks, due to the old default payees' payment method "check" and no one catching up with the issue, until metrics report is run. The AP Error and Individual Performance metrics are used to assess weak points in Accounts Payable processes and staffing issues.

All findings and statistical data made with metrics reports are discussed internally by managers and supervisors within the Accounts Payable department or, if need be, presented for review to higher level management, Controller or CFO. Remember that many decision makers will not be receptive to your performance improvement suggestions (no matter how good) without the quantifiable data.

## Systems Transitions and Upgrades

A commonplace process that many AP departments have gone through recently or plan for is a system upgrade process. Our times demand a more effective, efficient and real time customer service attuned financial processes that can no longer be supported by the old server-based accounting systems. SAS, cloud-based applications is the way to do business. I, personally, support the cloud but take it with a grain of salt: I don't fully own my data, my records. As long as I am paying the provider, as long as there's internet connection, I'm good. It's the standard these days, but I feel vulnerable.

The ERP systems allow two-way 24/7 interactions with vendors, customers, and other external and internal users, internal controls and processing work flows that both speed up and improve the quality of the financial and reporting and availability of the supporting documentation in electronic formats that is available from within the system. In the ERP system that I use I have immediate access to our payees W-9s and bank account information forms that are attached to the payees' master records. An e-mail may be attached to a journal entry to justify its processing or approval. Images of Purchase Requisition, Purchase Order, Receiving Report, and Invoice are attached to the respective AP records as e-documents. Often, an image is not required to begin with, since all the processing and authorizations were initiated and approved within the same system (e.g. Purchase Requisition, Purchase Order, and Receiving Report). Built in internal control rules and segregation of duties assure that the processing and approval runs along the predetermined 'check points' that provide for separation of authorization, recording and custody of transactions and records.

Using an ERP system has become the 'new normal' and the expected level of technical wherewithal for most of mid- to large-size businesses. Companies shop around for ERP systems and buy what they desire and can afford from SAP, Oracle, Microsoft and other vendors.

The conversion process can span years of analysis, design, specifications, planning and implementation of the new system. The AP process as it's been run in the old system often does not fully reference (or map) to the new system processes. In actual fact, the old system algorithms match only a small number of the ERP systems processes. Many of the AP procedures must be reanalyzed and reassessed to assure efficient processing, reporting and compliance utilizing the new system. It is a good opportunity to update and upgrade the existing AP processes and procedures.

Processing procedures are often rewritten for the new system's processes. Initially, there is a good deal of inertia and resistance to the new system's logic and demands, and I have experienced this myself. The transition often involves using both, new and old, systems simultaneously; one reason may be a safety parallel processing that backs up the new system's operations. Another is a timing reason; for example, all checks to void that were processed in the old system must be processed in the new system with journal entries, since there are no old checks in the new system, but only the beginning accounts balances.

My old legacy system (called *Computron*, used in the old days by Pfizer and A&E television networks, among others) had 1099 reporting codes specified in payees' master records. But the voucher entry process also allowed for 1099 codes overwriting. The old process allowed exclusion of a reimbursement for a New Year party cake paid to a royalty recipient, as one real life example. My new ERP system does not allow such payment modifications. The ERP system requires adjustment of the 1099 amounts if there's such a need. The seemingly lesser flexibility of the ERP process is actually a good control that prevents the overwriting of the payees 1099 codes. Do we end up with a New Year party cake reimbursement on form 1099?! It's not a perfect world; as I said before, the 1099 process is a tedious process not matter what accounting system is used.

With the great prospects of having a new system in place, there may appear a number of unexpected interdepartmental professional interactions issues. During the system transition that I have gone through I observed certain inter-office political power re-adjustments; the IT department, responsible for the new system customizing and implementation, quite logically *got strong* and influential. IT managers, none of whom are finance or accounting professionals, were instructing the finance department on the financial processes based on the new system's design and abilities.

There was a bit of the "buggy in front of the horse" situation because the accountants were told by the IT personnel how to run the accounting affairs based on what the system can do being in the 'out-of-the-box' shape. One advice that sounded more like a demand from the IT was not to use any information for the invoice number field in cases where there is no invoice number *per se*. The new system allows the *blanks* for the invoice number field. Later, I had to struggle during the 1099 review with thousands of invoice records that had no readily available invoice numbers (or rather invoice references in the invoice number fields) that were foregone based on the IT's blank invoice numbers suggestion (such references are usually made up by AP processors, "trip to Amherst, MA", "taxi cab/NASA meeting" or "Honorarium, 12-29-2014"), and serve much better a purpose than the blank space. There's a controversial element in the transition process and I hope that your finance department is strong enough in your company's hierarchy to demand and assume the full control of the financial processes establishment within the new system.

The new system must be initially run in the test mode. Then a production is rolled out to a limited segment of business, usually the most controlled cost center. Once the confidence that the new system is fully operational on the company-wide level is gained, it is released to all cost centers. The system should be closely monitored and many adjustments will be made to the 'live' system already in use. It is a reality that one cannot fully develop a new system in the test mode, unless it's a very simple system. The ERP's are not simple systems and fine-tuning and fixing of unexpected issues continues in the production phase. As I have mentioned earlier, it is a prudent process to upload the information processed in the new system back to the old system in case of a major unforeseen contingency that may render the new system inoperable.

No matter how careful, prepared, organized, and supported your new system roll out is, there are always glitches and unwelcome surprises associated with a new system implementation. Some result from different system logic and language, some are set up process issues, yet some stem from the inertia and emotional attachment to the old system's ways.

My last practical advice – embrace the new system. It is most likely that the new system is better than the old one. Ask to be the key departmental expert on it, offer to invest your extra time to the process. Be passionate about the new system, love it. This will make you engaged and excited. This will make you an irreplaceable company's asset for years to come.

*Intacct.* The most recent new system I have come into contact with is Intacct. Sage Intacct is a mid-size business ERP. The system is easy to navigate and enter data. The reports can be designed and customized to your specifications. Many reports are interactive (with 'drill down' function). Checks printing and ACH processing is easy. I was surprised to find out that an Intacct payee cannot have more than one remittance address – so I end up creating vendor IDs for the same business with different 'remit to' locations. More surprising was to learn that there is no true Cash Disbursement module in Account Payable to process wires and online payments: Debit expense, Credit cash in the same transaction. All cash disbursements are entered as 'invoices': Debit expense, Credit payable, and then 'closed' in a separate Bill Pay process: select open 'wire' invoice, select payment method 'record transfer'. Under this set up there is a possibility for such 'wire' or 'online pay' invoice to be also paid by check, if not flagged properly.

All AP transactions originate in Purchasing module. The Intacct AP logic if designed more for a distribution/warehouse type of operations, less so for a service company. The workflows are not as flexible as those found in SAP Concur – you cannot 'delegate' or 'approve and forward' a transaction in Intacct. Speaking of SAP Concur and Intacct – the two systems can be integrated and SAP Concur data uploaded directly into Intacct for payment (from Intacct) or reporting (if Concur-paid). My overall experience with Intacct is net positive – I like using Intacct much more than the previous system, MIP Abila.

When I think back about the accounting systems I used – Peachtree, Quickbooks, JD Edwards, Computron, Kuali, Peoplesoft, MIP Abila, Intacct – I realize how much such systems have advanced in the last twenty years and made the Accounts Payable work more efficient and fun. Get as much as you can for your AP operations from your accounting system, there are often functionalities that the administrators are not familiar with – inquire with your system can do for you (for example, use youtube).

# Processing Account Payable in PeopleSoft

## The most popular ERP of our days; true or false?

As much as you will disagree with me on this statement – PeopleSoft is the most popular, or let's say, most used, ERP system in our days. There are people who much prefer SAP for it being a strong accounting application; or Microsoft Dynamics fans who like the system's immediate compatibility with all other Microsoft products. I used to like QuickBooks, before the ERP days. I like PeopleSoft for the simple and less valid reason of my knowledge of the PeopleSoft system and years of experience with PeopleSoft.

Being an ERP, PeopleSoft got it all inside one system: workflows, email notifications, G/L, transactions processing, imaging capabilities, and compatibility with outside platforms to connect directly with outside parties. These are the technical features of the system. There is another less notable element that contributes to PeopleSoft's popularity; the software is being developed and sold by a domestic (US) vendor, Oracle Corporation. This is where PeopleSoft gets a lot of its competitive edge against SAP, the only other major ERP system. SAP is owned and marketed by a German company.

As an Accounts Payable specialist you are aware that buying restrictions and conditions often exist on what can be purchased and from whom: an almost non-exceptional rule for US governmental organizations and municipalities is to buy goods and services from domestic vendors. Anytime any state decides to upgrade its old main-frame system to an ERP, there's almost no need to decide between the two major ERP heavy-weights: PeopleSoft and SAP. Only a domestic vendor is allowed; and it is Oracle with PeopleSoft.

With such a critical mass of 'hostage' PeopleSoft users, all the federal, state, and municipal level governments, it's not surprising to see the snowball effect in place; there are trained users, system connectivity concerns for vendors that do business with government organizations, availability for a lower price given the number of PeopleSoft users.

It is surprising how SAP manages to survive in this anti-competitive environment to begin with. But SAP is surviving and thriving due to its being a robust ERP application.

Putting the marketing considerations aside, PeopleSoft is indeed a strong and powerful application. Even in appearance it looks very 'clean' and professional, without any fancy graphic that only distracts the user. There are some pages that remind me of QuickBooks' icons: requisition – PO – delivery – receiving – invoicing – RTV – payment. The data-mining is quick, search takes little time even when huge volumes of information are being worked through, queries are easy to write and run.

The computing and searching power of PeopleSoft obviously comes from Oracle Corporation being a major SQL language developer; Oracle had signed its first contract with the government (Department of Defense) to supply SQL-based programming products about 40 years ago. Oracle's procurement of SQL programming products to the feds has never stopped since then.

Another element of Oracle's products success may lie with its Chairman of Chief Technology Officer, Larry Ellison who has a celebrity status similar to that of Donald

Trump (this line was written in 2013). Larry is a *homeboy*, born on the Lower East Side in Manhattan; I would like him for that single reason, putting aside the fact that Larry and I are avid yachtsmen, great businessmen, experienced pilot (Larry), and billionaire (just Larry, not me).

I began this chapter with a rhetorical question: PeopleSoft is the most popular ERP, true or false? *PeopleSoft is the most popular ERP*, as far as I know. I know hundreds of people who use PeopleSoft, at different companies based in New York City. I know only one person, Greg H., who used SAP with Sanofi Pharmaceutical. I worked on PeopleSoft while managing AP with the City University of New York and New York University Medical Center.

## What PeopleSoft Can and Cannot Do for the Accounts Payable?

Can you 'work from home' three days a week, or work from a Florida beach if you are using PeopleSoft? No, you can't. You will not be able to enjoy the kind of work schedule that some IT folks utilize working from their remote homes and rarely showing up for work in a physical office. Your PeopleSoft application most of times will not be accessible via a browser over the internet, although you do access PeopleSoft through a browser in the office, but you work on your company's intranet, an internal computer network that connects you to the company servers.

PeopleSoft organizes the Accounts Payable operations within one system where all the information is entered into and accessed from. The system has the potential to make your Accounts Payable activities hassle-free, and headache-free; it connects all the players in the game in one virtual environment (even your vendors, if you connect them to PeopleSoft via an EDI system), it stores images of all relevant documents, it maintains the AP workflow to move the process along the lines, and it sends email alerts to the users when actions are needed.

It's a common saying about any machine or program that it is only as good as those people who use the system. But PeopleSoft does improve AP operations quality even with no change in quality of human work applied to Accounts Payable processes. One such improvement that any ERP has is the imaging capabilities; one of the 'head-aches' I mentioned just before used to be missing Accounts Payable paperwork. This was an annoying and persistent nuisance of the past: "Where's my travel reimbursement?! I submitted it two months ago!" – "Sorry, we'll surely find it (assertively)... maybe (in a hushed voice). Or, think the 1099 review already mentioned in the book; even with all the paper invoices in their right places in boxes in storages inside or outside the company, physically it took long time to get to see a piece of paper that held a key to whether report something or not on form 1099.

The workflow is another great advance that the ERPs and PeopleSoft in particular have brought about. If you are the next person to approve a transaction, you get an *action required* or *reminder* email, or you can just monitor your Action List to keep current on your required actions. You may set a proxy approver for the days when you are not in the office. There are some unexpected difficulties related to the workflow algorithm of PeopleSoft that has to do with *ownership* of a transaction; if a person who created a transaction or someone who must approve it next is not available, the transaction may get stuck in queue until IT department re-assigns the ownership of the transaction. That's why it is good to have good workers in place who never quit, get fired or retire; at list until there's another system upgrade.

Accounts Payable in PeopleSoft is without a doubt the next higher level of AP work, compared to the old computer systems used in AP. PeopleSoft allows you to concentrate on value-added processes and avoid being pulled into unproductive activities such as sending reminders to a department's head to approve a past due invoice. PeopleSoft does send such an email.

However, I can't help but think of the 'only as good as those who use it' statement in relation to PeopleSoft as well. It is quite obvious: if AP entries are processed carelessly, AP procedures not followed, systems operations not used as designed, there will be problems having a good Accounts Payable operation in place.

PeopleSoft does allow competent Accounts Payable processors to do a better job: process more transactions in less time, generate reports quicker, better communicate with suppliers and internal AP customers, better manage AP data.

For someone who is sloppy at what he does an upgrade to PeopleSoft or any ERP can provide little help, since the improvement is required in a different area.

## PeopleSoft's 'Nuts and Bolts' of Payables:

*Navigation of PeopleSoft*

You've been assigned a PeopleSoft user ID and password which bring you to the Home Page. You will have a number of menu options available based on your level of access. Some managers discourage their employees from using the Favorites option, I strongly advise to use it. Speed of access to various menus is often important when you have a vendor on the phone or just in need to get to the information quickly.

Your available options, menu folders, among other things may be:
- Accounts Payable
- eProcurement
- Procurement Contracts
- Purchasing
- Supplier Contracts
- Suppliers
- Travel and Expenses
- Worklist

Right off the bat, you should select the following menu options that you will be using on a constant basis (follow the menu path provided):

a. Regular Entry (to enter, review, and adjust various types of AP vouchers). Main Menu – Accounts Payable – Vouchers – Add/Update – Regular Entry

b. Purchase Orders (to review existing purchase orders). Main Menu – Purchasing – Purchase Orders – Review PO Information – Purchase Orders.

c.  Three-Way Matching Interface (to review matching of PO to Invoice and to Receipt). Main Menu – Accounts Payable – Review Accounts Payable Info – Interfaces – Purchase Order.

d.  Activity Summary (to review PO, receipts, invoices, matching, RTV (returns to vendor)). Main Menu – Purchasing – Purchase Orders – Review PO Information – Activity Summary.

e.  Supplier (to enter or review vendor information). Main Menu – Suppliers – Supplier Information – Add/Update – Supplier.

f.  Voucher Inquiry (to review detailed voucher information. A very useful page for investigating vouchers errors). Main Menu – Accounts Payable – Review Accounts Payable Info – Vouchers – Voucher.

g.  Receipts (to view receiving documents). Main Menu – Purchasing – Receipts – Review Receipt Information – Receipts.

h.  Purchasing Requisitions. Main Menu – Purchasing – Requisitions – Review Requisition Information – Document Status.

i.  Control Group (to 'unlock' old vouchers for modification). Main Menu – Accounts Payable – Control Groups – Group Information.

j.  Query Viewer (to run various reports). Main Menu – Reporting Tools – Query – Query Viewer.

Keep as many browser windows as you deem necessary for your work. To open a new window (and remain signed in), click on the New Window link. It will open a new browser window with the same menu as in the previous window.

Underscored links are rather important in PeopleSoft; many times information is not visible until you click on the View All link. This happened too many times in my department – voucher is not there, the PO line is not available, there is no receipt – all because people forget to expand the viewable information, and click on View All. Notice that various versions of PeopleSoft have the link either visible in your browser window, or may require you to scroll to the right to see that important link.

Another 'click on' item that holds important information is the inconspicuous *Expand Triangle*; you may find it many places, but most importantly for your Accounts Payable work, in the voucher entry or adjustment menus. The triangle appears next to the Copy From Source Document header and allows you to view copy options when entering different kinds of vouchers: Non PO Receipt, None, PO Receipt, Purchase Order Only (most used in the three-way matching type payments processing), Template, and Voucher (often used to process credit memos). The Expand Triangle on this screen shot appears mid-page followed by *Copy From Source Document* (voucher Invoice Information page).

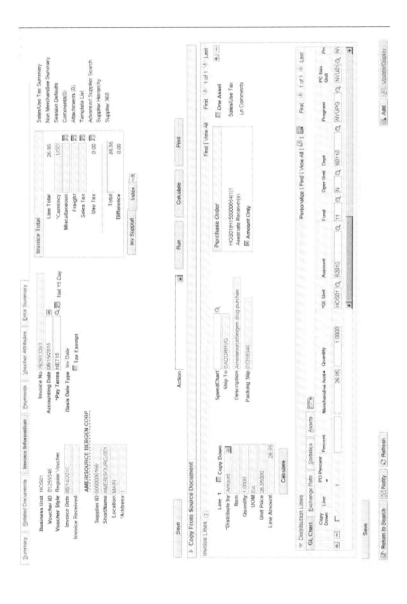

278

Let us review Voucher Entry (also, Change and Review page). As stated before, the menu path to it is Main Menu – Accounts Payable – Vouchers – Add/Update – Regular Entry. On the Voucher page you will see two tabs – Find an Existing Value and Add a New Value. We will research the Add New Value function later. Let us select Find an Existing Value now.

If your company is using more than one Business Unit you will be asked to identify that Business Unit. In case that there is only one Business Unit, if will be entered as a default. Enter then voucher number, or any other information you have or want to use. Options are: Voucher ID, Invoice Number, Invoice Date, Short Supplier Name, Supplier ID, Supplier Name, Voucher Style, Related Voucher, Entry Status, Voucher Source, Incomplete Voucher and various operators available for all these functions (=, begins with, contains, not =, <, >, <=, >=, between, in). You can use the search functions to run quick direct AP reports based on the available criteria. PeopleSoft is really good at running queries; you need to wait only seconds to get tons of information based of your search data. Remember that most custom made reports reside in Query Viewer.

Once your voucher is found, you access Regular Entry page with six tabs (menus) there: Summary, Related Documents, Invoice Information, Payments, Voucher Attributes, and Error Summary.

*Summary* page of voucher page. The page starts with the already mentioned Business Unit. Watch what Business Unit your voucher is in, in case there is more than one business unit. Next comes the voucher number, which you selected, or which was found based on other criteria entered on the search page. Voucher Style will be discussed later – it may be Regular, Adjustment, Reversal, etc. Next comes Supplier Name.

*Entry Status* may be one of the three: Deleted, Recycle, Postable (99% of time), or *blank* (all Quick vouchers).

*Match Status* is a line frequently looked at in a three-way matching environment. The options there are: Exception, Manually Overridden, Credit Note (manual change), Matched (this is what you want to see on all your vouchers), Dispute, No Match. All these statuses will be discussed in great details later in this chapter.

*Approval Status* is one of three: Pending Approval, Approved, or Denied.

*Post Status* changes from Not Posted to Posted.

*Budget Status* may be Valid or Error.

*View Related* drop-down menu has the following options to select from: Select and click Go to view related invoice information. [Quoted from http://docs.oracle.com/cd/E39583_01/fscm92pbr0/eng/fscm/fapy/task_ViewingVoucherSummaryInformation-9f7173.html] The system opens the inquiry pages in new browser windows, so you can review both the invoice and the related information at the same time.

- *Accounting Entries Inquiry*: Select to access the Voucher Accounting Entries inquiry page and view accounting entries for posted vouchers. If a voucher has not yet been posted, the page does not display accounting entries.
- *Payment Inquiry*: Select to access the Payment Inquiry page and search for related payments.
- *Purchase Order Inquiry*: Select to access the Purchase Order Inquiry page and search for related purchase orders.

- *Voucher Document Status*: Select to access the Voucher Document Status inquiry page to view related documents.
- *Voucher Inquiry*: Select to access the Voucher Inquiry page and search for related vouchers. [End of quote]

Next voucher tab, Related Documents, has Payment Details, Voucher Line – PO Information, and Receipt information.

The following page is the most used voucher adjustment page – *Invoice Information*. You will visit this page often when changing voucher information (before posting) or correcting match-exception errors. Remember to click on *View All* link to view all voucher lines. Within each voucher line box there is PO information (PO number, POs line related to this voucher line, and the voucher line's count within that PO line), and Associate Receiver information. In each line you can change the line's quantity, UOM (Units of Measurement), and unite price. You can enter voucher by copying POs lines or 'related' voucher lines – we will discuss this process later.

You can delete an individual line by clicking on (-) in the line's upper right corner; you cannot delete multiple lines – a voucher with 100 lines that need to be re-aligned on a PO is best deleted and a new voucher entered. An exclamation mark (!) in a triangle means that this voucher line has match exception error(s), which are explained in the last voucher tab – Error Summary. Remember that total amount is a sum of (PO) Line Total, Miscellaneous, Freight, and Sales Tax figures. On this page, you can adjust the Supplier ID and Address, which can be different from the Supplier ID on the Payment screen and does not affect the remittance information on check or ACH (the Payment screen selection governs the remittance).

*Payments (tab)*. There are few important items found here. Remittance information on this page is used to direct payments. Payment terms and due date (scheduled day) appear here. Method of payment, Check, ACH, wire, are listed as well. A much used action on this page is the Hold Payment check box; you must enter Hold Reason from the drop down list and enter a more detailed comment on Invoice Information page.

*Voucher Attributes* is a frequently misused page. I want you to remember this: do not use this page to change voucher match status when processing credits. Use the correct Match Exception Workbench Details page described in the following paragraphs. I only use this page to place a voucher in Match Dispute status, or remove that status, or assign Manually Overridden status to a voucher that fails to undergo a proper matching process.

*Error Summary* is a page that lists any matching errors that prevent a voucher from matching and being selected for payment. Errors are interrelated; an invoice with 2 items $50/each will have three errors if applied to a PO and receipt with 1 double $100 item, which is the same thing and is not an error per se. The errors will be extra quantity (2 instead of 1), wrong unit price ($50 instead of $100) and greater quantity billed vs. received (2 instead of 1 received). *Match exceptions* will be discussed in the following paragraphs.

I will not delineate all elements of PeopleSoft navigation as they are really common sense and easy to understand for any computer-literate AP specialist. I will list just two more instances where you need to be aware how to do the following: prepare a voucher to be adjust by a credit memo and change voucher dispute status to credit status directly.

In the three-way matching processing there are often cases of 'over-billing' – invoice prices exceeding POs prices agreed upon. Such invoices end up in match-exception (match exception will be discussed later in this chapter) and must be credited to allow a correct invoice (re-bill) to be matched against the PO. When a credit memo is entered (as Adjustment Voucher), the original voucher is first put in Dispute, then in Credit Memo status.

Oracle's manual on PeopleSoft, PeopleBooks, while describing the process correctly, led many AP departments into believing that the change of the original voucher must be done in the Voucher Attributes tab of the voucher. I have seen departmental instructions documents (created based on the PeopleBooks) with the procedures incorrectly documented upon inaccurate reading of PeopleBooks that caused many credits taken while the original invoice remaining in match exception. The situation repeated itself in hundreds of instances where goods were delivered; incorrectly, then correctly billed for; but the only payment document process was the Credit Memo taken against another unrelated payment to the same supplier.

This is an important point to understand: an overbill takes up the POs line and extra, remaining in match exception. A credit memo process against the overbill must adjust (reverse) the overbill and fully restore the PO to allow the rebill to be processed. For this process to run correctly, the original voucher is put in Dispute (when credit is entered), then in Credit Note status (after credit was matched, before the original voucher is matched), not on the Voucher Attributes screen.

The change to the overbill voucher is made on the Match Exception Workbench Details screen, which you access by clicking on the (Match Status) Exception link in the Summary (first tab) of the voucher (keep this Workbench screen open on the side for the time being). There, and only there, you should change the Voucher Match Action to Match Dispute first, and then to Credit Note. Make sure you click on the Apply button, to see Override in each of the Voucher Line Match Action line and then *Save*.

Match Credit Voucher manually first. Then change the original voucher, using the same Match Exception Workbench Details screen, to the Credit Note. Select Credit Note from the drop-down menu, click on Apply (to populate Override to each voucher line), and Save. Do not run the Matching on the original voucher; whatever previous errors were there on the voucher should now be overridden by the voucher adjustment process.

Mind you that in cases when you process a credit (adjustment style voucher) to reverse an overbill, the receipt information disappears from the three-way matching screen (PO Interface). This happens even after the receipt is reattached to the rebill (which initially has No_Receipt – Unmatched_Receipt_Exist error) and the rebill voucher is matched

As simple and immaterial this process appears, when there are credits that amount to millions of dollars in any given year, New York University Medical Center being one example, incorrect credits processing leads to 'taking' goods and credits, and not paying for either original or rebill vouchers. An embarrassing situation; if one does not know the correct matching process outlined above, the only cure for the situation is an ongoing manual overriding of match exception vouchers – a process frowned upon by all reasonable people, company auditors, and me, first and foremost. Continuous overriding of vouchers is admission of the inability to control the business process.

I will now describe one more situation involving a disputed voucher and the process to change its status directly to the Credit Note voucher. While gaining understanding of the process, you should get a bigger idea of how PeopleSoft payables menus are organized and linked together.

Let's say there's a voucher (invoice) that exceeds a corresponding PO amount. Some AP clerk had noticed the discrepancy and assigned to the voucher Match Dispute status (in the Voucher Attributes voucher tab/screed). If you entered a credit memo to offset this overbill voucher and matched that credit (always making sure that the credit and the original voucher get paid together; adjust the 'invoice dates' and 'payment terms' for that) you want to change your disputed voucher to Credit Note. Mind you, the Match Exception Workbench Details page was not used in the first place. It cannot be used now – Voucher Status: Dispute is not a click-able item.

In order for you to directly change a (long) disputed voucher to Credit Note, on the voucher's Summary, in the lower left corner in the drop-down menu, select Voucher Document Status, click on GO and find yourself taken to the Voucher Document Status screen. There you find Match Status as Match Dispute, click on Match Dispute, and change the status to Credit Note (Apply, Save, manually match the voucher).

When navigating PeopleSoft keep in mind that this is a browser housed application, and that a great number of useful details are just one click away from you behind a clickable link. I already mentioned View All and Expand Triangle. On the Invoice Information page there are 10 links in the upper right corner that have various menus helpful in your work. Invoice lines have clickable PO Number and Associate Receiver(s) links. Note this; while you are not authorized to process receipts according to duties separation, in the credit and rebill instances you will need to reapply a previously used receipt using this exact Associate Receiver (s) link. Remember this – even the PeopleBooks does not describe the process; once you enter credit and rebill, the original receipt applied to the overbill becomes 'handing', as I call. It is still the same item in the warehouse that was received, only there is a new invoice and voucher (rebill) to pay for it.

Errors on the rebill voucher is such situation are No Receipt Exists and Unmatched Receipt Exists. The End User does not need not process another receipt, since the original receipt is still valid for the merchandise and quantity. One of the common CPA tests questions has it – does a copy of PO sent to receiving has the item's price? The answer is: No. You can search (if you don't know the receipt number) for the receipt to apply to the rebill within the Associate Receiver menu – click on Associate Receiver Lines, enter Recv BU (Business Unit, if applies), Receipt Number, or click on the magnifying glass. Find the receipt and select it.

Every company that uses PeopleSoft has a test environment with a day delay volume of data that gets updated nightly. You can process any type of transaction without risk of affecting the production environment. I advise to take full advantage of that test environment and try every link, menu and process that you find there.

## Document Status Flow

A requestor, or end user, a person who is the 'forest' in the 'forest for the trees' proverbial expression, desires to buy something essential for business operations. The requestor creates a requisition that is submitted for approval. The approved requisition then appears in a buyer's queue.

The buyer is a person who negotiates pricing, gets competitive biddings auction-type process under way and ultimately issue a Purchase Order (PO). A purchase order is a 'big deal'. It ensures the supplier has the right for payment for the goods shipped. The supplier ships the goods, which are duly received by loading dock personnel, which know to accept the delivery based on a PO information in PeopleSoft. I used to be a truck driver back in the days. I do remember well – no PO, no unloading of the palettes.

When receiving takes place, the requestor can enter a 'receipt' of goods requested and received. The process covers two steps of the three-way matching process: (1) goods were duly ordered (PO), and received (Receipt).

An invoice for the aforementioned transactions comes in as a paper invoice or EDI invoice. The invoice is now in the 'three-way matching' pot: PO, Invoice and Receipt are compared and matched against each other to establish validity of ensuing payment. Discrepancy in the matching process creates a match-exception situation that will discussed later. Note that there is no need for physical signatures such as "Approved for payment, (date)" on a hardcopy of the invoice. The price and quantity had all been pre-approved on requisition and PO levels; the invoice approval is a mere check that the agreed upon price and the quantity shipped all tie-up on supplier's invoice that summarizes the transaction. Simple and clear.

### Three-Way Matching in PeopleSoft

There are three types of matching; two-, three-, and four-way matchings. Two-way matching compares PO and Invoice only, when the *Receiving Required* option for the PO is in *Optional* or *Do Not* status. Three-way matching compares (1) PO, (2) Receipt, and (3) Invoice when Receiving Required option has *Required* status and the Inspect box is not checked. When the Inspect box is checked and receiving is required, four items are compared (four-way matching) – PO, Receipt, (4) Inspection report, and Invoice.

In my practice, excluding the T&E and other reimbursements, two-way matching is required for about 25% of payments, four-way matching 5 %, and three-way matching about 70%. We will discuss the three-way matching as the most common matching type, and other matching types being variations of the three-way matching.

A PO may have different elements included on it and it affects the three-way matching process. A PO can be Amount Only: the quantity for Amount Only PO is always **1** (per line) and quantities on invoices and receipts applied to such PO do not matter. Only the amount matters. An Amount Only POs are used to purchase goods and services that are not measured in concrete units. Amount Only PO is really a mere budget limitation on a certain activity, for example a PO for Office Supplies for Fiscal Year 2017.

As already mentioned, a PO may not require receiving or require inspection, which changes the three-way matching to two- or four-way matching. A PO lists Item ID, Item Description, Category, Quantity, Unit Price, Unit Of Measurement (UOM), Shipping Code, Chartfield (which includes, GL Unit (Business Unit), Account (GL account), Fund, Operating Unit, Department, Program, PC Business Unit, Project, Activity, Source Type, Category, Budget Reference, Affiliate, Fund Affiliation, etc.), Tax details, Asset Information, and related Purchase Requisition information.

For 'quantities' POs (those that are not 'amount only') the following items must match: receiver's Item Description, quantity, and UOM matched to both PO and Invoice; invoice's Item Description, quantity, UOM (to both PO and receiver) and additionally price per unit to PO.

For *Amount Only* POs, what matters is, you guess it, only the amount; the amount of the receipt, invoice, and PO. Quantities are always '1' on all amount only individual documents.

There are Match Exception tolerance levels; discrepancy that you are willing to accept without investigating and correcting them. Usually it's 1-2% of quantity and amount discrepancy that is allowed. PeopleSoft will accept any other number that you deem appropriate. The tolerance level is a tricky business; I understand that 2%+ excess of 22% price per unit difference on a $1000 item ($22 per unit difference, time the quantity) is worth investigating. But a 50% difference on a $2 item, and I have seen many such POs, extra $1 per unit (times quantity), except when the quantities are substantial, is not worth investigating, working with supply chain management, requesting credits and rebills – the issue does not warrant the effort and the associated expenses.

There is time to match vouchers, and there is time to un-match vouchers. The un-matching process is less known and used, but is needed sometimes to re-do an incorrect matching. You can access the function by following this path: Main Menu – Accounts Payable – Review Accounts Payable Info – Vouchers – Match Workbench.

I will quote PeopleBooks now to provide certain rules and definitions. The information refers to the Match Status of a voucher, which appears on the Summary page of a voucher and can have the following status values: Ready, No Match, Matched, Exception, Credit Note, Dispute, and Overridden (Overridden changes to Matched after the matching process is run). [Quoted from http://docs.oracle.com/cd/E39583_01/fscm92pbr0/eng/fscm/ fapy/task_ViewingVoucherSummaryInformation-9f7173.html]

(Match Action Status) Displays the current matching status of the voucher. You can change the match status, but what you can change varies depending on where the voucher is in the matching process.

For example, before running the Matching process, you can change the matching status to No Match on a line-by-line basis; that is, you can indicate which lines require matching and which lines do not.

The User ID does not require match override authority to switch between a matching status of Ready and a status of No Match.

The match status values are:

*Credit Note:* Marks the voucher as being matched with a credit memo adjustment voucher.

*Dispute:* Indicates that the voucher is on hold from further matching processing.

*Exceptions:* A voucher that fails the Matching process initially has a status of Exceptions. In this case, you can select the Exceptions link on the Voucher – Summary page to transfer to the Match Exception Workbench Details page. Or you can override the match status here, provided that your user ID has match override authority.

*Matched:* Indicates that the voucher has successfully passed the Matching process.

*No Match:* Indicates that all voucher lines are flagged as Do Not Match. If no lines are flagged for matching, the system sets voucher matching to No Match. The system sets this value automatically when it copies voucher information from a purchase order or receiver. You can set this value manually as well.

*Overridden:* Enables the voucher to pass matching by setting the match status to Matched, even though the voucher does not match specified purchase orders or receivers. (Author's note: since properly matched and overridden vouchers after matching enter into Matched status, to find out which vouchers were overridden, you need to run a special report.) If you had previously set the status to Overridden, you change it back to Exceptions. (Author's note: the change can only be made if matching was not run on the voucher. Otherwise, you need to (possible un-post first) un-match the matched voucher and change the status.)

*Ready*: Marks the voucher as ready for matching so that it can be processed in the next time the Matching process is run. (Author's note: Matching process can be scheduled to be system-run and simultaneous, or can be processed manually, sequentially. The manual process differs from system-generated process; if the system matched two items on two different invoices to a one-item PO, the process is simultaneous, and both invoices end up in match exception (although only one invoice is 'extra'). Manual process allows you to select the correct invoice and manually match it to both receipt and PO; the 'extra' invoice will remain in exception until further investigation. The sequential manual matching is a better process that allows correct invoices to be matched, and even some non-existing (yes, that happens, too) match-exception errors to be resolved during matching. At New York University Medical Center where I worked, manual matching was (if projected to one person) a day-long permanent job that had to be done to overcome matching deficiencies of the system-run simultaneous matching process.)

Click Match Action History link to review match action history on the Match Exception Workbench Details page. Select to pay an unmatched voucher. You must have authority, defined in the user preferences, to do this.

What triggers the matching process? An invoice entry as a voucher; the voucher must be PO-related. The PO will determine whether the match will be two-way (no receipt or inspection required), three-way (receipt is required), or four-way match (both receipt and inspection are required). Once the invoice is entered and the voucher is saved, the combo is ready to undergo matching process, the voucher is in Ready status.

All matched vouchers are ready for payment selection based on due dates. All vouchers that failed matching must be corrected (most of times) or overridden (in exceptional cases). There must be a daily match-exception report run and subsequent daily review by departments and individuals responsible for match-exceptions corrections. Match-exception process is a subject of the next sub-chapter.

Below is *Activity Summary* page showing PO details, receipts, invoices, matching (PO dis-encumbrance) and RTV's. This is 'matching pot' as I call, where all things are put together; the "puzzle" icon leads you to details of all the documents in the pot.

When I copied this page I noticed that the PO has been over-matched, over-dis-encumbered. I now realized that I saved this screen shot because the receipts on one of the invoices were causing multiplication of dis-encumbrance amount projected through the invoice. It's a different story.

Activity Summary

| | | |
|---|---|---|
| Business Unit | 1 | PO Status Dispatched |
| Purchase Order | 30053166 | Supplier JOHNSON & JOHNSON HEALTHCARE |
| Merchandise Amount | 392.26 USD | Supplier Location ORTHO |
| Merchandise Receipt | 392.26 USD | |
| Merchandise Returned | 0.00 USD | |
| Merchandise Invoice | 374.72 USD | |
| Merchandise Matched | 444.96 USD | |

Lines — Personalize | Find | View All | First 1-4 of 4 Last

| Line | Item | Item Description | UOM | Qty Matched | Amt Matched | Currency Code |
|---|---|---|---|---|---|---|
| 1 | 210021 | MAGNESIUM 5 PACK/90 SLDS | PK | 16.0000 | 70.240 | USD |
| 2 | 210018 | BUBC 5 PACK/90 SLDS | PK | 16.0000 | 140.480 | USD |
| 3 | 148429 | PHOSPHORUS/5 300/PK SLDS | PK | 8.0000 | 117.120 | USD |
| 4 | 148458 | ACID URIC/5 SLDS 300/PK | PK | 8.0000 | 117.120 | USD |

Return to Search | Notify

## Match-Exceptions

Match-Exceptions is an ongoing concern for any company that utilizes invoice matching. It may come in different shape and form; back in the old paper days it would be a manila folders named 'No POs', 'No Receipts' in Accounts Payable department with incomplete for matching purposes batches of documents. I remember, early in 2000s receiving overnight UPS packages full of paper receipts from TYCO's manufacturing plan in Mexico and other packages full of paper POs from SCM (Supply Chain Management) center in California in my Secaucus, NJ AP office, where I was continuously laboring on a three-way matching puzzle completing it with the invoices received in my office.

There are no paper stacks in our days. A paper PO copy may be generated for some purpose. I now witness disappearance of paper receipts, which are being replaced by hand-held scanners linked to PeopleSoft receipts processing. Most of the invoices now, if not the EDI type, come as paper to a third-party invoice processor company (DigiScribe Inc.) located in Elmsford, NY with data processors located in the Philippines. This is the New York University Medical Center AP process; I am with the university at the time of writing this chapter. DigiScribe submits for uploads scanned images with invoice data entered as daily feeds.

There is no paper. There is no paper on my desk; just two monitors, keyboard and a phone. There is a daily match-exception report that is being reviewed by a number of designated individuals who are responsible for correcting match exceptions. Let's review some of them.

When talking about the three-way match exceptions, the errors, by definition, can only reside in three areas – *PO, Receipt and Invoice.*

Let's start with errors in receipts. Most of the times, the error is a non-existing receipt. This is often a big problem for any big organization since the persons who request and receive goods are usually not accountants, but a very different type of professionals. Processing a receipt is often times annoying for a requesting department process that needs to be reminded about. In contrast, processing of receipts at the loading dock or 'receiving' is a matter of a job duty.

The end-user (often the requestor, as well) 'receives' goods based on the underlining PO. PeopleSoft most used process for it is through accessing purchase orders which the end-user has initiated with purchasing requisitions. The menu path is Main Menu – eProcurement – Receive Items. As mentioned prior, only item description and quantity matter for matching of a regular PO. Item description and item price, not quantity, matter for 'Amount Only' receipts matching to PO and invoice.

Match-exception errors related to the receipts are most frequent ones - *No Receipts Exist*. Sometimes, a No Receipts Exist error comes with Unapplied Receipts Exist. This seemingly illogical situation, No Receipt and Unapplied Receipt, often results in quantities and price per unit differences between the PO and invoice liens, while being correct for all practical purposes (rebalancing of quantities and price per unit correct the situation if there are no genuine errors or discrepancies). The No Receipt – Unapplied Receipt combo often appears on rebill vouchers.

You can guess what other errors are based on what I said is being matched in PeopleSoft three-way matching: Invoice quantity not = PO quantity (Life To Date Voucher Qty > PO Qty + %Tolerance); Invoice quantity not = quantity received (Line qty not = recv qty with PO received % tol); Invoice price per unit not = PO price per unit (Converted Voucher Price <> PO Price +/- % Tolerance); RTV/Credit Adjustments are greater than the PO Line

Matched Quantity/Amounts; Invalid UOM conversion for PO (Units of Measurement are different on invoice and PO); PO is not dispatched (PO is not released by the Purchasing).

Some of match-exception items can be easily solved in the Accounts Payable department; these are those errors that resulted from incorrect data entry process. If a PO and invoice have multiple lines, the invoice can be erroneously entered line-by-line in the PO's line 1, or as a lump-sum in the PO's line 1. The right fix for it is simple re-distributing the invoice lines to the correct PO lines, provided that the invoice matches the PO. Technical aspect of the job may involve deleting all incorrectly distributed lines on the voucher (click on "-"of each voucher line), finding the PO, and selecting all PO lines to be copied to the voucher.

Note this element of the match-exception errors reporting; if you have a two-line PO with quantities 1 and $100 in each line, a correct two-line receipt, but invoice entered as 20 items at $10 (correct goods and quantities, but processed differently than the PO items by the vendor), the system will note (1) incorrect price per unit amount in line one, (2) incorrect quantity in line 1, and (3) quantity of the receipt (one for POs line one) not matching quantity of items billed for on the invoice (20).

Another 'popular' match-exception error is including the freight in the PO line; freight should not be put in the PO line unless such PO line was specifically set up for freight (or shipping and handling). Freight appears is a separate *Freight* box (there is also a similar by design *Miscellaneous* box) which is not included in the three-way matching process. I often times used the Miscellaneous box to write off minor PO to invoice discrepancies that exceeded the tolerance level; requesting a PO review to change an insignificant amount is often is counter-productive. Mind you that this action may be frowned upon by a more rigid management, and you may not be allowed to perform it.

Each PO line, both in PO and matching interface, has a Download icon; use it to download multiple-item PO lines to calculate total quantities and amounts.

Invoice applied to wrong PO, invoice lines applied to incorrect PO lines, invoice price per unit and quantity are not corresponding to those of the PO's (while being correct overall), non-invoices entered as invoice (statements, past-due letters, request for advance payment). These errors often happen due to remote invoice processing; invoice processing for New York University Medical Center is done in the Philippines, as one example, there is a pressure on the processor-company to process more – quality suffers as the result.

You should adjust all match-exception errors your department is responsible for and relay other match-exception errors to the supply chain management department (where POs are issued and maintained) and to end-users who process purchase requisitions, receipts, and RTV (return to vendor). The pressure is on the AP department to fix all the match-exception in expedient fashion even though the AP is not responsible for all match-exception. What the AP department is responsible for is for processing payments, and when payments are not processed, your company often gets put on credit hold, and this reflects poorly on the core business operations and your Dun & Bradstreet rating.

The AP Department often assumes the role of the proverbial *messenger* sending out requests to the SCM and end-user departments to adjust POs, a need to create a new PO, provide correct PO numbers, make POs 'amount only, provide credit memos for RTV's and overbills, and enter receipts. To be successful, the match-exception correction process requires a CFO's support and request for action from another departments' heads.

The process can also become quite tricky and a 'dead end', as I call it, especially in a big company, where extra goods may be requested in error and languish in the

297

warehouse unused, expire or become non-returnable. The end-user often does not underwrite (does not create a new payment requisition) to a buyer who dispatched a PO to a vendor in error the second time; I have seen such match-exception invoices being in limbo for years, still not resolved at the time of this writing. Remember, the older match-exception gets, the lesser chance of it being resolved properly. Time is not on your side. You may ask, how can you have an invoice unpaid for years? Well, I say, the big guys often get big breaks from small vendors which strive to do business. You think it's not fair to treat the little vendor this way? I do.

## Understanding and Entering Different Styles of Vouchers in PeopleSoft

In this section I will frequently quote *PeopleBooks* since I will be introducing to you something already described and it'd be silly for me to paraphrase it in an attempt to present it as my own writing. Quote Starts and Quote Ends will be denoted QS and QE.

The information can be found by using this web address:

http://docs.oracle.com/cd/E40049_01/psft/acrobat/fscm92fap y-b0313.pdf

[QS]

*Vouchers*. The lowest level of the control hierarchy is vouchers. Vouchers are supplier invoices with system applied defaults. You can enter them either manually using the online pages or automatically using the Voucher Build Application Engine process. Each voucher is assigned a unique – a voucher ID – either automatically or manually; the voucher ID provides a means for tracking all invoices, adjustments, and payments through the system.

*Definition of the Accounting Environment.* PeopleSoft Payables uses tables to store not only the data for business transactions but also the accounting environment and processing rules that drive the system and provide consistency while minimizing data entry. Before you can begin processing suppliers, vouchers, and payments, you must set up the accounting framework, which includes calendars, ChartFields, ChartField values, currency types, user profiles, general ledger journal information, and so on.

*ChartField Combination Editing.* You track payables transactions based on the ChartField combinations that you define when you set up ChartField combination editing in PeopleSoft General Ledger.

PeopleSoft General Ledger uses your accounts in combination with other ChartFields to create journal entries. In PeopleSoft Payables, ChartField combination editing provides a method to validate online and batch voucher entry accounting distribution information. By defining valid combinations, you can filter entries before you post them to ledgers, saving time and effort during reconciliation and closing. Although you employ ChartField combination editing rules during online and batch voucher entry, the PeopleSoft General Ledger Journal Editing Application Engine process (GL_JEDIT) performs the final validation of journal entries before you post them to the ledger. You can set up ChartField combination editing to reject vouchers with ChartField combination editing errors, recycle them, provide a warning, or perform no ChartField combination editing at all. You can set these options at the business unit, origin, control group, and supplier levels of the PeopleSoft Payables control hierarchy.

*Voucher Processing.* PeopleSoft Payables provides control over voucher processing and enables you to control voucher header information. The system:

• Checks for duplicate invoices.
• Calculates and confirms taxes.
• Converts the transaction currency to the base currency.
• Assigns default payment terms and calculates the payment due dates.

• Validates your suppliers against financial sanctions lists if financial sanctions validation is required.

You also have control over voucher line items. The system assigns numeric line numbers for you to ensure that each has a unique identifier. When you enter merchandise amounts on voucher lines, the sum of the line amounts must equal the gross voucher amount less the sum of freight, sales tax, and VAT entered on the voucher header. You can also define the sales and use tax and VAT at the voucher line level. In the event of an imbalance, you determine how the system responds—either rejecting or recycling vouchers until they are correct.

*Approving Vouchers.* All vouchers must be approved before they can be paid. There are three ways to approve vouchers:

• Matching vouchers to purchase order, receiver, and inspection information.
Matching occurs automatically based on the match rules—a set of rules and tolerances—that you define for a purchase order transaction. If the voucher successfully matches, it is available for payment. If the voucher does not successfully match and requires an adjustment, the system can automatically create a debit memo.
If a voucher does not pass matching, you can still pay it if you have selected the Pay Un-match Voucher option on the User Preference - Procurement: Payables page for your user ID. If do not select the Pay Un-match Voucher option, you can only pay vouchers with a Matched or *No Match* matching status.
• Routing vouchers through worklists and email using Workflow.
Workflow approval is most often used for vouchers that are not related to purchase orders, but it is not limited to that use. If you want, you can record a voucher as preapproved. The

301

voucher is not routed for approval, and it is available for payment immediately—provided that it has been matched or that matching is not necessary.
• Manually approving individual vouchers online.

*Posting Vouchers.* The Voucher Posting Application Engine process (AP_PSTVCHR) creates balanced accounting entries for vouchers. The system combines information entered for a voucher with other control information— offset accounts stored on the accounting entry templates and ChartField inheritance rules—to create the balanced entries. Vouchers do not have to be approved for accounting entries to be created.

You post vouchers through a batch process that you run periodically using Process Scheduler. You can continue to process new transactions online during posting.

PeopleSoft Payables also enables you to unpost vouchers—that is, you can back out the accounting entries made to accrue the liability and reopen the vouchers for amendment or closure.

Once vouchers are posted, the information created is available for distribution to other business processes, such as the Journal Generator Application Engine process (FS_JGEN), which converts payables accounting entries to general ledger journal entries.

*Payment Processing.* The payment processing included in PeopleSoft Payables enables you to create disbursements for transactions that flow through PeopleSoft Payables.

PeopleSoft Payables supports a number of payment formats: system check, automated clearing house (ACH), electronic funds transfers (EFTs), wire transfers, drafts, direct debits, and letters of credit. The system is delivered with several, ready-to-use EFT formats particular to local needs.

The PeopleSoft Payables Payment Interface also supplies a means for processing payments for transactions outside the PeopleSoft Payables system. This interface is used by PeopleSoft Treasury to make settlement payments and by PeopleSoft Expenses to make expense payments. The interface integrates with the PeopleSoft Financial Gateway functionality, enabling another means of electronic payment processing for EFT, ACH, and wire transfers. You can also use the interface to process payments for other in-house systems.

As part of the voucher entry process, the system schedules vouchers to be paid based on the pay terms and holiday options. If pay terms include discounts, the system also calculates a discount due date. You create pay cycles to group types of vouchers to be paid in a single payment run. For example, you might want to have one payment cycle for regular suppliers and another for employee reimbursements or check requests.

Each pay cycle that you create is essentially a reusable payment selection template that specifies the selection criteria the system uses to determine which approved vouchers should be paid. For example, you can select payments based on business unit, bank and bank account, supplier pay group, pay through date, and payment method, among others.

**Note:** During payment processing the system validates your suppliers against financial sanctions lists if financial sanctions validation is required. The system does not allow payments to suppliers who are potential matches to the financial sanctions lists.

*Payment Posting.* The creation of accounting entries for payments occurs during payment posting. As you post payments, the system generates corresponding accounting entries to relieve the liability, account for discounts earned (or lost), and generate an offset either to the designated cash account or to a PeopleSoft Payables clearing account if so designated at the bank account level. Like the Voucher Posting process, the Payment Posting Application Engine process (AP_PSTPYMNT) is a batch process that runs in the background.

*PeopleSoft Payables Control Hierarchy.* In PeopleSoft Payables, business units are the highest level of a hierarchy of defaults, called the control hierarchy, which facilitates both voucher entry and payment processing. As you formulate the PeopleSoft Payables structure, consider the five components of the control hierarchy that are key to PeopleSoft Payables.

*Levels of the PeopleSoft Payables control hierarchy.* Five components of the control hierarchy that are key to PeopleSoft Payables:
- Business Unit
- Voucher Origin
- Control Group
- Supplier
- Voucher

Default values entered at the business unit level appear automatically at the voucher level, unless you override the defaults with values stored at an intermediate level (namely, the voucher origin, control group, or supplier level). This hierarchy provides increased flexibility and control to fit unique business needs. For example, instead of requiring a PeopleSoft Payables user to enter the same default values repeatedly on vouchers, the system uses the control hierarchy to enter the predetermined values automatically. Then the user can override these values on the voucher.

When you enter default values and select processing rules at the levels that govern the control hierarchy, the system initially validates the information for you. The system then validates the data again during transaction processing to verify that it has the correct values assigned at the level that you designate.

*Business Units.* A PeopleSoft Payables business unit is an independent processing entity. Each business unit acts as a separate area of control, representing the primary level at which system tables can be controlled independently. Depending on the business requirements, you can set up business units to share core control tables such as calendars, payment terms, and suppliers. In the PeopleSoft system, TableSet processing handles this setup for you automatically, eliminating the need to maintain multiple sets of data for each business unit.

*Voucher Origins.* Each transaction entered into PeopleSoft Payables must have a valid origin, such as online or batch processing, that you define in the Voucher Origin table. You must have at least one origin, and each user must be associated with an origin. You can set up control values at the voucher origin level to override business unit defaults and automatically appear lower levels in the control hierarchy.

For example, if you have automated systems that pass information to PeopleSoft Payables—such as an electronic data interchange (EDI) interface—you might define an origin specific to those systems. Or you might set up and assign particular origins to individual data entry clerks, associating each voucher origin with a specific group of approved suppliers and allowing each data entry clerk to create vouchers for those suppliers only. For example, suppose that certain foreign invoices have distinct payment terms and other processing rules; you could set up a voucher origin with those default values and assign the origin to the data entry clerk who handles foreign suppliers.

*Control Groups.* Use control groups to maintain control over vouchers. Control groups enable you to:

• Post several groups of vouchers in one step.
• Divide large numbers of vouchers among data entry clerks while retaining centralized control over voucher processing.
• Use separate processing rules for a particular supplier's vouchers within a business unit.

*Suppliers.* You can define a set of suppliers for each business unit or share suppliers across multiple business units. You can also associate suppliers with other suppliers in the system and—if you use PeopleSoft Receivables— associate a PeopleSoft Payables supplier with a PeopleSoft Receivables customer for reporting purposes.

Suppliers can have multiple addresses and multiple locations. Addresses are the physical addresses of the supplier; a location corresponds to a unique way of doing business.

Use the location level to:
• Define payment terms and banking information for the supplier.
• Define a number of payment parameters that are used during payment processing.
• Generate separate checks for each voucher at the location level.
• Specify matching options if matching is used to approve vouchers for payment. At the location level, for example, you specify the number of days to delay discounted payment after the discount payment date has been reached—as well as the number of days to delay net payment after the net due

date has been reached. This provides additional payment flexibility based on how well you know suppliers.

For example, you can indicate how long a supplier typically waits for payment while still giving a discount. Maintaining supplier data is simple with PeopleSoft Payables. You can:

• Approve, inactivate, and reactivate suppliers.

• Record supplier information and conversations.

• Report on supplier activity and outstanding payment balances, as well as withholding and value-added tax (VAT) information.

[QE]

The next chapter describes the old-fashioned manual voucher entry. In PeopleSoft any manually entered voucher has origin status Online. I am not sure where the definition comes from, but it does sound misleading. You'd rather think of online invoice being an EDI invoice or any other type received via the Internet. This is not the case. Online = manual, in PeopleSoft.

# Entering and Processing Vouchers Online: General Voucher Entry Information

*Understanding Voucher Processing and the Voucher Life Cycle*

After you have set up all your control information, established your PeopleSoft Payables control hierarchy, and entered approved suppliers in the system, you are ready to enter vouchers into the system.

This section discusses one method of entering vouchers into the system: using the online Voucher component. The pages in this component are the equivalent of electronic voucher forms on which you can record invoice information from your suppliers in the PeopleSoft Payables database. You can also quickly copy the line item information from purchase orders and receivers from PeopleSoft Purchasing tables.

*Voucher Life Cycle*

[QS]
Vouchers go through several stages from initial entry to payment to posting. PeopleSoft Payables tracks these stages using various statuses for the following status types that relate to various actions and processes that can be run on a voucher:
• Entry status.
• Match status.
• Approval status.
• Budget status.
• Document Tolerance status.
• Post status.
• Payment status.
• Payment Post status.

When you first enter a voucher into PeopleSoft Payables, it has an entry status of Open. When you save the voucher for the first time, the system validates the input with information that is provided by default from the control hierarchy to ensure correct entries. If the voucher passes all validations, it goes into a Postable state. The system generates accounting entries when the Voucher Posting Application Engine (AP_PSTVCHR) process selects the voucher for posting. At this time, the voucher is available for distribution to the general ledger using the Journal Generator Application Engine (FS_JGEN) process.

If one or more of the validations fail, a couple of events can happen. For some edits, the system does not allow you to save the voucher until the error condition is corrected. For example, if you do not enter a date on the voucher header, you cannot save the voucher.

For other edits, you can choose less restrictive error handling, such as Recycle, which lets you save the voucher. However, you cannot post or pay the voucher until you correct the error. You set these rules at the business unit level of the control hierarchy and can override them at other levels: voucher origin, control group, supplier, and voucher. With duplicate invoice checking, for example, you can choose recycle error handling, which means that the system accepts the suspect vouchers but does not enable them to be posted or paid. To post and pay these vouchers, you must update the voucher with correct information.

Until a voucher has been reviewed for approval, or unless it is preapproved, it has an approval status of Pending. After that, a voucher can be approved or denied. A voucher cannot be paid unless it has been approved. However, if your business unit definitions enable you to, you can post a voucher even though it has not been approved for payment.

When you post a voucher in PeopleSoft Payables, the system creates balanced accounting entries to record the liability and sets the post status to Posted. When a voucher is in a posted state, you can make only limited changes to it. Essentially, you can change only descriptive information that does not affect the numbers on the voucher. To change the numbers on a posted voucher, you must first un-post the voucher to create reversing entries. This action puts the voucher back into a postable state, as if it had never been posted. You can then change the necessary fields.

A voucher can have one or more payment records selected for payment based on their scheduled pay date and other parameters. The payment status is Unselected, Selected for Payment, or Paid.


## Voucher Styles

PeopleSoft Payables provides various voucher styles, each of which addresses a particular objective:

*Adjustments*
Enter adjustment vouchers for credit or debit memos, or for relating one voucher to another. This style is also used for debit memo adjustment vouchers that are created by the Matching Application Engine process (AP_MATCH).

*Journal Voucher*
Enter vouchers for adjusting accounting entries.

*Prepaid Voucher*
Enter prepayments (down payments, progress payments, or deposits).

*Register Voucher*
Accrue an individual voucher for which the expense distribution is not known or not yet approved.

*Regular Voucher*

Enter standard vouchers (this is the default setting). This style is also used to enter purchase order vouchers and vouchers that require matching to purchase orders and receiving documents.

### Reversal voucher
Create a new voucher with reversal accounting entries and back out encumbrances.

### Single Payment Voucher
Enter a voucher for a one-time supplier without having to define the supplier in the system.

### Template Voucher
Create a voucher that can be used as a template for generating regular vouchers that share voucher data.

### Third Party Voucher
Enter vouchers for charges other than merchandise charges, for example, freight-only vouchers.

### Voucher Validation
When you save vouchers, many edits and processes occur automatically. Any problems that PeopleSoft Payables detects with a voucher are brought to your attention so that you can fix them immediately. Other edits that are specific to particular voucher styles, payment terms, and other circumstances are discussed in the sections about those styles and circumstances.

### Voucher Field Validation
The system performs a series of validation checks to ensure that you have completed all the fields correctly. Some of the validations that occur are:
• Duplicate invoice checking.
• Verifying the existence of a supplier ID.

• Verifying the existence of an invoice date and invoice ID.

• Balancing header amounts against voucher line amounts for both transaction and base currency amounts.

• Balancing voucher line amounts against distribution line amounts for both transaction and base currency amounts.

• Ensuring that the user ID that is approving the voucher is the same as the user who is signed in.

• Validating accounting distribution field values and combinations and error processing.

• Where appropriate, validating the calculation and proration of non-merchandise charges, such as sales and use taxes, value-added taxes (VAT), freight charges, and miscellaneous charges.

• Validating the bank ID, bank account number, and DFI ID [QE]

There is a lot in PeopleBooks about Online (manual) voucher entry process. But it really boils down to your knowledge of how to enter an invoice into the system either by copying a PO information (for PO-based invoices) or directly into chartfield (for non-PO invoices).

You need to get to Voucher screen by following Main Menu – Accounts Payable – Vouchers – Add/Update – Regular Entry path. Select Add a New Value tab.

1. First select the correct Business unit.

2. Voucher has NEXT value, to be assigned the next sequential number upon saving your work, or you can assign this number manually (I don't know why anyone would break the system's sequence).

3. Select Voucher Style. Voucher Styles are discussed separately. For most invoices, the correct style is Regular Voucher.

4. You can then skip to supplier ID, which is known to you most of times, or search for it. The supplier ID entered will populate the Supplier Name, Short Supplier Name, Supplier

Location, and will default the address number. (You will check the remittance number later.)

5. Enter invoice number.
6. Enter invoice date.
7. Skip other fields and click on Add.

The system takes you to invoice data entry screen with three tabs – Invoice Information, Payments, Voucher Attributes. For PO-based invoices, click on Copy From Source Document expand triangle (on the left) to make visible the Copy From drop-down menu on the right. Select Purchase Order Only – click Go. On Copy Worksheet screen select the PO Business Unit, type in PO number or find PO number using the magnifying glass icon. Once the PO number is found, or entered, expand the PO lines by clicking on View All.

Select the required/matching for your invoice lines, quantities, or amounts (select amount only for Amount Only POs). Click on Copy Selected Lines. Now the PO lines were copied to the invoice. Add Freight charges in the appropriate filed. When you click on the Calculate button, the system will show you Difference, which should be your invoice total. I do it this way. I then enter my invoice total amount in Total, click on Calculate again, and have the difference gone. Attach the invoice's image using the Attachment link.

Check the remittance address or ACH information, Pay Terms, or put invoice on hold, on the Payments page.

Save your work. You may write down the voucher number assigned to your entry at this time.

For a non-PO invoice, you won't copy any information, but enter it all manually. You need to know what Account, Fund, Operating Unit, Department, Program, etc. to enter when processing a non-PO invoice. All that information is entered and stored during the PO creating process; when copying a voucher from a PO, the information is copied to the voucher.

Now, let's go back to PeopleBooks to get more theoretical support and 'nuts and bolts' knowledge of what is going on behind the screen when you process a voucher.

By the way, how do you find out whether your PO is *Amount Only* or whether Receiving is required? If you inquire on a PO via Main Menu – Purchasing – Purchase Orders – Review PO Information – Purchase Orders, on the first screen in each PO line you will see an icon called Line Details. When you click on it, the Amount Only box appears on top, and Receiving and Inspection requirement on the bottom.

*Amount Only* PO line has always quantity of One, 1. If the quantity of POs line is more than 1, you know that this PO line cannot be Amount Only. Amount Only process is used for bulk items.

[QS]
If financial sanctions validation is enabled at the installation level, the system validates the supplier against financial sanctions lists upon saving the voucher. If financial sanctions validation is enabled at the bank level, no validation of the supplier is done during voucher processing unless you specify a bank for the remit supplier and the bank requires financial sanctions validation. The system updates the supplier's financial sanctions status on the Supplier Information component. If the system determines that the supplier is a potential match to a financial sanctions list, the system displays a warning message that the supplier is currently under financial sanctions review. You can proceed with saving the voucher; however, the system does not allow payments to suppliers with a financial sanctions status of Review or Blocked.

Click to enter comments for a voucher to explain payment schedules, issues with the supplier, or anything else that you need to document the invoice. Any comments that you enter in this field are meant for your reference only. You can enter up to 254 characters for a comment. If you exceed 254 characters, the system displays a warning message that it can save only 254 characters and truncates the message. The system displays the number of comments attached to the voucher. If no comment is attached, the system displays (0).

*Approval History.* Click this link to access the Approval History page and view the approval history for the voucher. Note: This link is only available for vouchers that are submitted for approval in the Approval Framework. (Author's note: it's been my observation that the Audit Trail or Change History is not a strong feature of PeopleSoft application).

*The Action Field.* When you have finished entering your voucher and saved it, you have three options for processing your voucher:

1. Perform budget-checking, matching, document tolerance checking, asset loading, posting, and journal generation on this and other vouchers in batch from the batch request pages for those processes.

2. Process the voucher on demand, directly from the Invoice Information page, using the Action field.

3. Process this and other vouchers in batch from the Voucher On-Demand Processes batch request page using on-demand process groups. The first option is generally the most efficient, but the second option is useful when you must process a voucher immediately, on demand. The third option is convenient when you want to perform multiple sequential processes, such as matching, asset loading, voucher posting, and journal generation, on a batch of vouchers.

If you want to process a voucher on demand from the Invoice Information page:

1. Save the voucher.

2. Select an on-demand process group in the Action field.

3. Click Run to initiate processing

*Copy from a Source Document.* PO Unit (PeopleSoft Purchasing business unit) and PO Number
If you want to copy all of the lines from a purchase order into the voucher, enter the PeopleSoft Purchasing business unit and the PO ID for the purchase order that you want to copy. Then click the Copy PO (copy purchase order) button. This option is available only if you are creating a regular voucher, template voucher, or third-party voucher.
Important! When copying a purchase order into a voucher, do not begin by entering non-merchandise and tax-exempt information on the add search page. Use the Copy PO button to ensure that the system provides these amounts by default to the appropriate fields.

*Voucher ID.* If you want to copy all of the lines from another voucher into the voucher, enter the voucher ID number that you want to copy. Then click the Copy to Voucher button. To copy individual voucher lines, enter a supplier and click the Copy from Worksheet link.

*Voucher to be Reversed.* If you want to reverse a voucher, select the voucher ID number of the voucher you want to reverse, and click the Copy to Voucher button. The system copies all information that is related to the selected voucher (such as voucher lines, distribution lines, freight, miscellaneous charges, and sales tax, and VAT information) into the reversal voucher.
This option is available only if you are creating a reversal voucher.

*Reverse.* Remaining Vchr Balance (reverse remaining voucher balance). Select to reverse only the unpaid voucher balance. This option is available only if you are creating a reversal voucher.

*Adjust PO/Restore Encumbrance (adjust purchase order/restore encumbrance).* Select to restore the encumbrance and to adjust the purchase order matched quantity or amount. This option is available only if you are creating a reversal voucher, and if the related purchase order has not been reconciled. If the related purchase order on the voucher line has been reconciled, this check box is deselected and unavailable for entry on the voucher line of the Invoice Information page.

*Copy From.* If you want to search for individual source documents to copy, to select a range of source documents, or to review individual source documents, select one of the values in this field to access the appropriate Copy Worksheet:

- Non PO Receipt
- None
- PO Receipt
- Purchase Order Only
- Template
- Voucher

*Invoice Lines.* Use the Invoice Lines scroll area to enter information for each line on the invoice: the merchandise amount, unit price, quantity, and description. Initially, at least one line appears automatically; enter as many additional lines as needed. The system assigns a line number to each voucher line that you add to ensure that each voucher line is unique.

*Distribution Lines.* For each voucher line that you enter, you must also enter the distribution information in the Distribution Lines grid. Each voucher line must have one or

more distribution lines. You can select the Copy Down check box on a distribution line to copy that line's general ledger business unit and ChartField values to new distribution lines.
[QE]

My next topic, *Adjustment Online Vouchers*, discusses a very useful and often confusing process of partial or complete reversal process. Adjustment style single voucher can reference many (!) original vouchers. Referencing means partial or complete reversal of a matched voucher; this is done do reduce an overbilled price, completely reverse an overbill invoice (and subsequently enter a rebill invoice), or register a supplier's cancellation of an invoice.

A very important concept to understand when processing adjustment vouchers in three-way matching environment is the restoring of POs quantities and amounts. If the adjustment does not reverse the original voucher, and does not restore encumbrance on PO, the PO remains matched to and reduced by the original voucher – this leaves no room for a correct invoice (rebill) to be matched to the PO. Always monitor Adjust Matched Values or Restore Encumbrance controls when processing Adjustment and Reversal style vouchers.

Logically, you rarely enter chartfields for adjustment of reverse vouchers; since you are un-doing a previously entered voucher, you always copy that voucher with a negative sign to have it reversed with all its original attributes.

## Adjustment Vouchers

[QS]

This section provides an overview of adjustment vouchers and discusses how to:
• Create adjustment vouchers.
• Create credit memo adjustment vouchers
• Adjust matched values.
• Reverse quantities or amounts for purchase order information.
• Reverse quantities or amounts for receipt information.


### Understanding Adjustment Vouchers

Use adjustment vouchers to adjust existing vouchers or to relate two vouchers to each other. You can manually enter adjustment vouchers or automatically create a debit memo adjustment voucher through the Matching Application Engine process (AP_MATCH). Enter adjustment vouchers to capture credits or to increase the initial voucher.

This section discusses entering adjusting information manually or copying the voucher that you want to adjust into the adjustment voucher. PeopleSoft Payables also provides the use of the Matching process to automatically create debit memos to resolve matching exceptions between the voucher and the purchase orders and receivers.

*Note:* If you are manually creating a credit memo adjustment for matching exceptions, use the copy function to copy the original voucher into the adjustment voucher. Run the Matching process to properly match the credit memo to the original voucher. This results in the credit memo adjustment voucher having a match status of Matched.


### Creating Adjustment Vouchers

To create adjustment vouchers:

1. Select Adjustments in the Voucher Style field on the add search page for the Voucher component (VCHR_EXPRESS), and click Add.

2. (Optional) On the Invoice Information page, in the Copy from a Source Document group box, enter the voucher ID of the voucher that you want to reverse in the Voucher ID field, and click the Copy to Voucher button to copy the entire voucher. These fields appear only for adjustment vouchers. *Note*: Source vouchers are regular vouchers and must have the same business unit, supplier SetID, and supplier ID as the adjustment voucher that you are creating.

3. (Optional) To copy individual voucher lines, enter a supplier on the Invoice Information header, and click the Copy From Worksheet link in the unlabeled group box above the Invoice Lines scroll area. This accesses the Voucher Worksheet page, where you can search for and copy voucher lines to your adjustment voucher. If you are adjusting a voucher that references a purchase order, you can update the prior quantity and amount matched against the purchase order by selecting the Reverse Qty/Amt field on the Voucher Worksheet page. You can also have the Budget Processor restore or liquidate the encumbrance budget by selecting Adjust Matched Values on the Voucher Worksheet page. Click Copy to Voucher to copy selected voucher lines to the adjustment voucher and return to the Invoice Information page.

*Note:* You can create an adjustment voucher by copying a regular voucher, regardless of the match status on the regular voucher. See Voucher Worksheet Page.

4. On the Invoice Information page, whether you use the Copy to Voucher button or the Voucher Worksheet page to copy voucher information to the adjustment voucher, the system populates the Related Voucher field on the invoice

line with the adjusted voucher's voucher ID to link the adjustment voucher lines to the voucher that you are adjusting.

*Note*: Copying source vouchers or voucher lines is optional. You can enter an adjustment voucher with no reference to another voucher. In that case, you do not have to enter a related voucher.

5. On the Invoice Information page, enter positive or negative adjustment lines as appropriate.
6. Access additional information for your adjustments on the remaining pages in the Voucher component. These pages are the same as those for regular voucher entry

## Creating Credit Memo Adjustment Vouchers

To manually create a credit memo adjustment for matching exceptions:
1. Place the original voucher on match hold by selecting Match Dispute in the Voucher Match Action field on the Match Exception Workbench Details page. No further match processing is done on this voucher until you change the match status.
2. Create an adjustment voucher for the credit memo invoice that you received from your supplier by copying the original voucher on the Voucher component.
3. Override the original voucher with a credit memo by selecting Credit Note in the Voucher Match Action field on the Match Exception Workbench Details page.
4. Run the Matching process. The Matching process applies the match status of Matched and the match type of Auto - Matched to the credit memo adjustment voucher if no other match exceptions exist. The Matching process applies the match status of Matched and the match type of Matched With Credit Note to the original voucher.

*Adjusting Matched Values*

If you select the Adjust Matched Values check box on the Voucher Worksheet page for any copied voucher lines when you create adjustment vouchers, here is what happens:

• Any adjustment line with the Adjust Matched Values check box selected forces the match status of the adjustment vouchers (MATCH_STATUS_VCHR) to be set to T for ready, even if the voucher total gross adjustment is negative.

• Adjustment lines have MATCH_LINE_OPT set to F for full match.

A full match adjustment voucher goes through matching, which performs purchase order adjustments for the credit lines and performs regular matching for the positive adjustment lines. If the check box is labelled Restore Encumbrance, then you are in a Commitment Control environment, and a related, unreconciled purchase order exists. If you select it, the system restores or liquidates the encumbrance amount in the budget ledger by the amount of the adjustment. The Budget Status field is changed to Not Checked.

If the check box is labelled *Adjust Mtch Value/Encumbrance*, then the voucher is subject to matching and Commitment Control, and selecting it causes both the matching status adjustment and the encumbrance restoration to occur.

*Reversing Quantities or Amounts for Purchase Order Information*

If you select the Reverse Qty/Amt (reverse quantity/amount) check box on the Voucher Worksheet for any vouchers when you create adjustment vouchers, here is what happens when the copied voucher is related to a purchase order:

1. The Matching process or Voucher Posting Application Engine process (AP_PSTVCHR) verifies that the credit adjustment of a voucher line does not exceed the purchase order schedule line total matched quantity (QTY_MATCHED and AMT_MATCHED in PS_PO_LN_SHIP_MTCH).

2. If the adjustments were to reduce the total purchase order matched quantities or amounts below zero, a system match exception occurs: the RTV/credit adjustments are greater than the purchase order matched quantity or amounts.

3. After the adjustments are validated against purchase order matched quantities or amounts, the following processing occurs:

    a. New rows are inserted into PS_PO_LINE_MATCHED with purchase order, receiver, and voucher line information, as well as credit adjustment values.

    b. PS_PO_LN_SHIP_MTCH is deleted for the same purchase order schedule line that was referenced on the credit voucher line.

    c. An insert is performed to PS_PO_LN_SHIP_MTCH by the addition of the matched quantity and amount for the same purchase order schedule line from PS_PO_LINE_MATCHED.

    d. Purchase order header match status (MATCH_STATUS_PO) for the same purchase order is updated to P for partial.

*Reversing Quantities or Amounts for Receipt Information*

If you select the Reverse Qty/Amt check box on the Voucher Worksheet for any vouchers when you create adjustment vouchers, here is what happens when the copied voucher is related to a receipt.

If any receiver information was found on the credit voucher lines, the system also adjusts receiver matched quantities or amounts:

1. The Matching process or the Voucher Posting process verifies the credit adjustment if a voucher line does not exceed the receiver ship line total matched quantity (QTY_MATCHED and AMT_MATCHED in PS_RECV_LN_SHP_MTH).

2. If the adjustments were to reduce the total receiver ship line matched quantities or amounts below zero, a system match exception occurs: RTV/credit adjustments are greater than the receiver ship line matched quantity or amounts.

3. After the adjustments are validated against receiver ship line matched quantities or amounts, the following processing occurs:

    a. New rows are inserted into PS_RECV_VCHR_MTCH with purchase order, receiver, and voucher lines information, as well as credit adjustment values. Note: If you undo matching for an adjustment voucher, the rows in PS_VCHR_RECV_MTCH are not deleted. The receipt information is still associated with the adjustment voucher.

    b. PS_RECV_LN_SHP_MTH is deleted for the same receiver ship line that was referenced on the credit voucher line.

    c. An insert is performed on PS_RECV_LN_SHP_MTH by the addition of the matched quantity and amount for the same receiver ship line from PS_RECV_VCHR_MTCH.

    d. Receiver header match status (MATCH_STATUS_RECV) for the same receiver is updated to P for partial.
[QE]

I will be honest with you and say that I do not understand the process described above: reversing quantities or amount for receipt information. I know from my experience that in a three-way matching environment, adjusting/crediting of the original voucher 'releases' the receipt. I use the term 'release'. The item's receipt remains in the warehouse (for rebill situations only, not RTV). The receipt is valid as far as the physical receiving of the item is concerned. The receipt is no longer associated with the adjusted original voucher. The receipt becomes 'released' for future matching. What's interesting is that the receipt disappears from the three-way matching Interface page where PO, invoice, and receipt all meet. Once you enter a rebill voucher for the same 'item in the warehouse' and the price is not matching the PO, you will get on your original attempt to match this rebill voucher a "No Receipt – Unapplied Receipt Exists" error.

PeopleSoft in its digital wisdom understands that there is a receipt in this particular "PO environment" – a hanging receipt that's been released from the adjusted voucher. To fix the problem there is no need to contact the receiver, end-user, loading dock, etc.; they had already received the item; they cannot do it again. You need to *point* the receipt to the new/rebill voucher. For that to happen you should open the Rebill Vouchers, find the Associate Receiver(s) on voucher information page (there is one for each voucher line), click on it and either search for the receipt of enter receipt number if know. Select it and save the change. The three-way match will now be passed.

Two-way matching situation does not present you with the 'released' receipt issue.

# Journal Vouchers

[QS]
Journal vouchers are used to adjust accounting entries for vouchers that have been posted and paid and for vouchers for which payments have also been posted.

For example, suppose a voucher has been entered using expense account 123000. The voucher has been posted and paid, and the payment has been posted, when you discover that the expense should have used account 456000. To avoid making a manual general ledger entry, which would cause PeopleSoft General Ledger and Payables to get out of sync, and to avoid un-posting the voucher, which involves correcting the voucher and then reposting it for payment, you simply enter a journal voucher. On the journal voucher, you reverse the amount to account 123000 and add the amount to account 456000, keeping PeopleSoft General Ledger and Payables in sync. Then you post the journal voucher without having to post a payment.

*Creating Journal Vouchers*

1. Select Journal Voucher as the voucher style on the add search page for the Voucher component and click Add.
2. Enter your new distribution lines. Journal vouchers are zero-amount vouchers; you cannot copy any source documents. Do not change any of the amounts on a journal voucher. You are using the journal voucher to back out accounting entries that were entered incorrectly.
3. (Optional) To link this voucher to the voucher that you are adjusting, enter a voucher ID in the Related Voucher field in the Invoice Information page header. Use the Related Voucher field to associate the journal voucher with the voucher for which accounting entries were entered incorrectly.
4. Access additional information for your journal vouchers on the remaining pages in the Voucher component.

## Reversal Vouchers

Reversal vouchers enable you to do several things. Primarily, reversal vouchers let you back out incorrect vouchers and start over. Suppose that you inadvertently enter the wrong amount on the voucher or reference the wrong purchase order. Rather than un-posting, undoing the match, and closing the voucher, you can simply enter a reversal voucher, and the system does the rest of the work for you. You can even enter a reversal voucher for a voucher that has already been paid.

*Important!* Normally, you should use the PO voucher close functionality instead of the reversal voucher functionality, because the PO voucher close functionality is more sophisticated and efficient. In general, use the Reversal Voucher feature only when your organization has existing reversal vouchers to manage.

Reversal vouchers also enable you to restore the encumbrance for actuals and budgets and reduce the purchase order's matched quantity or amount. If you are using the Commitment Control feature to check transactions against control budgets, you can use a reversal voucher to reinstate encumbrances, though using the PO voucher close functionality is more efficient.

If you use Matching and you opt to restore the encumbrance and reduce the purchase order's matched quantity or amount, the Matching process updates the purchase order and the receiver match status changes to Partial.

*Note:* The system provides a warning when you attempt to restore the encumbrance on a voucher that you have partially paid.

Reversal vouchers are similar to adjustment vouchers in all aspects except that:

• Reversal vouchers are designed to correct only a single voucher.

• When you create reversal vouchers by copying from a regular voucher, the freight, miscellaneous, sales tax/use tax, and VAT-related information from the regular voucher is copied to the reversal voucher.

• Reversal vouchers are always credit vouchers. All voucher lines and distribution lines of correction vouchers must have the reverse sign of the original voucher, and all voucher lines that reference a purchase order must be less than zero.

• The transaction currency of the reversal voucher must be equal to the source voucher.

*Note:* The system does not prevent users from reversing the voucher line, distribution line, or quantity and amount more than the original value, and no validation exists to check the reversal voucher gross amount. You can, however, enable security such that only authorized users can add and update reversal vouchers.

### Creating Reversal Vouchers

1. Select Reversal Voucher as the voucher style on the add search page for the Voucher component and click Add.

2. Enter the voucher ID of the voucher that you want to reverse in the Voucher To Be Reversed field. This field is located on the Invoice Information page in the Copy from a Source group box.

*Note:* Source vouchers must have the same business unit, supplier SetID, and supplier ID as the reversal voucher that you are creating. They must also be successfully budget checked and matched. You also can:

• Select the Reverse Remaining Vchr Balance (reverse remaining voucher) check box to reverse the remaining voucher balance. This field is used with partially paid vouchers. For example, suppose a voucher of 1000.00 EUR is to be paid in two instalments of 700.00 EUR and

300.00 EUR, and the first instalment has been paid. By selecting the Reverse Remaining Vchr Balance check box, you reverse the remaining 300.00 EUR. This is similar to closing the remaining balance; however, it also reverses the related encumbrance, un-matches the voucher, and so on. If you do not select the Reverse Remaining Vchr Balance check box, the system reverses the entire voucher.

     • If the voucher that you are reversing references a purchase order, and you are using Commitment Control, select the Adjust PO Amounts/Encumbrances check box to restore the encumbrance.

3. Click the Copy to Voucher button.

4. Save the reversal voucher. When you save the reversal voucher, the system automatically populates the Related Voucher field (in the Invoice Lines region) with the original voucher ID.

5. (Optional) Run the Budget Processor and Matching processes. If you have enabled Commitment Control or matching, you must run these processes after creating reversal vouchers.

## Single Payment Vouchers

When you must make a payment for a one-time supplier without having to create and store the supplier in the system—such as when you want to pay a rebate or refund—you can create a single payment supplier voucher. The system uses the settings that you establish for the single payment supplier to supply default information such as payment terms and taxes onto the voucher.

## Template Vouchers

If you receive multiple similar vouchers from a supplier, you can set up a template voucher to improve data entry efficiency. Use a voucher for a particular supplier as a model for other vouchers that you will enter in the future for that same supplier by creating a template voucher. You can also update this voucher as necessary. A template voucher is never paid or posted; it is used only as a model for other vouchers.

Once you have created and saved the template voucher, it is available for use during the entry of other vouchers for the specific supplier. When you create the new voucher, select Template in the Worksheet Copy Option field on the Invoice Information page. Click the Copy from template link to copy the appropriate invoice header, line, and distribution information from the source template voucher onto the voucher that you are adding.

*Creating Template Vouchers*

1. Select Template Voucher as the voucher style on the add search page for the Voucher component and click Add.
2. On the Invoice Information page, enter a Template ID and description. These fields appear only if you are creating a template ID.
3. (Optional) Click the Copy PO button or select the Worksheet Copy Option field below the Invoice Information page header to copy information from the appropriate voucher, purchase order, receiver, or other template.
4. Enter the remaining information for the template voucher that you are creating, using the Invoice Information and remaining Voucher component pages.
5. Save the voucher.

## Third-Party Vouchers

PeopleSoft Payables supports third-party vouchers, which are invoices that you receive that contain charges other than merchandise charges. No charges for merchandise are on these invoices. The merchandise is billed separately on another invoice.

Typically, these types of invoices occur for:
• Freight charges.
• Miscellaneous charges, such as insurance.
• VAT-only invoices.
• (IND) Customs duty (India only).

By using third-party vouchers for these types of invoices, you can link the charges on the invoices to a merchandise invoice and prorate them across the voucher lines of the merchandise invoice. Linking these freight and miscellaneous charges to the merchandise invoice enables the system to compute the landed cost for the merchandise.

*Creating Third-Party Vouchers*

1. Select Third Party Voucher as the voucher style on the add search page for the Voucher component and click Add.
2. Either on the add page or the Invoice Information page, enter the supplier that is to be paid. This supplier cannot be the same as the supplier for the source document that you copy in the next step.
3. Click the Copy PO button or use the Worksheet Copy Option field below the Invoice Information page header to copy information from the appropriate voucher, purchase order, or receiver. Note: To get vouchered amounts for third-party charges into PeopleSoft Inventory, you must copy these charges from a receiver. Otherwise, the charges will not be picked up by the Landed Cost Extract Application Engine process (LC_EXTRACT).

4. Enter additional voucher lines for the purpose of prorating the third-party charge to the distribution lines.

5. Complete the voucher using the remaining pages in the Voucher component.

[QE]

I want to mention something that just crossed my mind. Many times, there are other processes that interfere with your voucher entry of correction activities in PeopleSoft; payment batch processing, matching, etc. When such processes are run, you cannot change a voucher. I have noticed that a voucher that displayed another process running will remain with that process lock on it even after the process has ended – you need to close the browser and open another browser with the same menu to have the browser refreshed. Usually you have many browser windows open when working with PeopleSoft payables: I always have Voucher, PO, Interface, PO Activity Summary, Supplier and Query Viewer open on my computer.

Next we will quickly review a topic relevant to the voucher entry – deleting individual voucher.

## Delete Voucher

[QS]

Use the Delete Voucher page - Accounts Payable, Vouchers, Add/Update, Delete Voucher, Delete Voucher

*Note:* PeopleSoft Payables enables you to select only those vouchers that are eligible for deletion. The vouchers cannot have been posted or selected for payment, nor can any portion of the vouchers ever have been paid. PO vouchers with the Finalize checkbox selected cannot be deleted

Click to delete the voucher. The system prompts you to confirm your action. If document sequencing is enabled for the business unit, the system also prompts you to enter a deletion reason. If you choose to continue, the voucher is deleted from the database, and you receive another message verifying this. If you are using the Commitment Control feature, the Budget Processor process is automatically invoked after you confirm deletion.

Before saving the page, you can go to the Voucher Details page to view the details for the voucher.

Warning! Once you delete a voucher, you cannot retrieve it or undo the deletion. The data rows that are associated with the voucher remain in the tables so that you cannot reuse the voucher number.

*Note:* If you delete a voucher that was entered as a manual payment, the payment is not deleted; it remains in the system and can be applied to other vouchers. Vouchers associated with debit memo adjustment vouchers cannot be deleted unless all related vouchers are deleted first.

[QE]

Control Groups in PeopleSoft are similar to Batch Groups I remember using with JD Edwards mainframe system back in the days of old. Control or Batch group is a group of vouchers similar by style that are in the same batch. Instead of performing a particular action on an individual voucher, many times over, you can process the control group and all vouchers within it.

[QS]

Control groups are not a required component of the control hierarchy. They can, however, provide security options and determine workloads for data entry operators.

You can set up the system to process vouchers in groups to:
• Establish separate processing rules (different from those set up at the business unit and voucher origin levels).

• Specify when groups of vouchers should be posted or paid.

• Determine whether vouchers should be balanced or verified before they can be posted or paid.

• Divide vouchers among data entry clerks, including assigning a block of voucher numbers.

• Post several of these groups in one easy step. If you set up control groups, the system can:

• Check for control groups assigned for each user's ID.

• Select the earliest group in the queue for multiple groups. (You can override this feature if necessary by selecting the lookup button to the right of the Control Group field.)

• Track running totals.

• Automatically set the balanced group to Ready for Review status. The system displays a message offering to automatically update the status to Ready for Review when a group is in balance and the user saves the last voucher. Clicking *Yes* selects this option. Clicking No enables the user to manually update the status on the Control Group Update Status page.

• Select the next group in the queue each time that users finish a group.

• Provide auto-numbering. The system displays NEXT in the Group field until you save the page, and then the system increments by one the last ID number used to create the new control group ID.

*Note:* The system assigns control group IDs automatically if you select this option for the business unit. Alternatively, you can enter them manually. You set up control group auto-numbering on the Payables Definition - Numbering page. You can enter combinations of letters and numbers to provide additional identification for groups.

Supervisors can:

• Use the Run a Tape feature to ascertain the gross total and the number of invoices.

334

• Restrict PeopleSoft Payables users so that they can only enter vouchers in control groups.


## Quick Invoices

[QS]
Entry component (VCHR_QUICK_PNL) provides efficient data entry for large volumes of similar invoices and invoices for which you can use defaults to complete most of the voucher details. The Quick Invoice Entry component contains minimal online edits; default and edit processing are handled by the Voucher Build Application Engine process (AP_VCHRBLD). This makes the component easy to configure and upgrade and offers improved performance when saving data.

The Quick Invoice Entry component enables you to enter minimal invoice information, such as the business unit, supplier ID, invoice ID, invoice date, and merchandise amount. The Voucher Build process completes the other required fields for the voucher records using defaults from the PeopleSoft Payables control hierarchy. You can also use the Quick Invoice Entry component to copy purchase order and receiver information to create vouchers—either by copying purchase orders and receivers directly to the quick invoice at the time of entry, or by specifying key field information for the Voucher Build process to use in associating voucher lines with specific purchase order or receiver schedule lines. You can also set up session defaults that automatically populate voucher fields for an entire session, and you can override those defaults for a particular voucher.

The Quick Invoice Entry component comes with two templates: the complete worksheet and the simple worksheet.

The add and search page of both worksheets display the Freight Amount, Misc. Charge Amount (miscellaneous charge amount) and Sales Tax Amount fields. When you complete these fields, the system uses the values to automatically populate the worksheet's Balancing region.

Both worksheets display four invoice lines by default; the system automatically deletes any unused lines when you click Save. Use the Session Defaults page to modify the number of lines that display.

The complete worksheet enables you to enter more voucher line information than the simple worksheet. If you have a purchase order-related voucher and want to copy from a purchase order or receiver, select the complete worksheet. On the complete worksheet, you can enter multiple invoice and distribution lines. In addition, you can copy purchase orders (POs) and receivers to the voucher lines or specify PO and receiver default information for the Voucher Build process to use in locating POs and receivers for completing the voucher. The complete worksheet also enables you to limit the number of voucher lines and distribution lines called up when you open a quick invoice voucher in update mode.

The simple worksheet is the default worksheet. It provides minimal voucher header and voucher line entry, leaving it up to the Voucher Build process to use the session defaults and the PeopleSoft Payables control hierarchy to fill in the rest. The combined voucher line and distribution line facilitate data entry for supplier invoices that have a limited number of ChartField distributions requiring entry. You should use the simple worksheet for vouchers with no associated purchase order.

The simple worksheet also has these restrictions:
• A single distribution line per voucher line.
• No copying of purchase orders or receivers.

Both simple and complete worksheets enable you to:
• Enter and apply prepayment vouchers.
• Use on-demand processing functionality, running on-demand processes such as Voucher Build, Matching, Document Tolerance, Budget Checking, Voucher Post, and Journal Generate.
• Perform on-demand combination-edit and balancing functions above and below the invoice line level.

You can configure either worksheet to your organization's particular needs. You also use the Quick Invoice Entry component in the update/display mode for reviewing vouchers staged by the Voucher Build process to PeopleSoft Payables from external sources, as well as for correcting Voucher Build process pre-edit errors.

*Note:* If financial sanctions validation is enabled at the installation level, and the supplier has a financial sanctions status of Review or Blocked, the system displays a warning message that the supplier is under financial sanctions review.

You can save the voucher, however, the system does not allow payments to suppliers with a financial sanctions status of Review or Blocked. If you enable financial sanctions at the installation level, the system validates the supplier against financial sanctions lists (for example, the Specially Designated Nationals (SDN) list) when you attempt to save the quick invoice. The system does not perform validation during quick invoice entry if you enable financial sanctions at the bank level.

## Summary Invoice Processing

The Summary Invoice Entry component (VCHR_SUMM_PNL) enables you to enter minimal invoice and purchase order information, such as supplier, PO number, invoice number, invoice date, non-merchandise amounts, and gross amount, to create a voucher. You do not enter voucher line or distribution line information. The Voucher Build process builds the voucher from the selected purchase order and associated receipts.

Establish tolerance levels to validate the source document's merchandise amount against the invoice's merchandise amount. If the differences fall within the tolerance levels, the system applies the difference to a tolerance miscellaneous charge code specified on the Payables Definition - Summary Invoice page. This reconciliation allows the summary invoice to be balanced and the Voucher Build process to create a voucher. If the difference falls outside the tolerance levels, the system assigns the summary invoice a voucher build status of Tolerance. The Voucher Build process does not select invoices with a voucher build status of Tolerance. Use the Quick Voucher Entry component to resolve these differences.

To create a voucher using the Summary Invoice Entry component:
1. Enter invoice and purchase order information in the *Add and search* page or the Summary Invoice Entry page.
2. Copy receiver or purchase order information to the summary invoice. The system first searches for receiver information to copy. If it cannot locate this information, it then searches for and copies purchase order information.
3. Compare input invoice information with the purchase order and receiver information.

4. Save the voucher. Once you save the summary invoice, access the summary invoice using the Quick Invoice Entry component for further updating before the Voucher Build process creates the voucher.

5. Run the Voucher Build process. The Voucher Build process uses the same logic for copying a single purchase order and receiver information to the voucher as it does for creating vouchers from the Quick Invoice Entry component.

*Note:* The system does not copy sales tax, use tax, and value-added tax (VAT) amounts from the purchase order. You must enter these amounts. Also, if you enter freight and miscellaneous amounts, these amounts override any amounts that were entered on the purchase order.

Note that one PO line may require a receipt, another line of the same PO may not require receiving.

A situation that confirms that the receiver only considers the quantity is the following: when you get more items shipped than ordered (at the right price), you have three exception errors. Two relate to invoice to PO quantity and total price discrepancy, but only one quantity error is related to the receiver's discrepancy.

[QE]

## Spreadsheet Invoices

The spreadsheet voucher is a popular 'volume' processing of suppliers invoices in the absence of the EDI connection. Sending paper invoices is a cumbersome and expensive process. With an ERP system in place, there is no need to carry a piece of paper 'round the office collecting approval signatures on it and getting it entered in the system by an AP clerk, provided that the invoice does get lost along the way.

When there is an ongoing relationship with the supplier, you can agree that the supplier will enter all the billing information, most likely directly from the supplier's receivable system, into a preformatted spreadsheet. The spreadsheet is called **ExcelUploadforVoucher.xls** and has two worksheets: Template and Data Sheet. The Template has all the fields that you can configure for data entry. The Data Sheet is used to enter actual voucher data. The excel file can be found in the core\build\excel folder of the PeopleSoft software package.

The spreadsheet is the bridge between the supplier's receivables and your payables (EDI is a similar, but a more advanced 'bridge'). The supplier 'maps' its receivable module to properly upload invoice information into your spreadsheet. Your PeopleSoft system is already pre-mapped to receive the spreadsheet information. The process is rather interesting: your PeopleSoft file that the supplier completes with information is sent to you, the information is changed to an XML format and placed at a designated URL (use Generate XML and Post button). The PeopleSoft's process called *Integration Broker* (I called it *Interrogation Broker*) reads the URL with excel file information converted to XML format and (in the absence of any errors) begins vouchers building process.

XML upload converted off a spreadsheet is usually a one-way communication process, while EDI is a direct two-way communication. The spreadsheet voucher processing does not have the EDI implementation costs involved, it is more appropriate for smaller regular suppliers. And what about the absence of actual vendor invoices, with the logo, paper type, remittance portion? Who needs that paper?!

*Spreadsheet Voucher Processing*

[QS]

The Spreadsheet Voucher workbook lets you enter vouchers offline using Microsoft Excel and then import the vouchers into your PeopleSoft database. It supports regular voucher additions. Once you import the spreadsheet vouchers, the Voucher Build Application Engine process (AP_VCHRBLD) builds and edits the vouchers.

Note: The spreadsheet voucher process supports Microsoft Excel formats as input. If you use a non-Excel spreadsheet, you must convert the data file to a Microsoft Excel format before importing. Users uploading vouchers with Microsoft Excel 2007 must use the file with the .xlsm file type.

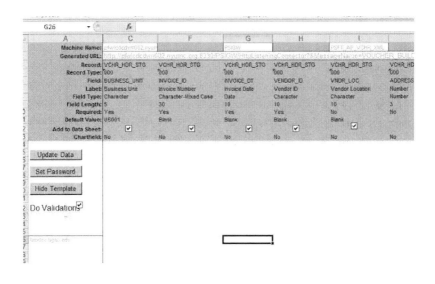

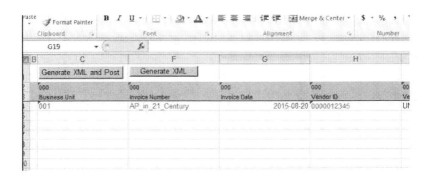

```xml
<MsgData>
- <Transaction>
  - <VCHR_HDR_STG class="R">
      <BUSINESS_UNIT>001</BUSINESS_UNIT>
      <VOUCHER_ID>NEXT</VOUCHER_ID>
      <VOUCHER_STYLE>REG</VOUCHER_STYLE>
      <INVOICE_ID>AP_in_21_Century</INVOICE_ID>
      <INVOICE_DT>2015-08-20</INVOICE_DT>
      <VENDOR_ID>0000012345</VENDOR_ID>
      <VNDR_LOC>UNITED HOI</VNDR_LOC>
      <ADDRESS_SEQ_NUM>2</ADDRESS_SEQ_NUM>
      <ORIGIN>ABC</ORIGIN>
      <OPRID>COSTAL</OPRID>
      <GROSS_AMT>100000</GROSS_AMT>
      <DSCNT_AMT>0</DSCNT_AMT>
      <SALETX_AMT>0</SALETX_AMT>
      <FREIGHT_AMT>0</FREIGHT_AMT>
      <MISC_AMT>0</MISC_AMT>
      <RATE_MULT>0</RATE_MULT>
      <RATE_DIV>0</RATE_DIV>
      <VAT_ENTRD_AMT>0</VAT_ENTRD_AMT>
      <DESCR254_MIXED>process as ACH</DESCR254_MIXED>
      <PO_ID>A000012345</PO_ID>
      <REMIT_ADDR_SEQ_NUM>0</REMIT_ADDR_SEQ_NUM>
      <ITEM_LINE>0</ITEM_LINE>
      <VCHR_SRC>XML</VCHR_SRC>
      <USER_VCHR_DEC>0</USER_VCHR_DEC>
      <USER_VCHR_NUM1>0</USER_VCHR_NUM1>
    - <VCHR_PYMT_STG class="R">
        <PYMNT_CNT>0</PYMNT_CNT>
        <PYMNT_MESSAGE>HOIST</PYMNT_MESSAGE>
        <PYMNT_GROSS_AMT>0</PYMNT_GROSS_AMT>
```

*Spreadsheet Voucher Flow:*

1. Enter the data into the spreadsheet voucher using a format that includes the minimum data requirements for a PeopleSoft Payables voucher.

2. Generate the XML and post the file from the spreadsheet voucher options. A Visual Basic (VB) macro built in the spreadsheet converts the spreadsheet data into an XML format that is readable by the Integration Broker. Also, a VB macro posts the file to a URL available to PeopleSoft systems.

3. Enter a valid user ID and password. Users are prompted to enter a valid user ID and password before the macro posts the file to the PeopleSoft system.

After you generate the XML and post your file, PeopleSoft systems:

1. Retrieves the data from the XML file and validates the data. If there are errors in the data the VOUCHER_BUILD message flags the data as being in error. You must correct the data using the application messaging error correction feature before the data can be processed successfully.

2. Copies the data into the voucher staging tables if there are no data errors.

3. Selects the vouchers based on the Voucher Build process run control parameters and builds and edits them.

4. Updates the voucher transaction tables.

5. Deletes the record from the voucher staging tables.

All data fields in the regular voucher entry process are included in the spreadsheet voucher. You can configure the voucher spreadsheet for the appropriate data entry required. However, certain fields must contain data to properly convert the data into an XML file.

Spreadsheet voucher edits exist in the spreadsheet, the VOUCHER_BUILD application message, and the Voucher

Build process. Valid data must exist in each stage of the process before further processing is performed.

*Spreadsheet Voucher Edits.* The spreadsheet voucher does not perform major editing. In addition to basic Microsoft Excel spreadsheet validation edits, the spreadsheet voucher edits include:
• Control Group ID always defaults to NEXT.
• Voucher Style always defaults to REG (regular).
• Voucher Source always defaults to XML.
• Voucher ID always defaults to NEXT.
• Required fields contain data. See Spreadsheet Voucher Data Fields.
• Voucher comments are 254 characters or less. (optional)
• All date fields are either empty or contain a valid date. (optional)
• Chartfields do not have a trailing space. For example, "DEPT ". (optional)

If one of these validations fails, the generate XML will stop immediately, and the error message will indicate you where and why the validation failed. The optional validations can be turned on or off on the Template page.
[QE]


## Evaluated Receipt Settlement (ERS)

Before we begin a discussion about Self-Billed Invoices, we need to learn what Evaluated Receipt Settlement (ERS) is. ERS is a process that builds vouchers based on the warehouse receipts. The ERS receipts must be priced and have extended merchandise amount, as opposed to the regular receipts that don't. To create ERS vouchers, you must identify the supplier location as an ERS supplier and set up the PeopleSoft payables business unit to allow ERS transactions. The voucher build process creates ERS vouchers from receipts that reference a PO, as well as non-PO receipts. For non-PO receipts, the process creates ERS voucher only for receipt lines that have price per unit, or priced receipts. The price per unit can be populated online from the item master or supplied by an external receipt load interface module.

*Understanding SBI Processing*

[QS]
PeopleSoft Payables supports SBIs. SBIs are invoices that are created from Evaluated Receipt Settlement (ERS) data that are sent to the supplier to provide tax details. Self-billed invoices contain all of the information that the supplier would have provided on an actual invoice. In business environments that use ERS and value-added tax (VAT), for example, there is typically a requirement to provide an invoice containing all the VAT details that can be returned to the supplier. Customers can send the supplier an SBI with all of the VAT details.

You can also combine data from multiple vouchers on one invoice to meet the requirements of businesses that process large volumes of receipts using ERS.

To create SBIs:
1. Create a receiver on the Receiving page.
2. Run the Voucher Build Application Engine process (AP_VCHRBLD) with the Evaluated Receipts (ERS) option selected as the voucher build interface on the Voucher Build page.
3. Review the voucher on the Voucher Summary page.
4. (Optional) Change SBI options on the Voucher Attributes page.
5. Run the Matching Application Engine process (AP_MATCH) from the Match Request page.

6. Run the Voucher Posting Application Engine process (AP_PSTVCHR) from the Voucher Posting Request page. (The voucher must be posted before running the SBI Application Engine process (APSBIPRC).
7. Run the SBI process in selection mode.
8. Review the SBI vouchers.
9. Run the SBI process in either commit mode or rollback mode.
10. Print the SBIs.

*Note:* When you build the ERS voucher using the Voucher Build process, the system populates the invoice number field with the packing slip number from the receiver.

*ERS Vouchers for SBI Suppliers.* When PeopleSoft Payables generates ERS vouchers for SBI suppliers using the Voucher Build process, the following actions occur:

1. The SBI flag on the appropriate voucher records is set to Y. The SBI process processes all posted and matched vouchers that are identified as SBI.
2. The SBI number is set to zero or blank.
3. The system determines the SBI numbering option based on the PeopleSoft Payables hierarchy. First, the system takes the option that is defined for the invoicing supplier using the location on the voucher. If the supplier is set to Default From Higher Level, the system gets the option from the PeopleSoft Payables business unit on the voucher. If the PeopleSoft Payables business unit is set to Default From Higher Level, it then gets the setting from the PeopleSoft General Ledger business unit.
4. The SBI in process flag is set to N and the SBI process ID is set to zero.

*SBI Voucher Status Summary.* Use the Voucher Summary page to review a voucher's SBI status before and after you run vouchers through the SBI process. Before processing the voucher through SBI, use the Voucher Attributes page to override the SBI Num. Option (SBI number option) field at the voucher level. After running the SBI process, use this page to review the SBI numbers for your vouchers. The SBI number is populated and appears only after the SBI process is complete.

If a voucher does not qualify for SBI, then the SBI Num. Option and SBI Number fields are unavailable for entry.

The Voucher Posting process creates accounting entries from vouchers. The system uses the accounting entry template and inheritance rules that you set up on the Accounting Entry Template and ChartField Inheritance pages to identify the offset accounts needed to create accounting entries. The entries include the expense distributions entered into the system, as well as additional entries for the payables offset, value-added tax (VAT) expense, non-prorated, non-merchandise expenses, and closure expenses. These accounting entries are then available for generating general ledger journals, using the Journal Generator Application Engine process (FS_JGEN). Vouchers must be entered, approved, and posted before you can send voucher information to the general ledger.

The Payment Posting process creates accounting entries from payment-related transactions, such as system-created payments, manual payments, drafts, electronic file transfer (EFT) payments, ACH payments, and cancelled payments. The Payment Posting process also creates realized gain or loss offsets when a transaction is entered in a different currency than the base currency and the rates have fluctuated between the invoice and payment dates. These accounting entries are then available to the Journal Generator process to pass to your general ledger.

There is a difference between running the Voucher Posting and Payment Posting processes and running the

348

Journal Generator process. Before you can transfer a voucher or payment to the general ledger, it must be associated with accounts. The posting processes create all accounting lines. Voucher accounting lines are created based on the distribution lines from voucher entry. However, proration of non-merchandise charges results in accounting lines that are different from what was actually entered in the distribution lines.

Here are examples of accounting lines that are created during the posting processes:
• Payables liability account.
• Discount earned.
• Discount lost.
• Late charge.
• Realized gains and losses.
• Use tax liability.
• VAT accounting entries.

The posting processes also assign interunit document sequencing numbers. To improve system processing time, each posting program calls the InterUnit Processor to function only when the following scenarios exist:

Voucher Posting process:
• The general ledger unit is different between the voucher distribution level and the voucher header level.
• The balancing ChartField value is different between the expense (DST) and liability (APA) line under the summary control posting option method. (This does not apply to the detail-offset posting option; in that method, balance ChartFields are always inherited.)

Payment Posting process:
• The general ledger business unit is different between the liability (APA) and the cash (CAS/CAC) lines.

• The balancing ChartField value is different between the AP liability (APA) and cash (CAS/CAC) lines.

*Note:* An exception to this process is when you post using the detail offset posting method. In this method, balance ChartFields are always inherited.

If you have selected multi-book accounting in the subsystem, the posting processes also post to the secondary ledgers in the default ledger group. If you set up multi-book accounting using non-translate ledgers, then the accounting entries are calculated from the transaction currency. If you are using translate ledgers for your multi-book accounting, then the accounting entries are calculated from the base currency of the primary ledger.

After you run the posting processes, vouchers and payments remain in the PeopleSoft Payables subsystem. Run the Journal Generator process to distribute the accounting lines to the general ledger.

[QE]

## EDI invoices

I have mixed feelings about the EDI invoices. Of course, it *is* the AP process of the 21st century. It makes so many former useful things non-existent: Pitney Bowes mail and postage machines, fax machines, scanners, the list goes on. Basically, your system is connected to your suppliers' systems. You are connected via data exchange platforms, which were already described in this book. The EDI platform that connects my PeopleSoft system to my suppliers' various systems is called GHX, Global Healthcare Exchange. The GHX does a number of data translations and conversions that allow my company to be in the same cyber-environment with the suppliers.

Many times I come across an invoice dated with the same date the PO was dispatched via GHX to a supplier. Goods get shipped almost immediately as well. It's this fast. No lost communication, ever. Unless there is disruption in the work of VAN (value-added network) used for EDI connections, or less frequently, internet.

When everything is honkey-dory, thousands of EDI invoices are processed without you noticing. But when an error kicks in, the damage may by extensive and a solution not easy.

I had a problem with suppliers making errors in PO numbers; not sure how, since the PO number were dispatched to the suppliers and remained a system item all along. The 'misspelled' PO would produce an invoice with another supplier items and the processing supplier invoice header. The PO validator took care of it.

EDI invoices are system-generated invoices and their images add no value to your understanding of a problematic situation, since all the data that appears on an EDI invoice comes from the system and carries no additional evidence of validity or other not-system details. "Did you check the invoice itself?" – "Neh. It's an EDI invoice."

Another area of my concern about the EDI system's performance is processing of purchase orders. PO dispatched by Supply Chain Management clerk to supplier two or three times results in two or three shipments and invoicing. The requestor had only request one set of goods. The warehouse receives two or three shipments. The requestor may claim from the warehouse what's needed, while the rest languishes unclaimed. The extra invoice does not pass matching, being PO extra items. To mend the situation, the buyer requests another purchase requisition from the end-user (requestor), and the requestor is not always willing to provide a new PReq – the extra goods may not be needed, there may be no funds to pay for extra shipments. Double dispatching is a very dicey situation; I spent quite some time working with the SCM tackling it.

With all the issues pertaining to the EDI process, it's still by far the most advanced and efficient method to process AP vouchers.

[QS]

To process EDI transactions:

1. Translate the EDI file. The translator converts the EDI transactions into a PeopleSoft business document format. A PeopleSoft business document is a layout that describes the fields—including name, type, length, format, short name, and long name—that make up the EDI file.

To translate a data file into a PeopleSoft business document, use a translation tool that prepares, parses, and maps the flat file into the PeopleSoft business document format. You can develop this tool yourself, or you can use third-party tools that are readily available.

2. Use EDI Manager to load the business document. EDI Manager uses a supplied EDI agent Structured Query Report (SQR) to import the electronic data flat file, translate the data using the PeopleSoft business document layout, and stage the data in the Voucher Staging tables in the PeopleSoft database. Use the Schedule Inbound EC Agent - Run Control Parameters page in EDI Manager to load the flat file with the invoice data into the staging tables.

3. Confirm that the data loaded into the staging tables successfully. Use the Business Document Summary page in EDI Manager to confirm that the status is Loaded.

4. Run the Voucher Build process to create voucher records and load them in the Voucher tables. Use the outbound AP_VCHR_MESSAGE_OUT EIP that was initiated in the Voucher Build process to send verification messages to the sender.

*Note*: In addition to delivering the outbound AP_VCHR_MESSAGE_OUT EIP as an application message, PeopleSoft also delivers it as a web service (VoucherOut). Enabling web services is discussed in the PeopleTools: Integration Broker.

Invoices that are entered into the system through EDI Manager might contain a blank space or the word Next in the Voucher ID field. The system automatically assigns voucher IDs for these vouchers during the Voucher Build process regardless of whether the PeopleSoft Payables business unit is set up for auto-numbering.

The Voucher Build process assigns match delay days to EDI transactions that require matching based on the PeopleSoft Payables hierarchy, business unit, origin, control group, supplier, and the ability to override on the voucher. If you do not define match delay days on the PeopleSoft Payables hierarchy, the Voucher Build process will not assign match delay days. As an example, if the match delay days are five days, the system adds five days to the entry date to determine the match due date. On the Match Request page, enter a date in the As of Date field to work in conjunction with the match due date. The Matching process selects only the vouchers that are ready to be matched as of that date. Match delay days are applicable only to EDI transactions and XML transactions. These types of transactions usually are processed in the system before the lines are received. Using match delay days enables you to wait to include these transactions in the Matching process.

When EDI transactions have been processed, they are deleted from the voucher staging tables. The Voucher Build process places any vouchers that receive pre-edit validation errors in the quick invoice entry tables for review and correction using the Quick Invoice Entry component.

*Voucher Build Minimum Data Requirements for EDI*

The following lists show the minimum sets of fields that the Voucher Build process requires when you supply the voucher header, voucher line, and distribution line information:

* Voucher header:
• ROW_ID
• BUSINESS_UNIT
• INVOICE_ID
• INVOICE_DT
• VENDOR_ID
• OPRID
• GROSS_AMT

* Voucher line:
• ROW_ID • BUSINESS_UNIT • MERCHANDISE_AMT • VOUCHER_LINE_NUM

* Distribution line:
• ROW_ID
• BUSINESS_UNIT
•LINE_NUM
•DISTRIB_LINE_NUM
• ACCOUNT
• MERCHANDISE_AMT

The particular fields that are required for any given run of the Voucher Build process can vary depending on the following circumstances:

• When you are trying to associate invoice lines to a purchase order, the supplier ID is optional and the distribution line should be absent.
The rest of the required fields vary depending on the Voucher Build code.

• When you are trying to associate invoice lines to a receiver, the distribution line should be absent and the rest of the required fields vary depending on the Voucher Build code.

You can build distribution lines from voucher line information without associating purchase order or receiver lines by specifying the general ledger business unit and account, at a minimum, along with any additional ChartField information, on the voucher line.
[QE]

## "Undo Matching" process

I want to dedicate a special paragraph to a much lesser known and used process of voucher un-matching. While matching is done on thousands of vouchers daily in my office, the process of un-matching was virtually unknown to people in my office until I raised the issue. There are instances when a voucher was matched to a closed receiver line, an adjustment voucher referred to incorrect original voucher (and matched), a voucher was processed incorrectly, but still match-able and matched. In all such cases, prior to my 'discovery' of the process, the problem was resolved by over-riding vouchers. Over-riding transaction is the last resort and can only be used in exceptional cases; if a problem can be solved by un-matching a voucher, a problem can no longer be qualified as 'exceptional'.

This is how you do it: un-post the matched voucher first, if it was already posted. Follow this path to the Match Workbench screen: Main Menu – Accounts Payable – Review Accounts Payable Info – Vouchers – Match Workbench. There select Business Unit, set Match Status equal to Matched, set Voucher ID equal to xxxxxx. Click on Search. The voucher to be unmatched appears on screen. Select Undo Match box, in the Action select Undo Matching and Run. The voucher is now unmatched; the link with the

PO and the receiver is now undone, and you can adjust the voucher again.

## All you need is Love and PeopleBooks

PeopleSoft and the extensions in form of EDI platforms, interactive vendor portals, eProcurement links to various supplier websites and catalogues is a huge universe. You can spend your life exploring it. It's a great software and I advise you to learn it the right way. Here's how: study PeopleSoft FSCM []: Payable (PeopleBooks) and make it your foundation of PeopleSoft knowledge. Not your company's procedure's about PeopleSoft use, or various forums. PeopleBooks is the book that you use with PeopleSoft. I have updated a number of established payables processes in well established companies; processes that didn't work because they didn't follow the PeopleBooks instructions precisely.

Here's the link to the PeopleBooks. You can also easily find it, google it, using *PeopleBooks payables* as the key words.
http://docs.oracle.com/cd/E40049_01/psft/acrobat/fscm92fapy-b0313.pdf

I've seen both *PeopleBooks* and *PeopleBook* in use, but the correct Oracle name for it is *PeopleBooks*.

# General Principles of the AP-Related Processes

## General Principles of Accounting

It has been my observation that many Accounts Payable discussions and publications concentrate solely on the Accounts Payable operations and rarely position the Accounts Payable department within a larger financial environment or business. The Accounts Payable process is often discussed as an operation on its own with no clear inter-relation with other financial activities. I believe that any Accounts Payable professional must have understanding of the general accounting principles and operations; how these principals and operations work and affect the financial activities of the business.

We must see the *forest behind the trees*, and this is why I decided to not only include a chapter on general principles of the AP-related processes in this book, but place it in the main body of the narrative, instead of the appendix, as originally planned. We, the Accounts Payable professionals, must know more of the accounting than just "use debits for normal invoices and credits for credit memos". In the 21$^{st}$ century the AP profession requires less technical and more analytical, judgmental and holistic approach skills to the Accounts Payable operations.

I will present a simple example of financial operations of a hypothetical business, explaining various accounting concepts along the way, which is the best method to learn and comprehend any new material.

*Once upon a time, on December 31$^{st}$, a corporation called RHYOLITE TOWNSHIP INC. was registered with the*

357

State of Nevada and sold 1000 shares of common stock to the public. The purpose of the corporation was publishing of business books and periodicals. The shares were offered for $700 apiece, but the expectations of the business were running high and the shares actually sold for $1000 apiece. The following journal entry is made:

**Cash (Balance sheet)**            **$1,000,000**
**Common Stock (Balance sheet)**            **$700,000**
**Additional Paid in Capital (Balance sheet)**      **300,000**

On the same day, December 31$^{st}$, RHYOLITE TOWNSHIP INC. borrowed $1,000,000 from the bank for 10 years, at 5% interest rate.
(I omit the present value calculations for simplicity purpose)

**Cash (Balance sheet)**            **$1,000,000**
**Bank's Loan (Balance sheet)**            **$1,000,000**

At the end of the year (suppose, RHYOLITE TOWNSHIP INC.'s calendar year is also its fiscal year) the accounting department of RHYOLITE TOWNSHIP INC. prepares three major financial reports: Balance Sheet, Income Statement (also not very correctly called Profit & Loss statement (P&L)) and Statement of Cash Flows. Balance Sheet is a summary of the company's assets, liability and equity on a specific date. The balance sheet is made of permanent accounts; these permanent accounts are not "eliminated" at the end of fiscal period (as is the case with the Income Statement accounts). The following is the balance sheet structure:

## *Assets = Liabilities + Equities*

| |
|---|
| **-*Assets* (Assets have normal Debit / left side balance)** |

**Equal:**

| |
|---|
| **-*Liabilities* (Liabilities have normal Credit / right side balance)**<br>**&**<br>**-*Equities* (Equities have normal Credit / right side balance)** |

An often used banking phrase "we credited your account" (added funds to it) is actually the opposite, from accounting standpoint, of what has happened to the cash account – when (accounting) cash balance is increased, the cash is *debited (cash is a balance sheet asset account with a normal debit balance; balancing credit is a liability if you borrowed the cash, or an equity if you invested your money, or a combination of the two).* **All assets accounts have normal debit balances.** The assets' (net) debits equal liabilities and equities' (net) credits.

On the *Income Statement* all revenue accounts have normal credit balances, and expense accounts have normal debit balances. Think about it in grossly simplified terms; when revenues exceed expenses (increase in credit balances) – they are balanced with more cash (or accounts receivable) on the debit side and otherwise.

*RHYOLITE TOWNSHIP INC.'s Balance Sheet <u>as of</u> December 31ˢᵗ, 20x1:*

### RHYOLITE TOWNSHIP INC.
#### Balance Sheet
*As of December 31ˢᵗ, 20x1*

| | | |
|---|---|---|
| *Assets: Cash* | $2,000,000 | |
| *Total Assets:* | <u>$2,000,000</u> | |
| *Liabilities: Bank's Loan* | | $1,000,000 |
| *Equities:* | *Common stock issued* | 700,000 |
| | *Additional Paid-In-Capital* | 300,000 |
| *Total Liabilities and Equities:* | | <u>$2,000,000</u> |

The purpose of the *Income Statement* is to measure a company's performance (to calculate net income or loss) over a specific period of time. The income statement has *temporary accounts*. In other words, Income Statement, instead of a single statement date, has "for the period ending" words - it calculates income (or loss) for a period of time. RHYOLITE TOWNSHIP INC., as a new company, has no income or loss "for the period ending December 31ˢᵗ, 20x1. Income Statement calculates *revenues* (credit side, balanced with AR or cash) and *expenses* (debit side, balanced with AP or cash), *gains* (credit side) and *losses* (debit side); revenues and gains when exceeding expenses and losses result in debit to Accounts Receivable or Cash, or Income (ITIDA, income before taxes, interest, depreciation and amortization).

The *Statement of Cash Flows* shows how a company manages cash. Since all private companies use accrual accounting (i.e. recognize revenues and expenses when they occur and not when they are paid for), it is very important to monitor the cash flows and assure that it approximates your company's net income or net loss financial results. Let's say that RHYOLITE TOWNSHIP INC.'s only service contract in a financial period will be paid under the contractual terms in the next financial period. While RHYOLITE TOWNSHIP INC. may have earned a hefty profit "on the books", has recorded revenue and accounts receivable, there are no cash receipts; with a solid net income RHYOLITE TOWNSHIP INC. may have a shortage of cash to pay for salaries, rents, supplies, debt financing, and utilities.

### RHYOLITE TOWNSHIP INC.
#### Statement of Cash Flows (indirect method)
*For year ended December 31st, 20x1*

| | |
|---|---|
| *Operating activities:* | |
| *Net Income (Loss)* | $ 0.00 |
| *Investing activities:* | $ 0.00 |
| *Financing activities:* | |
| *Issuance of common stock:* | $ 1,000,000.00 |
| *Loan proceeds:* | $ 1,000,000.00 |

| | |
|---|---|
| *Net increase (decrease) in cash:* | $2,000,000.00 |
| *Cash at beginning of year* | 0.00 |
| *Cash at end of year* | $2,000,000.00 |

*In the year 20x2 RHYOLITE TOWNSHIP INC. purchased land for $1,000,000 (paid cash, 100%) and a printing factory for $300,000 (paid 50% at time of purchase, with balance due on January 1 of next year, assume no interest).*

*RHYOLITE TOWNSHIP INC. **capitalizes** (treats as an item lasting and providing use to earn future revenues longer than the current fiscal period) both land and factory. Capitalization means future benefits to business, while expensing is paying for a current period's costs; this is a point, which I will reiterate several times more. Land does not depreciate (does not lose value), while a factory does depreciate (a factory does lose value based on usage and obsolescence). The useful life of the factory is 30 years. RHYOLITE TOWNSHIP INC. will depreciate (reduce the book value ($300,000)) of the factory using the straight line method over 30 years, which means that in accordance with the accrual accounting, RHYOLITE TOWNSHIP INC. will expense $10,000 of the factory's **carrying value** in each of the nest 30 years to match the reduction in value expense (depreciation expense) with revenues generated by the factory in those 30 years. We assume no residual value (after 30 years) for the factory. The yearly depreciation calculations are: 300,000-(Residual Value, 0) / 30 years =$10,000 per year.*

*A journal entry to record purchase of land and factory:*

**Land (Balance sheet)**      **$1,000,000**
**Factory (Balance sheet)**      **300,000**
**Depreciation / Factory**      **(0)**

**Cash (Balance sheet)**                         **$1,150,000**
**Accounts Payable (Balance sheet)**            **150,000**

There were two invoices submitted to the RHYOLITE TOWNSHIP INC.'s Accounts Payable department for payment, for land and factory. Land and Factory balance sheets accounts are marked to be debited in the payment documentation (the coding appears most likely in the PO documents).

RHYOLITE TOWNSHIP INC. buys printing supplies for $100,000/cash and prints its first set of books (all supplies are used up for books printing; assume no other but payroll-related expenses in order to manufacture books).

**Printing supplies (Balance sheet)    $100,000**
**Cash (Balance sheet)                           $100,000**

The Accounts Payable department is involved in processing various invoices that add up to $100,000 of printing supplies (paper, ink, binding materials and packaging materials).

The materials are converted to Inventory (books) assuming no other than labor input:

**Inventory (Balance sheet)      $100,000**
**Supplies (Balance sheet)                      $100,000**

RHYOLITE TOWNSHIP INC. sells all printed books to a local school district for $500,000 (payment terms- NET30). The following journal entries result based on AR billing:

*All books (the whole inventory) are sold:*

**Accounts receivable (Balance sheet)**    **$500,000**
**Cost of goods sold (Income statement)**   **100,000**
**Inventory (Balance sheet)**             **$100,000**
**Revenue (Income statement)**          **500,000**

*Payroll is paid next. Total payroll expense is $10,000 (more about payroll in the next chapter):*

**Wages expense (Income statement)  $10,000**
**Cash (Balance sheet)**                   **$10,000**
*(For simplicity, I omit accrual of the employer's portion of expenses)*
*The last business transaction for the fiscal period was the collection of $500,000 paid by the school district:*

**Cash (Balance sheet)**          **$500,000**
**Accounts receivable (Balance sheet)**     **$500,000**

*There were no other transactions in the year 20x2. Before RHYOLITE TOWNSHIP INC. prepares its financial statements, it needs to process the closing entries for year 20x2.*

*Closing entries reset all Income Statement temporary accounts to zero, record depreciation (also called Capital Consumption Allowance) and amortization, interest expenses, accrue payroll and other operating expenses not billed for by vendors. I will omit the closing of the revenue and expense accounts, which is a simple reversing of each Income Statement account into the Income Summary Account. I will show the year-end entries for the depreciation of the factory and portion of wages expenses, which are allocated to the current year 20x2, but not payable until the next year 20x3. Selected journal entries to record the December 31, 20x2 transactions are:*

**Factory depreciation expense (I/S) $10,000**
**Accumulated depreciation/factory (B/S)   $10,000**
*(Use a separate accumulated depreciation account, do not reduce Factory account directly; the net figure representing the carrying value of the factory is the net book value of factory. 300,000-10,000=290,000).*

**Accrued wages expenses (Income statement) $5,000**
**Wages payable (Balance sheet)                    $5,000**
*(For simplicity, I omit accrual of the employer's portion of expenses)*

*Interest expense on $1M (5%) is recorded and paid:*

**Interest expense (Income Statement)   $50,000**
**Cash (Balance Sheet)                          $50,000**

*On December 31st, 20x2 RHYOLITE TOWNSHIP INC. prepares the following financial statements:*

### RHYOLITE TOWNSHIP INC.
### <u>Income Statement</u>
*For the period ending December 31st, 20x2*

| | | |
|---|---|---|
| Revenue | | $500,000 |
| Cost of goods sold | (100,000) | |
| **Gross profit** | | **400,000** |

*Operating expenses:*

| | |
|---|---|
| *Wages expenses* | *(15,000)* |
| *Depreciation expenses* | *(10,000)* |
| *Total operating expenses* | *(25,000)* |
| *Non-operating expenses:* | |
| *Loan interest expense* | *(50,000)* |

**Net income before taxes**          **$325,000**

*RHYOLITE TOWNSHIP INC.'s accounting system or accountants will close all temporary Income Statement entries into **Income Summary** account, which in turn, will be closed to Retained Earnings (balance sheet) account. In other words, all Income Statement accounts will be zeroed out to net a "condensed" income statement's credit (net income) or debit (net loss); Net Income is in turn zeroed out (via Income Summary) to the Retained Earnings (permanent, Balance Sheet) account.*

*Here's the journal entry to close net income or loss, combined in one account (Income Summary) to Retained Earnings:*

| | |
|---|---|
| **Income Summary (I/S)** | **325,000** |
| **Retained Earnings (B/S)** | **325,000** |

A fine point: to record revenue, a company uses both Balance Sheet and Income Statement accounts:

Cash or AR:     $500,000 (Balance Sheet)

Revenue:                    $500,000 (Income Stm)

But only the Revenue is a part of the Income Statement. The balancing of the revenue happens in credit to Income Summary (for net income situation), when all other Income Statement accounts are closed (reversed, zeroed out), debited.

Revenue $500,000 (simplified)
Income Summary          $500,000

     Income Summary is then reversed and balanced with increase/debit to Balance Sheet account Retained Earnings (net income situation).

## RHYOLITE TOWNSHIP INC.
### Balance Sheet
### As of December 31st, 20x2

*Assets:*

| | |
|---|---|
| *Cash* | *$1,040,000* |
| *Land* | *1,000,000* |
| *Factory* | *300,000* |
| *Accumulated depreciation-factory* | |
| | *(10,000)* |
| *Total Assets:* | *$ 2,330,000* |

*Liabilities:*

| | |
|---|---|
| *Bank's Loan* | *$1,000,000* |
| *Wages payable* | *5,000* |
| *Equities:* | |
| *Retained earnings* | *325,000* |
| *Common stock issued* | *700,000* |
| *Additional Paid-In-Capital* | *300,000* |

    *Total Liabilities and Equities:  $ 2,330,000*

## RHYOLITE TOWNSHIP INC.
### Statement of Cash Flows (Indirect method)
*For the period ending December 31st, 20x2*

*Operating activities:*

**Net Income (Loss)**          **$325,000**

*Adjustment to reconcile net income to net cash provided by operating activities:*

Increase in wages payable   5,000 (did not affect cash)

Depreciation expenses      10,000 (did not affect cash)

**Net cash provided by operating activities:      340,000**

*Investing activities:*

Purchase of Land       (1,000,000) (did not affect income)

Purchase of Factory      (300,000) (did not affect income)

**Net cash provided by investing activities:    (1,300,000)**

*Financing activities:*          0

### Net increase (decrease) in cash: ($960,000)

Cash at beginning of year        2,000,000

Cash at end of year:        $1,040,000

The net income is reconciled to the change in the cash balance (accrual basis of accounting is converted to cash basis) by adding back expenses that did not affect cash *(payables, depreciation) and subtracting capital assets that did not affect income statement, but reduced cash. Note that the cash balance on the Balance Sheet "ties" to the cash amount at the end of the year based on the Statement of Cash Flows calculations.*

This simple example shows the complexity of the business' accounting cycle and the Accounts Payable function within it.

## General Principles of Payroll

Payroll is another form of the disbursement process, but with its own set of complicated rules and regulations. It is a good idea for any Accounts Payable professional to be familiar with the general payroll principles because Accounts Payable and payroll operations become at times overlapping, when remitting payroll taxes, processing payroll treaty portions for nonresident aliens (reported on form 1042-S, not W2) or funding outside payroll. Payroll operations may also present growth opportunities for Accounts Payable professionals, especially if your company is using an outside payroll processing provider (like ADP payroll services) when the payroll's funding is an AP function.

Just as with the general principles of accounting, learning basic principles of payroll is a smart professional investment. I will present in this chapter only the very basics of the payroll processing.

A new employee is hired by your company. Within three days she or he must complete form *I-9* (Employment Eligibility Verification) and form *W-4* (Employee's Withholding Allowance Certificate). This hypothetical employee has worked 40 hours in a first week and the pay rate is $25 per hour. We compute gross payroll, deductions and net payroll. The gross payroll is $1000 (40x25). The Employee's paycheck deduction include FICA taxes (**OASDI** (6.2%) – Old age, Survivors, Disability Insurance) and **HI** (1.45%) – Health Insurance), Federal Income Tax (calculated using the percentage method or the wage bracket method based on marital status and number of allowances (number of allowances is provided on form **W-4** by employee)), State Income Tax, Municipal Tax (when applicable), a portion of State Unemployment Insurance (if applicable), a portion of Health Insurance premium and Union Dues ( if applicable).

In case that the person's status is *Married* and three allowances are claimed (each allowance at the time of writing is $75), federal income tax (**FIT**) for $1,000 of weekly gross payroll (using the percentage method, see withholding table in the appendix) is $ 75.10 (do the math yourself, too). You can find the withholding tables at this address:

http://www.irs.gov/pub/irs-pdf/n1036.pdf

In our example, the **FICA** tax is $62 & $14.50 (6.2 and 1.45%), **State Tax** (assume 3% tax rate) is $30, **Municipal Tax** (assume 4% tax rate) is $40, state unemployment insurance - **SUTA**, employee's portion (assume 0.1% rate) is $1, health insurance / employee's portion is (hypothetically) $50 and union dues $20. The journal entry to illustrate the paycheck withholding is the following:

| | | |
|---|---|---|
| **Wages Expenses** | **$1,000** | |
| FICA payable / EE | | 76.50 |
| FIT payable | | 75.10 |
| SIT payable | | 30.00 |
| MIT payable | | 40.00 |
| SUTA payable | | 1.00 |
| Group Insurance Premium | | 50.00 |
| Union Dues Payable | | 20.00 |
| **Wages payable** | | **707.40** |
| | | **(paycheck amount)** |

Payroll payments must be distributed from a specially designated payroll bank's account, which is funded (from general business checking account) by the needed amount of net payroll to issue payroll payments.

| | | |
|---|---|---|
| **Payroll Cash** | **$707.40** | |
| **Cash** | | **$707.40** |

FICA taxes are shown separately for OASDI EE (employee's 6.2% portion) and HI-EE (employee's 1.45% portion) and OASDI-ER (employer's 6.2% portion) and HI-ER (employer's 1.45% portion) portions. *EE* stands for employee's portion of tax, and *ER* for employer's portion of the FICA tax. FICA tax applies to both employee and employer equally: it is a deduction on the employee's paycheck and also the same amount expense (6.2% and 1.45%) for the employer.

Now I will present the employer's portion of taxes related to the $1,000 gross payment. Employer's FICA taxes are the same as the employee's FICA taxes (as stated before). There are also *Federal Unemployment Tax / FUTA* (0.8% on first $7,000 earned) and *State Unemployment Tax / SUTA* (employer's portion), which can be as high as 5.4% and is based on the unemployment claims history. Employers take credit against FUTA based on their SUTA's rate. Some employer's may "fund" the actual unemployment claims, rather than paying state unemployment taxes. Not-for-profit organizations are exempt from FUTA and "fund" the SUTA. Our example's SUTA rate is 3.5%. The employer also pays 50% of health insurance premium on employee's behalf ($50). The journal entry to illustrate the employer's tax is the following:

| Payroll Tax | $169.50 |
| --- | --- |
| FICA / ER | $76.50 |
| FUTA | 8.00 |
| SUTA / ER | 35.00 |
| Group Insurance Premium | 50.00 |

You can understand from the example why many workers want to be classified as *independent contractors* (when opportunities present themselves) and not *employees* and some employers' propensity to classify employees as independent contractors (in less than obvious employment vs. independent contractor cases or by businesses with poor tax compliance). For the independent contractor, taxes are not withheld from payments, but reported on 1099 instead and are subject to various "write offs" on the contractor's tax return. For the employer, there is no payroll tax burden, health and pensions expenses liability when using services of independent contractors. Therefore, **this is one of the areas closely watched by the IRS – paying *de facto* employees as independent contractors,** and not paying payroll related taxes.

Use the *Twenty Questions Test* explained earlier to properly determine the employment status. Remember that there is *tax compliance* and *tax complacence*; you must be tax compliant no matter how strong the pressure to look the other way may be at times. There is yet another, independent contractor (IC) vs. employee test shown below:

1. *IC hires, supervises and pays assistants*
2. *IC plans the work*
3. *IC decides on work hours*
4. *IC performs services for different businesses*

5. *IC is paid for work done, not for hours worked*
6. *IC advertised service to the public*
7. *May incur profit or loss from operations*
8. *Buys tools and equipment*
9. *May be dismissed under the terms of contract*

You must understand that many *de facto* employees desire to be treated as independent contractors, or worse yet, scholarship or fellowship recipients. You must be able to properly discern all payroll payments as such (and refer them to the payroll department) when they are presented for payment to your Accounts Payable department for processing. And, you must argue from the position of knowledge any time the issues arise. *Knowledge is power!*

Many times payroll taxes and deductions are remitted through the Accounts Payable – now you know what they are for. Form 941 (Employer Quarterly Federal Tax Return) is used to account for the federal taxes withheld and remitted (similar to form 1042). Form 940 is Employer's Annual Federal Unemployment (FUTA) Tax Return. Form W-2 (Wage and Tax Statement) is furnished to employees to summarize payments and withholdings for calendar year. Payroll state tax forms vary from state to state.

Again, your company may not even be doing all the tax calculations, but have the payroll function outsourced to a payroll processing company. Nevertheless, it is a very good idea to know the inner workings of the payroll processing and payroll taxes implications on the Accounts Payable operations. Outside payroll management may present growth opportunities for the ambitious Accounts Payable professionals.

Outside payroll processing companies have been gaining popularity in the past years, especially with small and mid-size businesses. One of the largest and best known of such payroll processing companies is ADP Inc. (http://www.adp.com/). Outsourcing payroll may be more cost-effective and provide better quality of payroll output and expedite the release time. All a company needs to do is to collect new (or updated) employment information, send it electronically to the payroll processor and fund each payroll period (send required funds to the payroll provider) based on the payroll and tax calculations prepared by the payroll processor. The payroll processor distributes the payroll payments (direct deposits and checks), sends back to the company payroll registers and financial reports and does all the tax reporting with the government and employees on your company's behalf.

## General Principles of Excel

I have no doubt that each one of us is using the excel application on a daily basis. What I want to do is to make sure that we are all familiar with a number of advanced excel tools, which will help you streamline the processing of financial data and Accounts Payable reporting, make working with often times very voluminous AP records more fun and entitle you to be called an *advanced excel user*. I will discuss **Macros**, **Pivot Tables** and **V-look up** (and **H-look up**) excel features – all are great tools to work through Accounts Payable data to get the desired output. I will use sample excel data and present the concepts along the way. *Disclaimer: I am making a reasonable assumption that you know all the basic excel operations. The operations presented in this chapter are more properly called "advanced principles", rather than "general principles".*

First, for our exercise, you need to get a set of data to populate a blank excel file. Open new excel application and then go to the following website: http://www.noaa.gov/ (I use this website, knowing that the data is presented in a format that does not change over time and will produce similar results for readers in different geographic zones at different times. You will have a chance to check on your detailed local weather forecast as an added benefit to this exercise). Enter your zip code (upper right corner) in *Find Your Local Weather* window and click on *GO (I will underscore all clickable operations)*. Then click on the "*3 Day History*" link, which is located mid-page to the right. We will use this set of weather related data in our excel exercise. Highlight the area of this web-page from "*Date*" in the upper left corner to *"Precipitation (in.)"* in the lower right corner. *Copy* it. Copy it using the shortcut keys – press *Control* + *C* on your keyboard. Using short keys is a great way to speed up your processing of financial data. Moving the mouse cursor to the menu bar as well as "right-clicking" to select the *Copy* function takes too much time. ***Get a habit of using the shortcut keys*** – they allow for both hands' use in the documents processing. A few examples of the shortcut keys are shown below and a more detailed list can be found in the appendix.

| | |
|---|---|
| *Alt + F* | *File menu options in current program* |
| *Alt + E* | *Edit options in current program* |
| *Alt + =* | *Sum (of cells directly above)* |
| *Ctrl + A* | *Select all text* |
| *Ctrl + X* | *Cut selected item* |
| *Shift + Del* | *Cut selected item* |
| *Ctrl + C* | *Copy selected item* |
| *Ctrl + V* | *Paste* |
| *Ctrl + Z* | *Undo* |
| *Ctrl + P* | *Print current page of document* |
| *Ctrl + O* | *Open file* |

Now, in a new excel spreadsheet, point to cell **A2** (to select pasting from this cell and below) and *Paste* (Ctrl + V) the copied weather data. You may get 60 to 200 rows of data.

Let us create a new **Macro** now. Macro is a set of pre-programmed operations, which is recorded and then run on the same segment of the excel file. Find the *Developer* tab on top of in the excel menus. If you don't see it, go to *File-*

*Options-Customize Ribbon.* Find the *Developer* under *Main Tabs* and select it. Or, ask your IT staff to find it and add it to your excel menu. Within the Developer tab, find and click on *Record Macro*. I advise to assign a name that hints to what this macro does, or remember it as the default name *Macro1.* You can also assign a shortcut key to the macro: Ctrl + is already there, just add any letter in the box, let's say the letter "G". You can add a description as well. Click *OK*.

Delete columns **H** through **R**; highlight the columns by pointing the mouse cursor to letter **H** in the headings, and drag it through column **R**, right-click and press *Delete* (to delete columns H-R). You should have only columns **A** thru **G** left. Then highlight rows 2, 3, 4 and 5, right-click on the mouse and *Delete* – this operation leaves row 1 as your table's header. Delete rows 51 all the way down (highlight row 51, then press *Ctrl+Shift+End* and *Delete*), too. Select/highlight your whole data (cells A2 to G50). Go to *Home*, click on *Borders,* and select *All Borders*. Now click on the *Developer* tab and *Stop Recording*.

Delete all the data in the worksheet at this time – a quick way to do it is to press and hold *Ctrl+A* and *Delete*. Copy the weather information again from the NOAA's website again. Paste it into your excel spreadsheet (select cell A2 and then paste). Now press *Ctrl+Shift+G*. The macro did the trick! It formatted the data based on your pre-programmed commands.

Now comes my favorite part – *the buttons*. In the developer tab, click on *Insert*; in *Form - Controls* select the upper left icon (regular "grey button") and click on cell *A1*. You are now asked whether you want to assign any macro to the button. Select the just created *Macro1* and click *OK*.

Drag the row 1 border down, so that the button is not covering row 2. Don't you feel like a programmer now, seeing that cute little grey button in the upper left corner of your file?! *Delete all excel spread sheet data* yet again then copy and paste the same data from the website again (select cell **A2** to start pasting from). *Click* on the button. Do you see how clicking on it initiated your macro's formatting of the data? Doesn't it feel a bit like *magic*? It does, to me.

A button is better placed on the side of data, if you don't have too many columns with information. At this time point to the button, *right-click* on it, hold on to the button and *drag* it to the right from your table (into cell J1, confirm – *Move Here*).

I use macros to process daily AP reports, which must be reformatted in certain ways based on different criteria after I export financial data into the excel spreadsheet from a system-generated report. Preprogramming of editing of the repetitive and time-consuming tasks save much time and allows you to produce the desired reporting results, present your data in a very professional and user-friendly format and have it all done quickly.


The next excel-lent topic is the **Pivot Tables**. This is the most useful tool to analyze and sort through voluminous Accounts Payable system generated reports, filter out the needed data, by fields and types, sort data by one or two criteria. For example, how many checks were issued (among other types of payments) in the range of 0 to $1000 (among other payment ranges) and present it all in concise statistical format. We will now add column headers, which are required to properly process a pivot table, to our excel spreadsheet.

We will also add to this "weather report" a piece of hypothetical Accounts Payable information to make the exercise more relevant to the book's topic. In row 1, add the following headers for the six columns listed:

*(1) Number of Invoices Processed*
*(2) Time*
*(3) Wind*
*(4) Number of Checks Paid*
*(5) Weather*
*(6) Sky Condition*

(We are changing two headers from the original "weather report" format).

Highlight the table. Click on *Insert Tab* in the menu, find *Pivot Table* and click on the small black triangle to select *Pivot Table* – confirm the range selected, click *OK*. The pivot table should be placed in a separate worksheet. *Drag* the *Weather* from the *Pivot Table Field List* to *Row Labels* box below. You can also use another data filter, besides the *Weather*, which you would "drag" to the Column Labels. My data is not designed to have both Row and Column labels used, but you may *later* drag any of the remaining Pivot Table Field List items to Columns Labels and see what happens.

*Drag Number of Invoices Processed* from the *Pivot Table Field List* into the *Values* box below and *Number of Checks Paid* into the same *Values* box, too. Make sure the *values* for both *Number of Invoices Processed* and *Number of Checks Paid* are set to **Sum**. If no, (if *Sum* is not selected, but *Count* or *Average*, or other), click on little black triangle in each value (to reset, if need be), select *Value Field Setting* and reset to **Sum**. You may select various *Value Field Settings* for different purposes – at this time we need the **Sum** value. Check the results.

The zip code that I selected provides me with data that indicate that most invoices and most checks are processed on "Partly Cloudy" days. Next comes "A Few Clouds" days when the most work is done. Isn't it amazing? Check out your geographic area to find out when your Accounts Payable people work most productively. As I said before, reading Accounts Payable books may be fun. By the way, this is an example of the *Performance Metric* report.

To be considered an excel expert you must know the **V-lookup** ("V" for vertical) function. There is no tricking anyone in learning these three *excel* operations: Macro, Pivot Table and V-lookup and claiming the excel expert's crown. First, these are indeed very advanced and most used elaborate functions of excel. Second, once you get the taste of how powerful the excel application truly is, by learning these three functions; you will continue studying it and proceed to other advanced operations.

What does the V-lookup do? It searches for value in a column and returns another value in the same row (where the column value was found) from another column in the same table. H-lookup ("H" for horizontal) does the similar work searching for value in a row and returning another value in the same column from another row in the same table. Enough of theory - let us practice.

In column A, in cell **A52**, type the equal sign (=) and "*VLOOKUP*". Leave no spaces between any values. Open parentheses, type in any number that does appear in column A2:A50 (let's say "18") and select table's range. So far we have typed this much: *=VLOOKUP(18,A2:G50* - the system will search for the first occurrence of "18" in the column "A" of the selected range. Type number "6" in the formula next, which will direct the system to find value in *the sixth column* for the row where value "18" was found (if found) and type *False*, which directs the system to find the exact match for value "18" (and not to approximate). You must have the following formula in cell A51.

## =VLOOKUP(18,A2:G50,6,False)

The command directs the system to find first the exact (indicated by "False") occurrence of volume 18 in range A2:G50 and show value in column 6 in the same row.

Change "6" to "4" in your formula. This is column *4* labeled "Number of checks paid", but really is the *wind speed* from the NOAA's website table.

Let us add a logical test to the V-lookup formula created earlier. Change the formula so that you get the following logical task sentence:

## =IF(Vlookup(18,A2:G50,4,False)>20,"Storm","Quiet")

You have set a logical task for the system by asking to compare the value in column *4* for the first exact occurrence of today's date ("18"), comparing that value to "20" (which is our threshold for determining the wind as being Stormy or Quiet) and displaying the result in the cell with the formula. Note that it is possible to have your table in a different than the formula excel *worksheet*.

Let us make this scenario more *AP*-relevant, lest we forget what this book is about. Change the number in cell **A50** to *123456* – this is our AP check number. Let us think of column *4* value as *Dollar Amount*, and column *5* as

*Payee's Name* (you may rename the columns). Pretend that your task is to find in the tens of thousands of checks records in your AP report check number "123456" and display the payee's name only if the check amount is $1,000 and over, and do not display the name if the check amount is less than $1,000. Type check number "*123456*" in cell **A50**, "*1001*" in cell **D50** and "RHYOLITE TOWNSHIP INC. Company" in cell **E50**. Carefully copy to cell **A54** the formula below (note that there must be no "spaces" in the formula except in the "quoted" text sentences where "spaces" do not affect the formula's performance):

### =IF(VLOOKUP(123456,A20:G50,4,FALSE)>=1000, "Payee name is "&VLOOKUP(123456,A2:G50,5,FALSE)& "","Less than $ 1000")

Here we search for value "123456" in column A and compare the value in column "4" of the same row 50 (where "123456" is found) to our logical test of being equal or greater than $1000. The outcome is displayed based on the logical test results: if the value is equal or more than $1000, the outcome is "Payee name is (the name is shown as data in column "5" of the same row where "123465" check number was found). Otherwise, the system shows "Less than $1000". Change 1001 to 999 in cell **D50** to see the results change.

There are many variations of the V-lookup (and H-lookup) formulas and logical tests – all are very useful to sort and research voluminous Accounts Payable reports and extract the needed data. I hope I have ignited your interest in these excel operations and you will be professionally curious to research them further on your own. I stop my discussion of excel here, remembering that earlier in the book I have claimed, not entirely correctly, that this is "not a book on excel".

# Managing the Accounts Payable Department

Don's skip this chapter if you are not an Accounts Payable manager (yet). I offer suggestions that apply to any one in the Accounts Payable department. You will be an Accounts Payable manager one day, because you are interested in the AP processes so much that you decided to read this book and have advanced reading this book as far as this page. Your interest and determination prove the commitment to the Accounts Payable business and attest to your professional growth and success.

I will mention some basic and general work related requirements for running successful financial operations; and then will concentrate on the Accounts Payable specific areas. First, you must always appear as a professional finance person; dress, behave and talk professionally. Do not allow yourself any slack in look and behavior if you are not meeting with the company's president today. Do not allow yourself to think that the Accounts Payable work does not rise to the level of wearing white shirt, tie for men and dark suit as your professional business attire daily. You are often (and sometimes incorrectly) judged by your appearance. And, not less importantly, your appearance, and your perception of your appearance, influence how you behave and talk – the phenomena is called the *outside-in effect*. In a way, by dressing professionally, you set yourself for behaving in a more professional manner. It also eliminates your nightly pondering of what fashion item to dress in the next day. The *Casual Friday* dress code (and the associated behavior) is not for the serious professional people.

But, on the other hand, you must blend-in with the folks around you, especially your bosses, blend-in at a higher fashion end. Follow your boss's dress code and manners, if you can do it, if you can find it advancing to your professional growth.

This paragraph is rather short, but maybe the most important in the book – *Love your boss as you love yourself, try...* Be a reliable and trusted subordinate. Most of the bosses are bosses for a reason of merit, most of times. *Do unto your boss as you would've him do to you.* Listen. Nod your head. You have two ears and only one mouth. Don't interrupt. Smile. I feel like I'm teaching you the underlying foundations of success in business while you're standing listening on one foot. With this last one, yes, one foot: don't attempt to project your personal values on managers and peers. When feeling a disagreement with them, just whisper words of wisdom, *let it be*, and switch over to the apolitical and impersonal accounts payable activities.

Speak and write clearly in the *Standard English language*. Speaking and expressing your thoughts clearly is one of the most important qualities in any business environment. You may be the most knowledgeable, educated and hardworking person, but without being able to express yourself clearly, you set yourself to languishing in routine data-processing operations. The process works in the reversed way, too.

It is a good idea to take a class or read self-help books on how to write, speak and effectively communicate in the business environment. Buy and read *How to Write Effective Business English: The Essential Toolkit for Composing Powerful Letters, E-Mails and More, for Today's*

*Business Needs* by Fiona Talbot. Read a book about a non-verbal communications and body language (*Business Body Language: Learn How to Read, Lead, and Mange with Powerful Body Language* by Ben Night). Be physically fit, neat and courteous. You will set the tone in the Accounts Payable department and make others follow suit.

Set clear goals in the Accounts Payable department and monitor performance. Openly discuss any issues as they arise, try to foresee them. It is best to be direct and courteous when discussing performance or discipline-related issue. Hinting to an issue or other indirect communication will not address and correct the issue. Do not make issue a personal matter, concentrate on the effects of a person's actions and behavior on Accounts Payable processes and ways to address issues (do not say "*you* process most invoice data entry errors in the department", but say instead "we need to think of how to help you to improve *your* invoice processing"). Be there to help the person to be a professional who performs according to your department's standards and expectations. No one wants to be a "lousy worker" – it is a matter of creating the right environment for your employees to be high quality employees and team-players. Still, let the hopeless deadbeats go home, ASAP. Be a parent figure to your folks – be available to them, listen to them, stand up for them, take them out to local pizzeria and enjoy doing all these things.

Another very important Accounts Payable aspect is timeliness of AP processing and effective communication of all issues and errors. Do not allow any item to languish on your desk, in your emails, in your phone messages inbox, in the system's Approvals or Action lists. Many routine Accounts Payable errors may *mushroom* into interdepartmental and vendors-related problems, with other departments' managers getting involved and reporting complaints to the higher level. Review and act within reasonable and internally established time-frames on any issue and keep track-records of what you have done. Do not communicate any other than routine business matter verbally – have an audit trail of your decisions and actions.

Do not involve "outsiders" in your internal Accounts Payable reviews or discussions, interdepartmental arguments or conflicts. Maintain a good image of your department and your company on all levels.

I try to avoid the phone. All business consultants teach otherwise – pick up a phone and talk, they say. I pick up the phone when I happen to be 'less busy' and always listen to message and respond by email or phone. This advice is unusual, but I would not have been able to do my job had I always responded to all callers. Often I know that a caller is too bossy or too lazy to put an inquiry in email writing – and I, as AP manager, always need a trail of what was said, asked, and stated about the ongoing business – phone call leaves no such trail. I strongly prefer to receive business information in my inbox – available for future references. When you pick up a phone call you are forced to stop doing what you've been doing, have a small talk, jot down the information, research and call back the person, often more than once (phone tag). With that said, I always pick up calls from my bosses, that's no brainer (my vendors inquire with company departments).

The phone is an interrupter most of time, often questions asked on the phone do not pertain to your direct work and you end up being a middleman in unrelated communications. Emotionally-charged situations can be resolved faster over the phone – this is true, and I use the phone in such instances. I try not to get into such situations often - most of the AP communication exchange is financial information that must be transcribed – it is shared best via the email.

**Accounts Payable is a teamwork process**. You must establish a conductive for work and healthy ambiance in the department; nourish the attitude of comradeship, diligence, hard work and compliance. Monitor the workflow: always give praise where praise is due. Even praise individuals when they make minor errors in a way of repeating your high standard expectation of how they should perform.

Hire good people for your department – new employee selection process will make your AP life much more efficient and pleasant if you know how to detect the skill and behavior you look for and have the intuition to make right choices.

Never stop learning. Know your trade. Argue with conviction, which you gain with your increase of professional knowledge. Maintain a positive and friendly attitude when disagreeing, never make it 'personal'. Be ready to openly accept other's better idea.

Be on top of the Accounts Payable professional development; read books, attend conferences, be a member of a professional society, study to pass the CPA test. Yes, this is my universal advice to any finance processional – study to become a CPA. You may never pass all four parts, but the mere studying for the test takes you to the next professional level of Accounts Payable by virtue of gaining general accounting knowledge.

Be grateful for what you already have in life. Strive for more but do not forget to appreciate what is already had. I say, feel unsatisfied in the morning, but thankful in the evening.

And last, but not least – you must like your job. Here I admit I cannot offer any advice on how to do it. If you'd always dreamt of being a rock star, but have ended in the Accounts Payable department, you may have difficulties liking what you are doing. But, I believe, with age, we all come to the point in our lives when we ask ourselves – what am I? What am I good at? How useful am I? (I borrow the last question from my kids' favorite *Thomas & Friends* cartoon). How do I contribute best to my family, company, country' success? What do I do to be a valuable and contributing member of the commonwealth?

Well, not by strumming your old Fender Strat onstage with other drunken musicians. The answer is your hard work, improvement of the professional knowledge, personal skills, character traits, health and appearance. The learning and improvement process never ends. You must not let it end and believe that your personality had been *set in stone* at certain age and whatever shortcomings are there in your character, are there to stay - this is not true. Believe in a constant improving of yourself and aspire to be the best you can be. And, enjoy it!

*Epilogue*

Twenty-four years ago, I sent via Western Union a $100 transfer to my then girlfriend, Irene. $100 required 20 hours of work on an Islamorada, FL resort. Hard and monotonous work under the hot and humid Florida Keys Sun. I added a message to the transfer - *I mad about you.* You'll say – *mad about you* and just $100!? Well, yes, both…

A good Western Union lady pointed out that I should correct the memo to *I'm mad about you*, which I did. (The line comes from a song by Sting.) I've been thinking of those Islamorada days so frequently as of late, while working on the eleventh edition of this book. It feels so surreal; 12 hours of dull labor each day, beer by the trailer at night where I lived with a bunch of noisy and unruly pals, lightnings on the gulf side, dark settling over from the Atlantic. *I mad about you – I'm mad about you.* Fast-forward 24 years. Professor Irene S. is my wife and I am a CPA.

I am surprised by the volume of information and number of different topics in this book on Accounts Payable. Many times, I have shortened the dry payables discourses to keep the presentation readable given the limited time allowed by our professional and personal lives.

The specialization of Accounts Payable presents many opportunities to be a part of the financial process and actively participate in the building of your company's growth and success. It allows for employment stability, professional development and career growth. And, while it may not be as dynamic as some other *exotic* professions, it has the added benefit of existential permanency and demand for the AP skills since it will exist as long as there are monetary transactions in the business operations.

The profession is changing with the world. There is less or no need for the old-type invoice *keying-in* skills; AP information is more often submitted by vendors as e-invoices, or cost centers users, who upload or prepare the AP data for your Accounts Payable system through the remote (web-based) access sites. There are fewer people involved in the AP process in our days, it is true. Those who are involved no longer need to deal with repetitive and manual tasks.

The present and future Accounts Payable professional is more concerned with analytical, statistical and qualitative management of data, as well as the usual payments processing and cash management. There is now a higher level of engagement for modern Accounts Payable professionals when they must access business needs, arrange for the required AP processing mechanisms, integrate various systems, be involved in review, approval, payments processing and monitoring of the systems workflows to maintain compliant AP operations and find areas where the processes can be improved further.

The 21st century business environment calls for more educated, trained and intellectually curious and proactive Accounts Payable professionals who take advantage of the amazing processing tools that the modern technology offers. But no matter how great Accounts Payable systems may by, they are only as good as the people who use them. The modern systems actually allow for a greater magnitude of error, with all the automations of Accounts Payable processes in place, if used improperly or with inadequate knowledge. There has been no program developed yet that can substitute a competent Accounts Payable professional and there never will be, not even in our technologically advanced and innovative 21st century business environment.

I hope that this book added to your knowledge and appreciation of the Accounts Payable profession. I hope that the book will help in your professional growth, development, and success. God Bless America. Let there be peace and love in the 21st Century. May God bless us All.


Sincerely,

Costa Levi P, CPA
New York City, 2019

# Appendix

# The Six *A.S.P.I.R.E.* Accounts Payable Principles

-**A**P. Aspire to be the best AP professional: read, research and attend everything that applies to the AP profession. Improve your professional image in substance and appearance.

-**S**ystems. Strive to work with the ERP or AP systems that approximate the ERP's functionalities when making employment choices.

-**P**aper. Eliminate paper processing where possible.

-**I**maging. Use easily-accessible imaging system for storing the AP documentation.

-**R**educe paper checks processing to the absolute minimum.

-**E**rr on the side of under-paying and over-reporting when in doubt.

## A.S.P.I.R.E. to be the Best you can be!

# US Bank Holidays 2019 - 2020

| Observed Holidays | 2020 | 2019 |
|---|---|---|
| | | |
| New Year's Day | January 1 | January 1 |
| Martin Luther King, Jr. Day | January 20 | January 18 |
| President's Birthday | February 17 | February 18 |
| Memorial Day | May 25 | May 27 |
| Independence Day | July 4 | July 4 |
| Labor Day | September 7 | September 2 |
| Columbus Day | October 12 | October 14 |
| Veterans Day | November 11 | November 11 |
| Thanksgiving Day | November 26 | November 28 |
| Christmas Day | December 25 | December 25 |

*Note: Do not use bank holidays, Saturdays, or Sundays to calculate required lead days for payments.*

# INTERNAL REVENUE CODE § 1441

Section 1441. Withholding of Tax on Nonresident Aliens

(a) General rule

Except as otherwise provided in subsection (c), all persons, in whatever capacity acting (including lessees or mortgagors of real or personal property, fiduciaries, employers, and all officers and employees of the United States) having the control, receipt, custody, disposal, or payment of any of the items of income specified in subsection (b) (to the extent that any of such items constitutes gross income from sources within the United States), of any nonresident alien individual or of any foreign partnership shall (except as otherwise provided in regulations prescribed by the Secretary under section 874) deduct and withhold from such items a tax equal to 30 percent thereof, except that in the case of any item of income specified in the second sentence of subsection (b), the tax shall be equal to 14 percent of such item.

## (b) Income items

The items of income referred to in subsection (a) are interest (other than original issue discount as defined in section 1273), dividends, rent, salaries, wages, premiums, annuities, compensations, remunerations, emoluments, or other fixed or determinable annual or periodical gains, profits, and income, gains described in section 631(b) or (c), amounts subject to tax under section 871(a)(1)(C), gains subject to tax under section 871(a)(1)(D), and gains on transfers described in section 1235 made on or before October 4, 1966. The items of income referred to in subsection (a) from which tax shall be deducted and withheld at the rate of 14 percent are amounts which are received by a nonresident alien individual who is temporarily present in the United States as a nonimmigrant under subparagraph (F), (J), (M), or (Q) of section 101(a)(15) of the Immigration and Nationality Act and which are--

(1) incident to a qualified scholarship to which section 117(a) applies, but only to the extent includible in gross income; or

(2) in the case of an individual who is not a candidate for a degree at an educational organization described in section 170(b)(1)(A)(ii), granted by--

(A) an organization described in section 501(c)(3) which is exempt from tax under section 501(a),

(B) a foreign government,

(C) an international organization, or a binational or multinational educational and cultural foundation or commission created or continued pursuant to the Mutual Educational and Cultural Exchange Act of 1961, or

(D) the United States, or an instrumentality or agency thereof, or a State, or a possession of the United States, or any political subdivision thereof, or the District of Columbia as a scholarship or fellowship for study, training, or research in the United States.

# Most Used Excel Shortcuts

*("+" means "and"; press Alt key and equal sign key for the first shortcut below)*

| | |
|---|---|
| Alt + = | Sum of the above cells |
| Ctrl+A | Select All |
| Ctrl+B | Bold |
| Ctrl+C | Copy |
| Ctrl+D | Fill Down |
| Ctrl+F | Find |
| Ctrl+G | Go to |
| Ctrl+H | Replace |
| Ctrl+I | Italic |
| Ctrl+K | Insert Hyperlink |
| Ctrl+N | New Workbook |
| Ctrl+O | Open    File |
| Ctrl+P | Print    File |
| Ctrl+R | Fill Right |
| Ctrl+S | Save    File |
| Ctrl+U | Underline |
| Ctrl+V | Paste |
| Ctrl W | Close |
| Ctrl+X | Cut |
| Ctrl+Y | Repeat |
| Ctrl+Z | Undo |
| F1 | Help |
| F2 | Edit |
| F3 | Paste Name |
| F4 | Repeat last action |
| F4 | Switch between absolute/relative references |
| F5 | Go to |
| F6 | Next Pane |
| F7 | Spell check |
| F8 | Extend mode |
| F9 | Recalculate all workbooks |
| F10 | Activate Menu bar |
| F11 | New Chart |
| F12 | Save As  File |

| | |
|---|---|
| Ctrl+: | Insert Current Time |
| Ctrl+; | Insert Current Date |
| Ctrl+" | Copy Value from Cell Above |
| | |
| Ctrl+' | Copy Formula from Cell Above |
| Shift+F1 | What's This? |
| Shift+F2 | Edit cell comment |
| Shift+F3 | Paste function into formula |
| Shift+F4 | Find Next |
| Shift+F5 | Find |
| Shift+F6 | Previous Pane |
| Shift+F8 | Add to selection |
| Shift+F9 | Calculate active worksheet |
| Ctrl+Alt+F9 | Calculate all worksheets |
| Shift+F10 | Display shortcut menu |
| Shift+F11 | New worksheet |
| Shift+F12 | Save File |
| Ctrl+F3 | Define name |
| Ctrl+F4 | Close File |
| Ctrl+F5 | Restore window size |
| Ctrl+F6 | Next workbook window |
| Shift+Ctrl+F6 | Previous workbook window |
| Ctrl+F7 | Move window |
| Ctrl+F8 | Resize window |
| Ctrl+F9 | Minimize workbook |
| Ctrl+F10 | Maximize or restore window |
| Ctrl+F11 | Inset 4.0 Macro sheet |
| Ctrl+F12 | File Open |
| Alt+F1 | Insert Chart |
| Alt+F2 | Save As          File |
| Alt+F4 | Exit     File |
| Alt+F8 | Macro dialog box |
| Alt+F11 | Visual Basic Editor |

# Sample ACH/EFT *NACHA Flat* file format
(Source: www.treasurysoftware.com)

Sample ACH / NACHA file

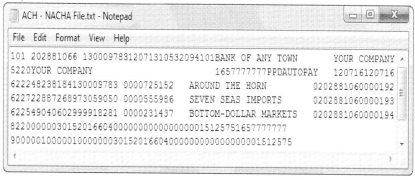

# Sample ACH/EFT *XML* file format

```xml
<?xml version="1.0" encoding="UTF-8" ?>
- <achPayments>
  - <ach disbursementNbr="101">
      <processCampus>XX</processCampus>
      <processId>00000538</processId>
    - <bank code="1002">
        <accountNumber>123456789</accountNumber>
        <routingNumber>021000021</routingNumber>
      </bank>
      <disbursementDate>2013-11-07</disbursementDate>
      <netAmount>137.52</netAmount>
    - <payee id="IanGilan1" type="V">
        <payeeName>IAN J GILAN</payeeName>
        <line1Address>BANK OF AMERICA LOCKBOX SERVIC</line1Address>
        <line2Address>111111 COLLECTION CENTER DRIVE</line2Address>
        <city>CHICAGO</city>
        <state>IL</state>
        <zipCd>60693</zipCd>
        <country>United States</country>
        <achBankRoutingNbr>021000322</achBankRoutingNbr>
        <achBankAccountNbr>333222555666</achBankAccountNbr>
        <achAccountType>22</achAccountType>
      </payee>
```

# IRS forms

| PAYER'S name, street address, city or town, state or province, country, ZIP or foreign postal code, and telephone no. | | 1 Rents<br><br>$ | OMB No. 1545-0115<br><br>2**019** | Miscellaneous Income |
|---|---|---|---|---|
| | | 2 Royalties<br><br>$ | Form **1099-MISC** | |
| | | 3 Other income<br><br>$ | 4 Federal income tax withheld<br><br>$ | Copy 1 |
| PAYER'S TIN | RECIPIENT'S TIN | 5 Fishing boat proceeds<br><br><br><br>$ | 6 Medical and health care payments<br><br>$ | For State Tax Department |
| RECIPIENT'S name | | 7 Nonemployee compensation<br><br>$ | 8 Substitute payments in lieu of dividends or interest | |
| Street address (including apt. no.) | | 9 Payer made direct sales of $5,000 or more of consumer products to a buyer (recipient) for resale ▶ ☐ | 10 Crop insurance proceeds<br><br>$ | |
| City or town, state or province, country, and ZIP or foreign postal code | | 11 | 12 | |
| Account number (see instructions) | FATCA filing requirement ☐ | 13 Excess golden parachute payments<br><br>$ | 14 Gross proceeds paid to an attorney<br><br>$ | |
| 15a Section 409A deferrals<br><br>$ | 15b Section 409A income<br><br>$ | 16 State tax withheld<br>$<br>$ | 17 State/Payer's state no. | 18 State income<br>$<br>$ |

Form **1099-MISC**     www.irs.gov/Form1099MISC     Department of the Treasury - Internal Revenue Service

405

| Form **W-9** | **Request for Taxpayer** | Give Form to the |
|---|---|---|
| (Rev. October 2018) | **Identification Number and Certification** | requester. Do not |
| Department of the Treasury Internal Revenue Service | ▶ Go to *www.irs.gov/FormW9* for instructions and the latest information. | send to the IRS. |

**1** Name (as shown on your income tax return). Name is required on this line; do not leave this line blank.

**2** Business name/disregarded entity name, if different from above

**3** Check appropriate box for federal tax classification of the person whose name is entered on line 1. Check only **one** of the following seven boxes.

☐ Individual/sole proprietor or single-member LLC    ☐ C Corporation    ☐ S Corporation    ☐ Partnership    ☐ Trust/estate

☐ Limited liability company. Enter the tax classification (C=C corporation, S=S corporation, P=Partnership) ▶ _____

**Note:** Check the appropriate box in the line above for the tax classification of the single-member owner. Do not check LLC if the LLC is classified as a single-member LLC that is disregarded from the owner unless the owner of the LLC is another LLC that is **not** disregarded from the owner for U.S. federal tax purposes. Otherwise, a single-member LLC that is disregarded from the owner should check the appropriate box for the tax classification of its owner.

☐ Other (see instructions) ▶

**4** Exemptions (codes apply only to certain entities, not individuals; see instructions on page 3):

Exempt payee code (if any) _____

Exemption from FATCA reporting code (if any) _____

*(Applies to accounts maintained outside the U.S.)*

**5** Address (number, street, and apt. or suite no.) See instructions.

**6** City, state, and ZIP code

Requester's name and address (optional)

**7** List account number(s) here (optional)

*Print or type. See Specific Instructions on page 3.*

---

**Part I**    **Taxpayer Identification Number (TIN)**

Enter your TIN in the appropriate box. The TIN provided must match the name given on line 1 to avoid backup withholding. For individuals, this is generally your social security number (SSN). However, for a resident alien, sole proprietor, or disregarded entity, see the instructions for Part I, later. For other entities, it is your employer identification number (EIN). If you do not have a number, see *How to get a TIN*, later.

**Note:** If the account is in more than one name, see the instructions for line 1. Also see *What Name and Number To Give the Requester* for guidelines on whose number to enter.

Social security number

☐☐☐ – ☐☐ – ☐☐☐☐

**or**

Employer identification number

☐☐ – ☐☐☐☐☐☐☐

---

**Part II**    **Certification**

Under penalties of perjury, I certify that:

1. The number shown on this form is my correct taxpayer identification number (or I am waiting for a number to be issued to me); and

2. I am not subject to backup withholding because: (a) I am exempt from backup withholding, or (b) I have not been notified by the Internal Revenue Service (IRS) that I am subject to backup withholding as a result of a failure to report all interest or dividends, or (c) the IRS has notified me that I am no longer subject to backup withholding; and

3. I am a U.S. citizen or other U.S. person (defined below); and

4. The FATCA code(s) entered on this form (if any) indicating that I am exempt from FATCA reporting is correct.

**Certification instructions.** You must cross out item 2 above if you have been notified by the IRS that you are currently subject to backup withholding because you have failed to report all interest and dividends on your tax return. For real estate transactions, item 2 does not apply. For mortgage interest paid, acquisition or abandonment of secured property, cancellation of debt, contributions to an individual retirement arrangement (IRA), and generally, payments other than interest and dividends, you are not required to sign the certification, but you must provide your correct TIN. See the instructions for Part II, later.

| Sign Here | Signature of U.S. person ▶ | Date ▶ |
|---|---|---|

# US Nonimmigrant visas

| | |
|---|---|
| A Visa | Foreign Government Officials (A1, A2 and A3) |
| B Visa | Temporary Visitors |
| B-1 | Visitor for business |
| B-2 | Visitor for pleasure: tourism, sightseeing, visiting relatives |
| C Visa | Foreign Nationals in Transit (C1, C1-D, C2, C3 and C4) |
| D Visa | Crewmen (D1 and D2) |
| E Visa | Treaty Traders and Investors (E1 and E2) |
| F Visa | Academic Students |
| F-1 | Student |
| F-2 | Spouse or child of F1 student |
| G Visa | Foreign Government Officials to International Organizations (G1- 5) |
| H Visa | Temporary Workers |
| H-1B | Engineers, scientists, specialty occupations, models, etc. |
| H-1C | Nurses working in health professional shortage areas |
| H-2A | Agricultural worker |
| H-2B | Temporary worker: skilled and unskilled |
| H-3 | Trainee |
| H-4 | Spouse or child of H1, H2 or H3 |
| I Visa | Foreign Media Representatives |
| J Visa | Exchange Visitors |
| J-1 | Exchange visitor |
| J-2 | Spouse or child of J1 |
| K Visa | Spouse or Fiancé of US Citizen |
| K-1 | Fiancé |
| K-2 | Minor child of K-1 |
| K-3 | Spouse of US citizen |
| K-4 | Child of K-3 |
| | |
| L Visa | Intra company Transferee |

| | |
|---|---|
| L-1A | Executives, managers |
| L-1B | Specialized knowledge |
| L-2 | Spouse or child of L-1 |
| M Visa | Non-Academic Students |
| M-1 | Vocational, language, or other non-academic student |
| M-2 | Spouse or child of M-1 |
| N Visa | Special Immigrants (N-8 and N-9) |
| NAFTA Visa | North American Free Trade Agreement |
| NATO Visa | North Atlantic Treaty Organization (NATO1 to NATO-7) |
| O Visa | Workers with Extraordinary Abilities |
| O-1 | Extraordinary ability in science, arts, education, business or athletics |
| O-2 | Alien accompanying O-1 |
| O-3 | Spouse or child of O-1 or O-2 |
| P Visa | Athletes and Entertainers (P1, P2, P3 and P4) |
| Q Visa | International Cultural Exchange Visitors (Q1, Q2 and Q3) |
| R Visa | Religious Workers (R1 and R2) |
| S Visa | Witness or Informant (S-5 and S-6) |
| T Visa | Victims of Severe Form of Trafficking in Persons (T1 to T4) |
| TN Visa | Trade visas for Canadians and Mexicans |
| TD Visa | Spouse or child of TN |
| TPS Visa | Temporary Protected Status |
| TWOV Visa | Transit Without Visa (Passenger or Crew) |
| U Visa | Victims of Certain Crimes (U1 to U4) |
| V Visa | Certain Second Preference Beneficiaries |
| V-1 | Spouse of LPR with I-130 pending since before 12/21/2000 |
| V-2 | Child of LPR with I-130 pending since before 12/21/2000 |
| V-3 | Dependent child of a V-1 or V-2 visa holder |

# SAP Concur Travel Expense System

## New User Manual

1. After a Concur account has been created, a welcome email will notify you to set up a permanent password.
2. User ID is user's business email address. User ID (cLeVI@AP21C.com) <u>is not</u> case-sensitive, the password <u>is case-sensitive</u>.

3. Your next Concur activity must me *Deposit Account* set up. This process enables SAP Concur to make direct deposits to your bank account.
Click on Profile, Profile Settings (upper right), then Bank Information (mid-left).


Enter your bank account information. SAP Concur will validate your bank account, which takes two business days. Before the account is validated, a Concur report cannot be submitted, but can be prepared.

4. Prepare and submit one report per month immediately after month-end, before the 10th of the following month. To create a new report, click on **Expense** link (top), then **Create New Report**.

The best naming practice is to simply assign month-year as the report's name: OCTOBER 2018. *Note that all Concur fields with red shading must be completed.*

# Create a New Expense Report

Report Header

| Report Name | Report Date | Business Purpose |
|---|---|---|
| NOVEMBER 2017 | 12/03/2017 | |

<u>Receipts: All reimbursements must be accompanied by Transaction Receipt (or Itinerary Receipt for Egencia bookings) that shows names of seller and buyer, details of purchase, and method of payment. Credit card statement is not a valid receipt, but it can be used to add payment info to a transaction document.</u>

*Receipts can be paper or electronic. Some receipts (or, broadly speaking, transaction confirmations) may be emails, web-site check out pages, etc. You must be able to capture receipts in the pdf format. A paper receipt is scanned manually. Any online, on-screen transaction confirmation can be PDF'd using functions such as Microsoft Print to PDF, Print to File, or saved as PDF files. All Egencia (company's travel agent) documents are transferred to a linked Concur account of the same user.*

*!**The best way to capture receipts is by using SAP Concur phone application**! Download the app on*

*your cell phone by finding SAP Concur in Play Store (Android) or App Store (Apple). Sign in to the app with your existing Concur log in. Take pictures of receipts with the app camera: the system fist validates the quality, then sends all receipts to user's Concur <u>Available Expenses</u>. The available expense listing reminds the user of the expense that need to be included in a report. It is very easy to select all available expenses and included them in a new or existing report. Concur's optical character recognition (OCR) function allows reading and completion of many transaction fields, which otherwise are filled out manually.*

AVAILABLE EXPENSES

| Expense Detail | Expense Type | Source | Date ▾ | Amount |
|----------------|--------------|--------|--------|--------|
| Business Meeting over Meal | Business Meeting over Meal | | 10/16/2017 | $672.80 |
| Business Meeting over Meal | Business Meeting over Meal | | 10/16/2017 | $222.99 |

*All transactions, except Personal Car Mileage, require transaction receipts that shows names of seller and buyer, details of purchase, and method of payment. Credit card statement is not a valid receipt, but it can be used to add payment info to an incomplete transaction document.*

*Submit all receipt separately, do not combine them by expense type.*

5. (Continuing about creating a new report.) Select Expense Type from the available list. Transaction date (date of purchase) is often different from the Event Date. Include in your monthly reports all business transactions you paid for in that month.

Business Purpose must state the event that triggered your payment.

Vendor name and city are required fields. Payment type always remains 'cash/out of pocket".

You may enter a comment if need be.

6. Attach a document that supports your payment for the described transaction:

Your pre-saved receipts are in your computer's designated folders, or (those process with *ExpenseIt* app and Egencia) in Concur's Available Receipts.

Learn how to send receipts from your email directly to your Concur account visiting this web page:

http://assets.concur.com/concurtraining/cte/en-us/cte_en-us_exp_available-receipts.mp4

- If there's an attachment in your email (to receipts@concur.com), the attachment will be the available receipt in Concur.

- No attachment – the email information/text is showing in the uploaded     Concur document.

7. Hotel bills must be 'itemized', i.e. amounts broken down by number of nights, times room rate and application taxes. The number of nights is calculated based on Check-In and Check-Out dates that the user must enter.
If you have a hotel bill with different nightly rates, use the Itemization function to enter the most common rate. There will be a difference to adjust - adjust the entered rate(s) with other daily rate(s) for specific days.
Enter incidental hotel expenses after you entered the room rates - use itemization function for that as well (select appropriate, other than Room Rate and Tax, expense type).

*Workflows: your report, after you submit it, goes to your manager for review (there may be a bookkeeper review before manager review), then to the Finance department. All reports fully approved by end of business on Tuesday get paid the following Friday. The payments are made by direct deposit to your bank account.*

*Manager of Finance Approver may request more information about a report or transaction. A complete report or individual line(s) may be returned to user for adjustment. The adjust report or line(s) (individual lines will be assigned a new report name Addendum: [Original Report Name]). The report must be submitted, and then approved by all managers again.*

8. Cell phone and internet monthly allowances are assigned on the case by case bases. The reimbursement amount is the lower of the actual bill or the allowed monthly limit.

9. If you are using company Amex card, all transactions processed with that card are listed in the Concur-Expenses: Available Expenses. The list is a welcome reminder to be reimbursed for the business purchases made (there should be no personal purchases with company Amex). Select *all* transactions or individually to be included in a new report.

Amex receipt by itself is not a valid supporting document – attach transaction receipts to matching Amex receipts.

You must strive to clean up the available Amex expense on the 'rolling' monthly basis: submit all prior month's qualified transactions. The current month's Amex transaction will remain listed until included in a new report early next month. There should be no un-reported Amex transactions older than 40 days.

Paying off Company Amex card statement balance is the card-holder's responsibility.

*Example of an available expense generated by Amex transaction:*

AVAILABLE EXPENSES

| | Expense Detail | Expense Type | Receipt | Date ▲ | Amount |
|---|---|---|---|---|---|
| ☐ | OFFICE DEPOT 2567 LAKE WORTH FL | Undefined | 🙂 | 04/27/2017 | $354.91 |

*Note that a Concur report must show a flow of events in the prior month: an airfare purchase is followed by a taxi ride to airport, a taxi ride to a hotel, meals at conference, possibly Business Meetings Over Meals (names of attendees required), possibly Car Rental (gas receipts, tolls and parking may accompany car rental), taxi rides back to airport and home.*

*If you use your personal car, select personal car mileage and enter Way Points (travel points). The system will calculate miles and reimbursement amount due to you. Gas receipts cannot be submitted with Personal Car Mileages, while tolls and parking can.*

9. Read Company Notes on SAP CONCUR home page. Following the guidelines will allow for an organized and expedient report processing and payment.

11

10

9

8

7

6

5

4

3

2

1

0

Made in the USA
San Bernardino, CA
29 August 2019